MAKING THE LATINO S(

LATINX HISTORIES

Lori Flores and Michael Innis-Jiménez, editors

Series Advisory Board
Llana Barber
Adrian Burgos Jr.
Geraldo Cadava
Julio Capó Jr.
Miroslava Chavez-Garcia
Kaysha Corinealdi
María Cristina García
Ramón Gutierréz
Paul Ortiz

This series features innovative historical works
that push boundaries in the study of race, ethnicity,
sexuality, gender, migration, and nationalism
within and around Latinx communities, premised
on the view that Latinx histories are essential to
understanding the full sweep of history in the United
States, the Americas, and the world.

A complete list of books published in
Latinx Histories is available at
https://uncpress.org/series/latinx-histories-2/.

Making the
·············· Latino South

A HISTORY OF RACIAL FORMATION

Cecilia Márquez

The University of North Carolina Press

Chapel Hill

*Published with the assistance of the Authors Fund
of the University of North Carolina Press.*

Designed by April Leidig
Set in Calluna and Sancoale Slab by Copperline Book Services

Manufactured in the United States of America

Cover art courtesy stock.adobe.com/simonmayer.

Library of Congress Cataloging-in-Publication Data
Names: Márquez, Cecilia, author.
Title: Making the Latino South : a history of racial formation / by Cecilia Márquez.
Other titles: Latinx histories.
Description: Chapel Hill : The University of North Carolina Press, 2023. |
    Series: Latinx histories | Includes bibliographical references and index.
Identifiers: LCCN 2023008283 | ISBN 9781469676043 (cloth ; alk. paper) |
    ISBN 9781469676050 (paperback) | ISBN 9781469676067 (ebook)
Subjects: LCSH: Latin Americans—Southern States—Social conditions—20th
    century. | Hispanic Americans—Southern States—Social conditions—20th
    century. | Latin Americans—Race identity—Southern States. | Hispanic
    Americans—Race identity—Southern States. | Latin Americans—Southern
    States—Ethnic identity. | Hispanic Americans—Southern States—Ethnic identity. |
    Racism—Social aspects—Southern States. | Southern States—Race relations—
    Social aspects.
Classification: LCC F220.S75 M377 2023 | DDC 975/.00468073—dc23/eng/20230310
LC record available at https://lccn.loc.gov/2023008283

To my family:

Jaime Márquez, Janice Shack-Márquez,

Bianca Márquez, and Annise Weaver

CONTENTS

ILLUSTRATIONS

ACKNOWLEDGMENTS

This project began more than a decade ago, in 2010, at the Student Nonviolent Coordinating Committee's (SNCC) Fiftieth Anniversary Conference. I am first and foremost thankful to the members of SNCC who taught me the power of telling history.

I could not have completed this book without the financial support of several institutions, which made it possible for me to travel, research, and write. Thank you to the German Historical Institute, the Smithsonian Latino/a Studies Predoctoral Fellowship, the American Council of Learned Society/Mellon Foundation, the Institute for Citizens and Scholars (formerly Woodrow Wilson Institute), the Summer Institute for Tenure and Professional Advancement, and the NYU Humanities Center.

I am grateful to the audiences at the conferences and institutions where I presented my work: the American Studies Association, the Organization of American Historians, the Southern Labor Studies Association, the American Historical Association, the Labor and Working-Class History Association, Georgia Southern University, and the Smithsonian National Museum of American History.

I am immensely grateful to Dr. Allison Dorsey at Swarthmore College who was my first intellectual mentor and taught me that the classroom could be a space for social change. Also, at Swarthmore I was fortunate to be part of the Mellon Mays Undergraduate Fellowship program, which was, and remains, a constant source of support. I benefited greatly from my time as an intern at the Institute for the Recruitment of Teachers (IRT) and am especially grateful for the mentorship and guidance of Monica Martinez and Ernest Gibson III.

At the University of Virginia, I had generous and gifted peers who helped me find joy both inside and outside of our work. Thank you to Clayton Butler, Benji Cohen, Jonathan Cohen, Mary Draper, Erik Erlandson, Leif Fredrickson, Shira Lurie, Rachel Moran, and Tamika Nunley. In Charlottesville I was lucky to know Katy Meinbresse, Wyatt Rolla, and Cherie Seise who made central Virginia home. I was also lucky to be a part of the Living Wage Campaign at UVA, a group of people who taught me a great deal about what it was to fight for a better world. Lawrie Balfour, Brian Balogh, Claudrena Harold, and Elizabeth

Varon were among the wonderful faculty at UVA who shaped my vision of history. It was at UVA that I also met my adviser and friend, Grace Hale. She has been my fiercest advocate, most dedicated reader, and kindest supporter. This book is a testament to her abilities as a teacher and mentor.

I am forever indebted to the Department of Social and Cultural Analysis (SCA) at New York University (NYU) where I worked for three years. I had the amazing luck of having Philip Harper, Carolyn Dinshaw, and Julie Livingston as mentors throughout my time in SCA. I learned so much from my colleagues at NYU about how to do the work we do with ethics and a commitment to justice, thank you to: Mike Amezcua, Liz Ellis, Irvin Ibarguen, Mireya Loza, Jennifer Morgan, Crystal Parikh, Mary Louise Pratt, Renato Rosaldo, Dean Saranillio, Nikhil Singh, Pacharee Sudhinaraset, and Simón Trujillo. I was able to benefit from a Manuscript Workshop funded by NYU Center for the Humanities, which brought together several NYU faculty members as well as Matthew Frye Jacobson and Julie Weise who both read my manuscript in full and whose insight made this a better book. I am especially grateful for the Latina faculty I met at NYU who taught me so much about scholarship, friendship, and mentorship: Cristina Beltrán, Arlene Dávila, and Josie Saldaña Portillo. Marty Correia and Kate Conroy, there are no words to express what our friendship has meant, most of all for bringing me Annise Weaver. Some colleagues transform into friends, and I am lucky to count Thuy Linh Tu and Heijin Lee among my friends who read my work, listened to my anxieties, and brought brightness to my days. Robyn d'Avignon, your friendship infused my life in New York with joy and made all of this possible.

In 2019, months before a global pandemic, I returned to the South to complete this book. My colleagues and friends at Duke University have been important parts of making Durham home and bringing this book project across the finish line. My colleagues in the History Department at Duke quickly became my new intellectual home. I am especially grateful to Juliana Barr, James Chappel, Calvin Ryan Cheung-Miaw, Thavolia Glymph, Evan Hepler-Smith, Reeves Huston, Gunther Peck, and Pete Sigal. I am indebted to several colleagues who read pieces of the manuscript and offered critical insight, including Nicole Barnes, Sarah Bruno, Sam Daly, Alicia Jimenez, Javier Wallace, and Emily Yun Wang. The Franklin Humanities Institute funded a book workshop that gathered Patrice Douglass, Sally Deutsch, Wesley Hogan, Adriane Lentz-Smith, Timothy Lovelace, Nancy MacLean, and Orin Starn along with outside readers Stephen Pitti and Natalia Molina. The comments from these readers helped me finally see light at the end of the tunnel. Several undergraduate re-search assistants assisted in completing this work and I am especially grateful to Hen Kennett, Isabel Lewin-Knauer, and Catherine Howard. My colleagues Jolie Olcott and Sally Deutsch both read this manuscript in its entirety more than once—their fierce mentorship for me as a junior faculty member has been a beacon. Patrice Douglass and Leo and Lathan D'Agostino became the core of our community in Durham, North Carolina, and their friendship throughout the pandemic kept us afloat.

I am fortunate to write alongside several amazing people at Duke University. These fellow writers saw me through every ache and pain as well as every joy and celebration of this project. Thank you to Jennifer Ahern-Dodson for your leadership of the Faculty Write Program; Monique Dufour for your consistent and human-centered support of faculty; and Adam Rosenblatt, Amy Sayles, Karin Shapiro, Melissa Simmermeyer, and countless others for walking along-side me as fellow writers. Cristina Salvador came to Duke and led the charge to start the Latinx Faculty Writing Program, and, with support from Duke's Office for Faculty Advancement, this group has become a constant source of accountability, support, and snacks.

Since I first met my editor, Mark Simpson-Vos, when I was still in graduate school, he has remained a perpetual cheerleader for this project and had faith it would come together even when I waivered. Jessica Newman stepped in as my developmental editor at a crucial time in the book process, and I am grateful for her editorial prowess and sense of levity when it came to tackling thorny issues.

Throughout my time working at the intersection of Latino history and Latino studies, I have had the immense fortune of getting to know several colleagues whose interventions and guidance are embedded in this book. A special thanks to Gerry Cadava, Perla Guerrero, Cindy Hahamovitch, Mike Innis-Jiménez, and Julie Weise, who have served as guides in how to work in this profession with intellectual rigor and a commitment to developing future generations of Latino scholars. This field has also given me many colleagues whose own research and friendship have shaped this book: Sophia Enriquez, Pablo Jose López Oro, and Yami Rodriguez. Sarah McNamara and Yuridia Rámirez have been devoted friends and colleagues since graduate school, and I am honored to have my work situated alongside theirs.

Mia Fortunato, Max Beshers, and Stephan Lefebvre have been constant com-panions on this journey from the earliest days of my PhD program through the completion of this book. Together we have built special connections that have withstood relocations, changes in jobs, and life's many challenges. Their friendship has sustained me in ways that are hard to express.

I am also grateful to the friends and family I gained through my marriage. I am especially thankful for Suzanne Hoyes for being the best hype-woman I could ask for, and to Shereé Dunston and Liz Espinoza for their friendship and support. I am also endlessly appreciative of the love and encouragement I have received from the Weaver/Arringtons who welcomed me into their Scrabble games, their road trips, and, most importantly, their family.

Thank you to my extended Shack family who kept me distracted with laughter during my long archival visits to Georgia and Texas: Richard, Jamie, and Bodhi Bubb; Landon Bubb; Lawson, James, Henry, Jackson, and Lincoln Little; Barbara Shack; and Lynda and George Streitenberger. Thank you for always having a place for me to stay and a family to come home to. My grandmother, Ruth Shack, has long been my hero. From her I learned to love art and to fight for justice.

My family's love is etched all over this book. My sister, Bianca Márquez, is a force of nature. She has listened to me lament setbacks and celebrate accomplishments all while remaining a constant source of positivity and humor. Every day she dedicates her life to progressive politics and combatting climate catastrophe. As I remain mired in history, she gives me hope that we can build a better future. Our relationship is truly the greatest gift I could ever ask for.

I first learned history from my father, Jaime Márquez, who taught us Jewish history with butcher paper and magic markers. He is a true intellectual who filled our home with books and lively dinner conversations. Day in and day out I watched him dedicate his life to ensure that my sister and I could achieve whatever we dreamed. I hope this book, and the life that I have made, serves as proof that his hard work has not been in vain.

My mother, Janice Shack-Márquez, has been an indefatigable source of love my entire life. From a very young age, she tried to teach me to be "good enough" and let go of perfectionism. As with many of life's best lessons, it took me too long to see the genius behind this—the fact that I was able to complete this book is evidence I've finally internalized her shared wisdom. Through it all, she has been my strongest champion, most dedicated editor, and a pillar of strength that holds our family together. I aspire to live a life as full of joy, love, and creativity as the one she has built.

Annise Weaver, building a life with you has been the greatest adventure. At the beginning of the pandemic, we moved our lives into a two-bedroom apartment in an unfamiliar city. Sharing a (too-thin) wall as we worked from home, I learned so much about what you do. Your relentless commitment to building healthy communities, to equity, and to racial justice remains a ceaseless wonder. There are no words to express the gratitude I feel for all the ways you have loved and supported me. When I think about this book, I am grateful for what it has helped make possible—it brought me to New York where I found you, and it took us to Durham, North Carolina, where we made a home with Junior. Our love is my greatest source of inspiration and endurance.

MAKING THE LATINO SOUTH

T he Soto family left San Antonio, Texas, in the late 1950s and moved to Rosedale, Mississippi, in search of better jobs and a better life. Daniel Soto, the family patriarch, was a trained electrician unable to find work in Texas—a fact he attributed to being Mexican. "We were trying to get out of Texas," his wife Alice Soto said, describing the decision to join her sister and brother-in-law who had already moved to the Mississippi Delta. Of his grandparents' experiences, Soto's grandson Richard Enriquez said, "There just wasn't a lot of opportunity for Mexicans down there [in Texas]." Like so many other Mexican and Mexican American people, the Soto family likely faced racial discrimination in Texas that took the form of residential segregation, limited job opportunities, separate and unequal accommodations, and daily encounters with racism.[1]

The Soto family was hopeful that the Mississippi Delta would offer more promising prospects. They were right. Daniel Soto quickly found steady and good-paying work in Rosedale, Mississippi. In Texas, Daniel was making thirty-five dollars a week and had to work multiple jobs; Alice worked for fifty cents an hour doing housework and babysitting. In Mississippi, Alice Soto remembered, "We were rich! He was making sometimes over one hundred dollars a week." In Texas, their high school–age daughter, Mary, was rejected by white students, while in Mississippi she quickly found friends among her white peers.[2]

In contrast with Texas, the Soto family found a new kind of racial acceptance in Mississippi. "[People were] very nice, very sweet, very friendly, very helpful," Alice remembered. "We didn't feel like outsiders at all."[3] The Latino community in Mississippi, unlike Texas, was small, as was the case in many southern states in the mid-twentieth century. The Sotos were part of a tight-knit Mexican community organized around the Catholic church. They gathered along with family and others in the Mexican and Mexican American community in each other's living rooms to share food, music, and revelry.

While arriving in Mississippi meant the Soto family had found greater economic opportunity, it also meant they had to learn a new set of rules regarding racial interaction. As in Texas, Jim Crow laws created separate and unequal

accommodations in nearly all facets of life. Mississippians had to choose between "white" and "colored" water fountains, hospitals, neighborhoods, and
store entrances. Although the Soto family was acquainted with their own version of Jim Crow in Texas, Mississippi's racial order functioned quite differently.
In Texas, "white" entrances were not for Mexicans, so when the Soto family
arrived in Mississippi, they initially used "colored" entrances; this was, after all,
the heart of Dixie during the height of Jim Crow.

The Sotos first confronted Mississippi's Jim Crow laws in a restaurant. Their
daughter Mary Enriquez (née Soto) described the experience: "Coming from
Texas [we were] used to not mingling. . . . You knew where you belonged and
you didn't cross the line." Because of their time in Texas, the Sotos initially used
"colored" entrances. They were immediately redirected to "white" entrances
by Black and white patrons alike. Describing one of these encounters, Alice
Soto said, "The Black side sent us to the white side, we didn't even know why."
When she asked, they said, "This is the Black side, you go to the white side."[4]
In the 300-mile sojourn east, the Soto family had gone from using "Mexican"
or "colored" facilities in Texas, to "white" ones in Mississippi. Their acceptance
in white spaces was not because Mississippi of the 1960s was a more racially
progressive space than Texas. Instead, it was because race worked differently
in this place.

The Sotos were not alone in contending with the complexity of Jim Crow.
When Manuel Aguirre, a Mexican American man born in Iowa, was transferred
to West Virginia during World War II, he recalled seeing something he "had
never seen before." "You couldn't sit no places," he recalled. "Whites and Blacks,
everything whites and Blacks. I went in the whites, I wasn't Black."[5] In his retelling, Aguirre chose "white" accommodations, not because he identified as
white, but because he was not-Black. While he was not "passing" as white, the
stories of non-Black Latino people like the Sotos suggest that white and Black
southerners did see them as racially distinct.[6] However, it was their perceived
non-Blackness rather than any claim to whiteness that afforded them access to
white spaces in segregation.

Jim Crow was surprisingly expansive for non-Black Latino people like
Aguirre and the Soto family; the same could not be said of Black Latino people
in the South. During World War II, Manny Diaz, an Afro–Puerto Rican soldier
from New York City, was stationed in Biloxi, Mississippi. While on furlough,
he and a group of friends went to a bar where the bartender refused to serve
him in the white section. Rather than be subjected to Jim Crow, Diaz left the

bar. Moments later he was followed by his friends, who had absconded with an empty beer bottle that they used to shatter the bar window before running away. Although the military may have categorized Diaz as "white," he was "colored" to the Biloxi bartender.[7]

When Latino people encountered Jim Crow, southern people and southern institutions sorted them into Black or non-Black. The South, therefore, laid bare an internal classification among Latino people as Black/not-Black.[8] The definition of whiteness (or non-Blackness) was capacious and could include non-Black Latino people like the Soto family and Aguirre. That capaciousness, however, had firm boundaries guarding against Black inclusion. The combination of the system of Jim Crow and the small numbers of Latino people in most of the South at this time meant that non-Black Latino people experienced relative racial freedom, whereas Black Latino people experienced none of that flexibility.

The acceptance of non-Black Latino people into white spaces was not a reflection of a racially progressive approach to *Latinidad* (or Latinoness). Instead, it was a deep commitment to the preservation of the anti-Blackness at the heart of Jim Crow.[9] The inclusion of non-Black Latino people should be seen as an extension of, rather than a challenge to, the project of white supremacy in the South.

Although non-Black Latino people like Aguirre and the Soto family used white entrances, attended white schools, and lived alongside white people in the Jim Crow era, this provisional whiteness would ultimately prove fleeting. Fifty years after the Soto family moved to the Southeast, life would look very different for those Mexican, Mexican American, and Latino people who migrated to the Deep South.

By the 1980s, southern states were home to thousands of Latino people as Latino immigrants arrived in huge numbers.[10] Since the 1980s, the US South has seen some of the fastest-growing Latino populations in the country. Between 1990 and 2000, this migration reached its peak as immigrants from Mexico and Central America flocked to the region. In that decade, the size of the Latino population increased by nearly 400 percent in North Carolina, 337 percent in Arkansas, 300 percent in Georgia, and 278 percent in Tennessee. In this time period, seven of the ten states with the fastest-growing Latino populations were below the Mason-Dixon Line. Alabama, South Carolina, and Tennessee all had more than 150 percent growth in their Latino populations during this time.[11]

As a result of this rapid demographic change, economic fluctuations in the region, and geopolitical shifts across the globe, the friendly welcome the Sotos received in Mississippi was gone by the new millennium. In the early 2000s, Mississippi was home to one of the most draconian anti-immigrant laws in the nation. Along with Georgia and Alabama, Mississippi passed harsh legislation that strove to make life as difficult and dangerous as possible for the thousands of new Latino migrants in their states. Undocumented immigrants were targeted for detention and deportation in all facets of daily life—at their children's schools, in hospitals, at traffic stops, and at their workplaces. The legislation authorized local police officers to question those who they suspected of being in the state "illegally"—a category that local officials seemed to interpret as synonymous with Latino.

Making the Latino South examines how non-Black Latino people lost their access to white privilege over the second half of the twentieth century. From the vantage point of living in the South in the 1940s, it may have appeared that non-Black Latino people would follow the Italians and Irish in becoming white. However, the confluence of demography, economics, and global politics thwarted that development.

This book is, therefore, less a history of "Latino" communities in the region and more a story of how this diverse group came to be seen as "Latino" and how southerners ascribed meaning to that categorization. By examining the evolving racial position of Latino people in the South between 1945 and 2010, *Making the Latino South* uncovers a very different timeline of Latino identity and community formation than elsewhere in the country. While most histories of Latino people put the development of Hispanic or Latino identity as early as the 1920s or 1940s, *Making the Latino South* shows that many parts of the South did not have coherent "Hispanic" racial categories until the 1980s. World Wars and the Great Depression, both of which played a massive role in Latino identity development elsewhere in the country, shrink in importance in the South. By the 1970s, as many of the biggest cultural and legal battles for Latino civil rights had already occurred elsewhere in the country, things were just starting to change for Latino people in the South.

Making the Latino South tells a new history of race in the post-1945 US South, one that uncovers the central role of Blackness in creation of the category of "Latino." This book shows that Latino populations (and other southerners) were often sorted into Black and non-Black. This resulted in the incorporation of non-Black Latino people into a provisional whiteness and of Black Latino people into Blackness. In telling the southern history of Latino people, this book casts new light on several of the most important moments in the history of race in the United States: Jim Crow, the civil rights movement, free trade, immigration, the September 11 terrorist attacks, and the economic recession.

Moving chronologically across the second half of the twentieth century, *Making the Latino South* examines how the racial position of Latino people in the US South changed over time. Traveling through Georgia, North Carolina, Alabama, Mississippi, South Carolina, Washington, DC, and other southern locales, it traces how, over this period, non-Black Latino people went from being racialized as "provisionally white" before the 1970s, to "hardworking immigrants" in the early 1990s, and eventually to being cast as "illegal aliens" in the post-9/11 period. Looking at the social, cultural, and political history of these populations, this book shows that race transformed dramatically for Latino people in the South between 1945 and 2010.

This shift was the most evident in many of the southern states that social scientists called "new destinations."[12] These southern new-destination locales are the geographic core of this book: Georgia, North Carolina, Alabama, Mississippi, South Carolina, and Washington, DC. These places all have in common small Latino populations in the postwar period followed by massive growth in the 1980s and 1990s. Because of this focus on sites with relatively small Latino populations before the 1980s, Florida and Texas appear throughout, embedded in the migration stories of many of those like the Sotos, but they are not central to the geography of this book.[13] Ideas about race were not, of course, hermetically sealed across state boundaries, and in parts of Texas and Florida, the racial landscape certainly looked much like it does in the rest of the Southeast. However, by focusing on the states with smaller Latino communities in the second half of the twentieth century, this book is able to trace how race was made and remade as demographics, politics, and social movements retooled the southern landscape.[14]

By tracing the shifting racial categorizations of Latino people from the 1940s to the present, we can see how race and racism are formed and reformed under demographic, cultural, social, and economic pressures. Race, as this book shows, was a category formed through several "racial projects."[15] Racial projects are different ways of representing, explaining, and defining the meaning of racial categories. Jim Crow, for example, sought to reestablish racial distinctions unmoored in the wake of emancipation. Years later, the creation of the "hardworking Hispanic" would legitimize hyperexploitation of Latino laborers under the guise of a celebration of the fictitious racial predisposition of Latino people to hard work. What it meant to be white, Black, or Latino was a historically and geographically constituted category, or as historian Thomas C. Holt writes, "Neither race nor racism can live independently of its social environments, the times and spaces it inhabits."[16] Race, therefore, was an embodied set of practices, an ideology, an identity, and a culture. It was an assemblage of social constructions with very material consequences.[17]

In the parts of the South examined in this book, Latino presence, in any sizeable amount, would be relatively new and would arrive onto a landscape built on Native American genocide and racial slavery, the results of which continue to shape the contemporary economic and political climate.[18] Despite that continuity, the South is a complex and ever-changing space with competing and overlapping political, cultural, social, and economic worlds.[19] The same region that has been home to some of the most violent white supremacist terror has also been the fertile ground from which emerged the most politically creative and effective social movements for social change.[20]

Making the Latino South interrogates how non-Black Latino people have lived within the category of whiteness and its connected logic of white supremacy. It examines how they simultaneously chafed against, benefited from, and participated in this southern system of whiteness. By focusing primarily on non-Black Latino people, the contours of southern racial ideologies become clear. Non-Black Latino people, who are often cast as "disruptive" to the Black/white binary, instead reveal the boundaries of whiteness, Blackness, and Latinidad. In fact, this history shows that this population of Latino people were not always as disruptive to the racial binary as imagined.

This book suggests that those who want to move "beyond" the Black/white binary underestimate the resilience, persistence, and capaciousness of that binary. Faced with an ostensibly non-Black, non-white population, those in the South found that their racial binary could bend to include Latinos without breaking. Southern Latino history suggests that whiteness, rather than a fixed category, has historically held a diverse range of non-Black people. Introducing Latino people to the history of the South shows that Latino people, before the mid-1970s, fit into racial binaries rather than disrupting them. *Making the Latino South* argues, therefore, that it is not possible to move "beyond" the Black/white binary, as many scholars are eager to do, without fully contending with the structural role that Blackness and anti-Blackness played in how race was made in the South.[21]

The stories of southern Latino people also allow us to think critically about Latino racial identity in the region. Instead of fixating on whether Latino people fit into a "binary" racial system, the South demands that we instead think critically about how this bimodal racial system has long incorporated Latino people—not as white people, not with a requirement to pass, but as Black and non-Black Latino people who were marked as racially distinct while at the same time being integrated into whiteness and Blackness. The South, therefore, shows how ideas about Latino people are made across time and space, and how anti-Blackness undergirds Latino racial formations.

Although Latino populations' racial position changed in the mid-1970s, what endured was the separate and unequal experiences of Black and non-Black Latino people. *Making the Latino South* probes this fracture around race within the Latino community. Looking at Latinos in the context of Jim Crow exposes the ruptures that divide this community along lines of race and color. In fact, reading Latinidad through the lens of southern history, at times, renders the category of Latino completely incoherent.

Latino Racial Formations

Because this project spans from the 1940s to the 2010s, we can categorize the Latino community in myriad ways. In this book, I use the term "Latino" to describe the diverse group of people from various Latin American origins in the United States. The use of "Latino" as a term, however, did not emerge in most places until the 1970s when largely Mexican and Puerto Rican populations were forming common cause against segregated housing, underresourced schools, and hyperpolicing.[22] Since then, this community has been described in several ways: Hispanic, Latino/a, Latin@, Latinx, and Latine.[23] The term "Latino" would certainly feel strange to those in the United States in the 1940s; in fact, it may even feel strange to members of that community today. It is my hope, however, that "Latino" allows the most people possible to see themselves reflected in the stories this book documents.

Latino as a category is not completely self-evident and contains important internal contradictions.[24] I want to make clear my conflicting investment in the term "Latino." It is a term that I use, and it is a term that this history challenges. "Latino" has long frustrated racial categories because of the varied people under the umbrella of Latinidad. Nowhere is that more evident than in the US South, where the racialization of some of the people in this diverse group has changed so much over this period, whereas others have faced anti-Blackness throughout this time.

The category of "Latino" has been critiqued by scholars and activists as a term rooted in the denial of Indigeneity and Blackness.[25] Scholars and activists argue that "Latino," as it exists in the contemporary imagination, represents a largely mestizo (racially mixed) population and eschews those members of the community who are Black and Indigenous.[26] The history of Latino people in the South affirms and extends this argument by demonstrating how the category of "Latino" is internally fractured along lines of race.

In the South, and in this book, the majority of the Latino people are of Mexican descent. However, these stories also include the histories of Latino people with origins in Puerto Rico, Central America, and South America. Of course, these Latino populations were often understood through the lens of Mexicanness because of the predominance of that population. But it is the shared experiences of these groups across divides of national origin that makes it necessary to think collectively about them as Latinos.

Given the predominance of Mexican and Mexican American populations, the long history of *mestizaje* looms large over the question of Latino racialization. Mestizaje, a Latin American racial ideology that sought to "improve the race" through racial mixture, was, at its core, focused on the erasure of Black and Indigenous Latin Americans. In this way, mestizaje, and many other Latin American ideologies of race, shared underlying white supremacist logic with US racial systems even if its goals for achieving these ends were quite different.[27] Latino migrants, therefore, came to the United States with their own deeply held ideas about race, color, and power. Those ideas were extended in the United States. As a result, "non-Black Latino" and "Black Latino" become important distinctions in this book project to examine not only how race operated in the US South but also how hemispheric forms of anti-Black racism are embedded in this story.[28]

Even with the necessary modifiers, the term "Latino" retains importance for the purposes of this project. The history of Latino people in the South suggests that the category "Latino" is both a project of Black and Indigenous erasure *and* a category that captures the shared experiences, communities formed, and linked identities of a group of people.[29] The use of the term acknowledges these overlaps and connections. Non-Black Latino people were racialized, and, at the same time, Black Latino and Indigenous people were subject to particular forms of oppression because of the racism they faced both from outside and within the Latino community.[30] The experiences of Black and Indigenous people, therefore, consistently reveal the boundaries of the category of "Latino." Turning to the South uncovers the limits of Latinidad and how Blackness in particular disrupts notions of unity.

The Latino South and the Work of Racial Binaries

Before the 1970s, most non-Black Latino people lived in the South as provisionally white. Some were easily welcomed, whereas others used what historian Julie Weise has called "the Mexican strategy" to claim—rather than eschew—their foreignness as a shield against racism by asserting cultural resonance between Mexico and the US South. For instance, in the early 1940s, when Lillian Marguerite Hollingsworth introduced her future husband Oswaldo Ramírez, a Mexican American man from Texas, to her self-described WASP (White, Anglo-Saxon, Protestant) family, she found little resistance. Lillian attributed the broader social acceptance of her husband and their marriage to the compatibility of "southern" and "Latin" culture. "In truth," Lillian said, "the Southern culture is very similar to the Latin culture." She noted that in both cases, patriarchal values policed the gender and sexuality of young people. "The girls are always chaperoned when there was high school dances," Lillian commented. "Parents were around. . . . Families meant a great deal." Additionally, Lillian maintained that family was central to both cultures. She said, "Families in the South [mirrored] the Latin community, that closeness."[31] In Lillian's assessment, these shared values linked southern and Latin culture and made Oswaldo such an easy fit into her family. Oswaldo Ramírez was able to make space in whiteness, not by attempting to erase his Mexicanness, but instead by showing the overlaps between "Latin culture" and the southern culture of Jim Crow.

Scholars have long debated whether the entrée into whiteness that some Latinos experienced reflected a strategic claim to whiteness or a deeply held belief. Some argue that, rather than an identification as white, this whiteness was a tactical way to fight against anti-Mexican racism.[32] Others emphasize Latino people's place in the long history of immigrants (both white and non-white) distancing themselves from Blackness as part of an aspirational path to whiteness.[33] Some scholars stress that the possibilities of whiteness that may have been present in the midcentury were foreclosed by the end of the 1960s, when growing Chicano, Puerto Rican, and Latino identities took hold in social movements.[34] Others still, recognize the yawning gap between the legal position of many Latino people as white (specifically Mexicans after the Treaty of Guadalupe Hidalgo in 1848, which guaranteed full citizenship and, by extension, legal whiteness) and the social realities of being Latino.[35] In this book, I suggest that the quest for whiteness remains elusive for many non-Black Latino people, both historically and contemporarily. However, their stories also suggest that, in the

South, successfully distinguishing themselves as "not Black" was the most important entry marker into many of the entitlements of whiteness.

With an emphasis on how the category of "Latino" developed in relation to Blackness, I also extend arguments that race is a relational formation. In this framework, race is a category necessarily defined by its relation to other groups. "Race," scholars Daniel Martinez HoSang, Natalia Molina, and Ramón A. Gutiérrez write, "does not define the characteristics of a person; instead, it is better understood as the space and connections between people that structure and regulate their association."[36] Similarly, Latino racialization is best understood in relation to other racial groups in the South during this time.[37] Latino southerners were racialized based on their proximity to or distance from Blackness rather than in isolation. Put differently, Latino people were racialized by Black and white southerners based on whether they were Black or not Black.

As the Ramírez family shows, this provisional whiteness was not about "passing" for white; rather it was a distinct category that did not conflict with access to many white institutions. Latino people were not assuming, and did not need to assume, "white" or Anglo identities to access these white spaces—they could come as they were. In 1943, when Juan Rivera applied to attend Duke University in Durham, North Carolina, administrators found themselves at an impasse trying to classify the Puerto Rican applicant. Dr. Joseph C. Robert, the assistant dean of the graduate school, responded to concerns about Rivera, noting, "When it comes to the man and his color I do not know whether or not he is white, but he says he is white. . . . You can obviously see," he continued, "that he is not entirely so. His skin is dark." However, Roberts noted that "sometimes their type has been accepted in the south [sic] as dark Spaniards." Despite his dark skin and "lively" hair, Rivera was admitted to Duke.[38]

Non-Black Latino people's provisional whiteness, Rivera's admission at Duke shows, was unstable and not a foregone conclusion. At times, their racial categorization was fleeting; it was shaped by their class, their Catholicism, their color, and their language. Although non-Black Latino individuals' ability to access some white spaces (e.g., country clubs, fraternal organizations) was limited, they were able to find footholds in the most critical institutions of whiteness in the Southeast: attending white schools, living in white neighborhoods, and intermarrying into white families.

Black Latino people had a very different experience of the South. Bob de Leon, an Afro-Puerto Rican from New York, was warned about Jim Crow by his older brother before he went to the South for military training. "Bob," his older brother said, "you're going to go into a situation . . . where people don't know the difference between Puerto Ricans and Negroes . . . so be careful. You're gonna have a lot of trouble."[39] His brother was right; Jim Crow did cause de Leon "a lot of trouble."

Black Latino people's confrontations with Jim Crow stood in stark contrast to the non-Black Latino people who often acquiesced to the racial order. Running late to catch a plane in Columbus, Georgia, de Leon ran into a bathroom without paying attention to the Jim Crow signage. Apparently, he had entered the white bathroom and was followed in by a state trooper who loomed over him as he relieved himself. De Leon responded to the state trooper's intimidation by saying, "You see something you like?" As the state trooper reached for his gun, one of the petty officers came in and retrieved de Leon to board the plane. Turning back, he watched the "huge state trooper putting his gun back into his holster" and thought, "He could have shot me."[40] In another incident, de Leon was mistakenly drinking from a "white" water fountain and was approached by a cop. De Leon, dressed in military uniform at the time, noticed the "white" sign as the cop arrived next to him. The police officer said, "You're not from around here, are you, boy?" De Leon responded by moving to the "colored" water fountain and then turned to the police officer to say, "You know, it tastes the same. I don't notice a difference, do you?"[41] The officer reached for his gun, but de Leon was able to defuse the situation and leave unscathed. Whether de Leon did or did not continue to earnestly make the same "mistake" of using white accommodations, his open defiance of white police authority when told to leave was a dangerous form of activism.

Examining Black and non-Black Latino people side by side lays bare the extent to which Latino subjectivity was defined not in relation to whiteness but instead to Blackness. In this book, therefore, I demonstrate how Latino people in the South were always understood through the register of Blackness. Blackness, in this text, is both a lived reality and a constellation of connected ideas. It is a set of real human experiences of Black southerners who daily moved through the South's racial order and who would lead social movements to dismantle de jure and de facto forms of discrimination. It is also diasporic in the way that Black migrants both forged community and movements and were simultaneously subsumed into many forms of the separate and unequal world of the South.[42]

Whiteness, like Blackness, has always been more than a comment on someone's physical appearance.[43] Like other racial categories, whiteness is a historically and geographically constituted category that was porous despite claims of purity.[44] Additionally, even as I show that "whiteness" could make space for non-Black Latino people, it remained a category defined by the strict policing of Blackness. Whiteness could remain somewhat fluid as long as it was tightly guarded against Blackness.

My framework for thinking about both whiteness and Blackness is also deeply influenced by those writing about the "afterlife of slavery" and its enduring role in shaping our contemporary racial landscape.[45] The legacy of racial slavery in the South looms large in the definition of these racial categories. Just as racial categories were forged in the United States in the transport and control of the labor of enslaved persons of African descent, it was the absence of racial slavery as a result of abolition that caused a reconstitution of racial and labor control through Black Codes, the spread of convict lease labor, and the institution of Jim Crow laws as methods to enshrine white supremacy and impede Black resistance.[46]

Race in the US South, once defined as free (white) and unfree (Black), was consecrated in Jim Crow under which divisions in public accommodations managed new meanings of racial difference. In the 1970s and 1980s that racial order would morph into a new "colorblind" regime of mass incarceration, police violence, and hyperexploitation under capitalism.[47] Blackness and the denial of Blackness forged in slavery continue to structure race in the South. This experience is drawn into sharp relief in the history of Latino communities in the South, whose differential experiences across lines of Blackness and non-Blackness demonstrate the diasporic reach of slavery's afterlife.

Jim Crow generally refers to the system of white supremacy from the late nineteenth century to the mid-twentieth century that managed racial difference in the postemancipation United States. The abolition of slavery removed racial distinctions between Black and white that had previously been defined by free and unfree.[48] Jim Crow, therefore, sought to reaffirm those racial boundaries that had become unmoored in the wake of abolition. Jim Crow, while traditionally associated with the US South, was not uniquely southern.[49]

The Jim Crow system operated on many levels. It was simultaneously a set of laws managing racial separation, a violent system of lynching and murder, a cultural practice enshrining racial hierarchy, a sexual regime that sought to preserve imagined white racial purity, a visual economy that marked the southern landscape, and a routine that influenced nearly every facet of southern life.[50] As a result, Latino southerners were regularly confronted with the nature of Jim Crow.

Although they were certainly acquainted with the white supremacist views that pervaded Latin America, this kind of stark separation was new to many.[51]

When Fernando Castro came to study in North Carolina from Costa Rica in the 1950s, he was surprised to find this intense segregation. In North Carolina, Castro sat in the back of the bus, as he often did in Costa Rica, only to find the driver urgently motioning to him. His limited English made the interaction challenging, but the driver clearly wanted him to know that he could not sit in the back of the bus and needed to move to the front.[52] The glaring separation was foreign to Castro, but he quickly learned through interactions with those like the bus driver. In moments like this, Latino people like Castro were learning how Jim Crow operated as they actively participated.

These encounters with Jim Crow offer a window into the way Latino people were racially sorted in this period. Jim Crow, a system ostensibly organized around Black and white racial difference, was in fact also managing a diverse group of Latino, Asian, and Native American people.[53] *Making the Latino South* uses the histories of Latino people in the South as a way to understand how those living in this era grappled with the racial diversity that existed in the region during the early twentieth century. It shows how Jim Crow was simultaneously capacious in its incorporation of non-white/non-Black groups and rigid in the tight boundaries managing Blackness.

Race and the "Nuevo South"

It was both push and pull factors that drew Latino people to the South starting in the 1970s and accelerating in the 1980s and 1990s. Economic crises in Mexico and civil wars in Central America pushed Latino people to come to the United States. Latino people were also drawn to a more peaceful life away from urban centers like Los Angeles, freedom from tight immigration enforcement in places like California and Texas, and access to some of the abundant jobs they heard about from friends and relatives who had already migrated to the South. Roshell, a Latina college student in Alabama, remembered that her family wanted to escape the fear of violence, the noise, and the immigration restrictions of Los Angeles. In 2003, only two years after moving from Mexico to Los Angeles, Roshell's parents relocated the family to Alabama. Los Angeles had "too much going on," she remembered. "They didn't want to raise the family there."[54] A combination of limited jobs for her father in California and the slower pace of life drew them to Alabama.

Southern industry also actively sought out Latino workers, offering incentives to existing Latino employees for every person they could recruit.[55] By 2002, southern companies like Gold Kist poultry were purchasing billboard space in

Tijuana, Mexico, advertising "*Mucho Trabajo en* Russellville, Alabama" [There's plenty of work in Russellville].[56] As southern manufacturing and food processing sectors continued to expand while other parts of the country saw slower economic growth, the South became an appealing place for Latino migrants.

During this period, race began to change for Latino southerners. The category of "Hispanic," which had been rarely used in the South before the 1970s, was beginning to cohere. By the 1980s and 1990s Latino people's provisional whiteness had been replaced by Hispanicness. As a result, at the exact moment that previously small southern Latino populations expanded into thriving and settled communities, the Southeast was beginning to coalesce with the Sunbelt—California, Arizona, and Texas—where anti-immigrant, and specifically anti-Mexican, racism had long flourished.[57]

It is perhaps surprising, then, that Latino people were not initially absorbed into western and southwestern ideas about race. Instead, in the 1980s and 1990s South, the "hardworking Hispanic" replaced what had formerly been a provisionally white racialization. Many southerners, particularly white southerners, in the 1980s and 1990s imagined Latino people as industrious, family oriented, and religious. This new racialization marked a departure from earlier forms of Latino racialization.

Before the 1970s, with some notable exceptions, there simply were not enough Latino people to meaningfully impact agricultural labor throughout the region. However, as weak labor and environmental standards drew manufacturing and food processing to the South in the 1970s and 1980s, there were a growing number of jobs, and Latino workers became the "lifeblood" of many of these industries.

The production of this category of "Hispanic" also served an economic utility. Race, both within and outside of the US South, has long been a tool to manage labor under capitalism.[58] In previous eras, the preservation of anti-Blackness through social and legal mechanisms of control served to immobilize Black workers and communities and cement their ties to plantations, sharecropping regimes, and prison labor systems. In this new era, Latinos came to occupy many of the same jobs Black southerners had previously held. As the southern economic system was becoming increasingly reliant on Latinos, it also became important for manufacturing and food processing companies to control the Latino labor population. The veneration by many southerners of the "hardworking Hispanic" naturalized a new kind of hyperproduction required by late twentieth-century and early twenty-first-century corporations.

By the early 2000s, the increased segregation, policing, and detention of non-Black Latino populations began to parallel much of what Black southerners were also facing. It seemed that for many non-Black Latino people in the messy middle, their racial position had shifted closer to that of Blackness, while remaining distinct. Importantly, Black Latino migrants faced both the increased vulnerability of being targets of anti-immigrant legislation and the enduring cruelty of anti-Blackness at the heart of the project of policing in America. The same fractures within Latinidad that existed in the pre-1970s South continued after large-scale migration. Many more non-Black Latino people were identifying with and finding community with their Black neighbors.[59] However, the abiding significance of Blackness in structuring race in the South produced specific challenges faced by Black Latino individuals that were rarely captured in emergent Latino social movements.[60]

Additionally, the modifier "hardworking" in the phrase "hardworking Hispanic" was doing important work to distance non-Black Latino communities from southern Blackness. Those praising non-Black Latino people often did so with thinly veiled comparisons to Black communities that were always in the shadows of this praise: non-Black Latino people were hardworking, whereas Black people were lazy, and non-Black Latino families celebrated family values, whereas Black families were dysfunctional.[61] Even if the majority of non-Black Latino people had moved decidedly away from any identification with whiteness, they maintained distance from Blackness.[62]

If race was changing quickly for Latino people, so too was racism. By the early 2000s, Latino populations were increasingly targets of racist and xenophobic attacks by right-wing politicians. The anti-Latino racism that had long existed outside of the region had finally caught up to southern Latino communities. As spokesperson for a Republican politician Lance Frizzel was quoted saying, "Regardless of the size of the local illegal immigrant population or a region's proximity to the US-Mexican border, in this election year 'every state is a border state.'"[63] As a result of the terrorist attacks on September 11, 2001, and the 2008 Great Recession, Latino people became villainized as "illegals," threats to national security, and drains on welfare resources and limited job supplies.

Book Structure

The book is organized chronologically with five chapters, each of which is centered around population movement and how Latino migrations—both large and small—uncover new truths about race in the US South. The first three chapters establish what provisional whiteness meant for Latino migrants before the mid-1970s. Chapter 1 examines Latino people in the 1940s in Washington, DC, focusing primarily on the case of Karla Rosel Galarza—a girl who was kicked out of a "colored" vocational school for not being Black. The story of Karla and her family's time in Washington, DC, opens up a broader understanding of the experiences of the larger Latino community in the District at the time. I argue that in this moment, Latino people were sorted into Black and not-Black. Non-Black Latino individuals accessed a "provisional whiteness" that gave them access to white Jim Crow institutions, whereas Black Latino individuals were Jim Crowed along with other Black populations. Black Latino and non-Black Latino people, this book shows, had very different experiences of race and Jim Crow.

Although non-Black Latino people were given access to parts of white society and provisionally accepted as white in most spaces, many white southerners remained deeply concerned with preserving and maintaining racial hierarchy, especially as growing Black freedom movements were challenging this system. Chapter 2 looks to South of the Border, a Mexican-themed rest stop opened in 1949 and situated between North and South Carolina. This chapter examines how white southerners used and transformed national scripts about Latinoness as a way to negotiate their anxieties about the swelling activism across the Southeast that would become the civil rights movement and, ultimately, end Jim Crow. As white locals surrounding the South Carolina rest stop felt the pressure of civil rights activism changing their world, they turned to fantasies about Mexicanness as a way to revel in the pleasures of racial subjugation.[64]

Chapter 3 takes the civil rights movement as its focus. It looks at Latino activists who traveled south to participate in the civil rights movement—more specifically, those working with the Student Nonviolent Coordinating Committee (SNCC). This chapter shows that in the Deep South of the 1960s, in a moment when war was being waged over the future of race, Latino communities were racialized much like Latino people in Karla Galarza's 1940s Washington, DC—non-Black Latino people were seen as racially distinct, but provisionally white, and Black Latino people faced Jim Crow alongside African Americans. This meant that non-Black Latino populations occupied a fraught and eventually contested space in southern civil rights organizing as the movement became increasingly focused on Black self-determination over the course of the late 1960s.

Chapter 4 serves as a crucial pivot in this historical narrative. It was in the post–civil rights movement era that Latino people first emerged as a cohesive non-white racial group and moved from provisionally white to racially other when they became "Hispanic." This coincided with a rapid increase in Latino migration to the region to work in the expanding manufacturing and food processing sectors. Although Latino people had always been racially distinct— that is, they were never passing as white—in the 1980s and 1990s, they lost privileges of whiteness and emerged as a marginalized racial group in the region. As this chapter shows, this initial racialization contained the veneer of a positive welcome. Racialized by their employers as "hardworking Hispanic immigrants," Latino migrants began to lay claim to their new southern home as they embraced and extended the category of "hardworking."

Chapter 5 represents yet another moment of transformation—as perceptions of Latino people changed from hardworking immigrants to "illegal aliens." This chapter looks at the first two waves of anti-immigrant legislation enacted in the South to show how race changed for Latino communities in 2001 after September 11 and again during the Great Recession in 2008–9. During this period, Latino people shifted from being seen as "hardworking" to "illegal" and were subjected to a proliferation of laws that made daily life more dangerous all over the country—but especially in the Southeast. Despite the many changes in Latino racialization over the second half of the twentieth century, both color and Blackness continued to structure racial hierarchies within the Latino community.

The history of Latino people offers a new and complex way of understanding the history of race in the South. Latino populations were victims of, participants in, and on the frontlines of fighting white supremacy throughout the history of the US South. Latino people were implicated in all parts of southern history, both radical and racist. They were fighting Jim Crow, they were benefiting from Jim Crow, they were profiting from Sunbelt expansion, and they were being exploited by the growing food processing and manufacturing sectors in the region. It is not a monolithic past, and it is one that refuses simple narratives about race. Rather, it is a more tangled web of alignments and realignments with racial categories in the region. Latino people have all of these southern legacies and get to choose which legacies they want to mobilize as they imagine their southern futures.

■ ■ ■ ■ ■ ■ ■ ■ ■ ■ ■ ■ ■ ■ ■

CHAPTER ONE

Not a Negro

Latinos and Jim Crow in 1940s Washington, DC

On April 12, 1947, *Chicago Defender* writer Joe Shephard wrote a front-page story in one of the largest Black periodicals in the country about a challenge to segregation in the nation's capital. The article, "Girl Jolts D.C. School System," told the story of the strange case of, as he put it, "Jim Crow in reverse." This case, he continued, "resulted in the barring of a white girl from a Negro vocational school." Shephard wrote, "Miss Karla Rosel Galarza, 22-year-old daughter of the educational adviser to the Pan American Union, is a native-born American of Mexican descent. . . . [She] entered the Margaret Murray Washington Vocational School in February to take a course in dress designing under Miss Cordelia Wharton." A month after her arrival at Margaret Murray Washington, Dr. Garnet C. Wilkinson, the assistant superintendent in charge of "Negro" schools in the District of Columbia, called Karla in for a meeting where he told her that "she was not eligible to attend that school because of her race." Shortly after that meeting, she was formally expelled from the school because she was, as Wilkinson put it, "not a Negro."[1]

Karla was, in fact, not Black, but her whiteness was still suspect to many. Shephard, for example, calls her both "white" and "of Mexican descent" in the same story. Karla Galarza was the stepdaughter of Ernesto Galarza, a famous farmworker organizer and Popular Front writer, whose star was on the rise when his family moved from California to Washington, DC, in 1947. Despite news reporting and suspicions of the school board, she was, in actuality, white. Karla's mother Ruth Mae was white and her biological father, who passed away when she was a year old, was also white.[2] Karla was later adopted and raised by Ernesto Galarza. No evidence suggests, however, that anyone on the school board or in the local media knew this fact. In addition, no evidence suggests that Ernesto Galarza shared this information. As a result, many assumed Karla was the biological daughter of Ernesto Galarza. Presumed to be Mexican

Karla Rosel Galarza.
Associated Press.

American, Karla and her family navigated the school expulsion with no known mention of her natal whiteness.

Unlike other desegregation cases, this was not a clear-cut issue of someone attending the "wrong" school. Given the assumption by many that Ernesto Galarza was her father, a fact he seemingly never refuted, she was a presumably Mexican American student being kicked out of a "colored" school and placed into a "white" school. Her story ran counter to the dominant narrative of Latino education in the 1940s, which highlighted Latino students as victims of segregated school systems in places like California and Texas.[3]

Of course, Karla's exclusion from the Margaret Murray Washington Vocational School paled in comparison to that of the Black students in Washington, DC, who had been shut out from educational opportunities their entire lives. Examining Karla's story is not an effort to reclaim her as a civil rights icon, to extoll the struggles of non-Black Latino people in the District, or to suggest this mirrors in any way the very real forms of segregation many Black people were facing in Washington, DC, and non-Black Latino people were facing elsewhere in the country. Instead, her story helps to uncover how southern racial hierarchies evolved to incorporate non-Black Latino people in the nation's capital.

Alongside the stories of other Latino people who lived in the District in the same moment, the Galarza family, school officials, local and national media, and activists all struggled to resolve the internal contradictions in the racial discourse surrounding the Karla Galarza case. The Galarzas entered a world that was ostensibly sorted into "Black" and "white" by laws, daily practice, and consumer culture. However, the growing Latin American population (along with migrants from other nations) revealed the dual capaciousness and rigidity of this racial system in the face of Black and non-Black Latino arrivals.

The Latino history of 1940s Washington, DC, shows how Latino people were racialized under Jim Crow, what their relationship to the color line was, and why their racialization differed so considerably from their Latino counterparts elsewhere in the country during this time. Washington, DC, in the 1930s and 1940s was, as Clinton Howard, the great-nephew of a Howard University founder, referred to it, "the most southern city north of Richmond."[4] Although the city differed from many states in the South, its history with slavery, emancipation, Reconstruction, and Jim Crow produced important political, economic, and social similarities with the rest of the region.[5] Those in the District, as was the case with many other southern cities at the time, had little history with Latino populations and, as such, were in the midst of defining how Latino people would fit into the South.

Karla Galarza and her experiences in 1940s Washington, DC, mirrored those of a diverse group of Latino people, including Venezuelans, Bolivians, Costa Ricans, and Mexican Americans. These new populations collided with the Jim Crow system that governed the District. Tracing Karla's story alongside actual Latino people shows how non-Black Latino people were understood through a mosaic of racial categorizations, including color, phenotype, ancestry, family, language, citizenship, and, perhaps most important, their proximity to or distance from Blackness.

The Galarza family, like many of the ambassadorial class, were part of a much smaller migration than the kinds of labor migrations traditionally associated with Latino history. Unlike many other Latino communities in the United States at the time, this was a fairly diverse population in terms of country of origin. Latino people of Mexican and Caribbean descent seemed to represent the largest population, but there was also a contingent from Central and South America. They generally came for prestigious careers, but non-Black Latin American migrants also came to attend southern universities, were able to enroll in white schools, and were able to access social spaces Black people could not.[6] For the Galarza family, and other members of the District's Latino elite, their class background certainly shaped their ability to access whiteness, but class alone does not explain the inclusion of non-Black Latino people into provisional whiteness.

The stories of these Latino populations in the South are representative of only a small fraction of Latino people in the United States at this time. The 1940 census indicates that Latino people were living throughout the Washington, DC, metropolitan area, including in segregated white neighborhoods.[7] This included at least 720 "white [individuals] of Spanish mother tongue" in 1940.[8] Although it is likely that inconsistent census records have undercounted the total number of Latino and Latin American people in DC, it never paralleled the larger-scale migrations seen in other parts of the country. Juana Campos, for example, remembered there was only one "Latin grocery store," Casa Peña, when she arrived in the 1940s, and it largely catered to the diplomatic community.[9] Although another grocery store, La Sevillana, would open a few years later, the Latino world at this time was a far cry from the Washington, DC, of the 1980s and 1990s that contained a robust, and growing, Latino population.

Washington, DC, however, was not alone as a southern city with a growing Latino population. Other southern port cities like New Orleans were also home to a rising international population, which included a diverse group of Latino people. Like Washington, DC, New Orleans had a noted concentration of white-collar workers: nearly 45 percent of the Mexican-descent population was working in white-collar jobs in 1920 and 32 percent in 1930. Historians have found that Mexicans and Mexican Americans lived as "Europeans" in those cosmopolitan urban centers.[10]

Black and non-Black Latino people were incorporated into, rather than disrupting, the racial logic of Jim Crow.[11] Non-Black Latino people, like Ernesto Galarza, were afforded a similar "provisional whiteness" that made it possible for them to benefit from the "wages" of whiteness: they lived in white neighborhoods, they went to white schools, and they were able to accrue the associated benefits of whiteness. This provisional whiteness also included the delicate dance many Latino people in the South had to perform to be racially legible as well as the moments of racial exclusion they experienced in some social situations. Some faced discrimination within those white schools and neighborhoods or found themselves excluded from certain white social spaces.

Black Latino people, however, had very different experiences of Jim Crow than non-Black Latino people. Instead, they found that their Blackness, rather than their Latinidad (or Latinoness), was the most important factor shaping their racialization. This is not to say that their being Latino did not matter; it was just that their Blackness mattered more. In this chapter, I illustrate the central role of Blackness in shaping racial formations in the region. Rather than lingering on the question of whether non-Black Latino people were "white," I show that Latino people did not need to be white to access key benefits of whiteness—they just needed to be not-Black.

Latin American immigrants were not unfamiliar to racial hierarchy from their countries of origin.[12] Latino people also brought racial ideas with them from Latin America to the United States.[13] Each Latin American country had its own particular racial composition and history that resulted in distinct forms of inclusion and exclusion, but they shared with the United States a history of anti-Black and anti-Indigenous racism rooted in legacies of slavery and settler colonialism.[14] Although Jim Crow posed a new kind of strict separation with which they may not have been accustomed, the underlying beliefs about race and power were not entirely foreign. For those immigrating from Latin America, the strict racial separation in the Jim Crow South was new for many. When Juana Campos arrived in Washington, DC, in the 1940s, she recalled that "people . . . were separated like tuberculosis patients, Black and white apart."[15] These rigid forms of separation had to be learned by the new Latino immigrants to the city.

For non-Black Latino people, their encounters with Jim Crow showed that Washington, DC, stood in stark contrast to the experiences of non-Black Latino people elsewhere in the country.[16] Non-Black Latino people in DC were experiencing a provisional whiteness, while nascent Chicano activism was beginning to foment in the West and Southwest. The Mexican and Mexican American community in California at this time also fought against school segregation. Most notable among these battles was *Mendez v. Westminster* (1947), which would strike a decisive blow against the segregation of non-Black Mexican and Mexican American pupils in schools.[17] *Mendez* ruled that Sylvia Mendez, the school-age daughter of Gonzalo Mendez, could not be segregated into remedial "Mexican" schools as had been the practice in many California communities.[18]

In a remarkable confluence, 1947, the year of the *Mendez* decision, was the same year that Karla Galarza was kicked out of Margaret Murray Washington Vocational School for being "not-Black." At the moment Mexicans and Mexican Americans in California were fighting in the federal courts in *Mendez* to get out of segregated "colored" schools, Karla was being forcibly placed into a "white" segregated school.

The experience of Latino people in Washington, DC, also ran counter to the many Latino communities reshaping urban centers in the 1940s.[19] Those in New York, Chicago, and other urban centers faced residential segregation and racial violence.[20] Although Latino people were often racialized as non-white in US cities, they had a wide range of experiences.[21] As a result, during this time, Latino people in urban centers began organizing into social movements to combat the racism they faced.[22]

Ernesto Galarza was part of this growing cohort of Mexican American activists and intellectuals who were confronting the issues of race, labor, and inequality for Mexican Americans in the United States. Galarza graduated college and eventually earned both a master's degree and a doctorate.[23] Despite his elite education, Galarza learned about residential and labor segregation firsthand when his family struggled to find decent housing and he labored as a farmworker alongside Mexicans and Mexican Americans in the fields of California.[24]

Ernesto Galarza. Courtesy Special Collections and College Archives, Occidental College, Los Angeles.

During his graduate education, Galarza became an increasingly important Popular Front labor intellectual as he published pieces about the brutality of agricultural labor for Mexican Americans in the West and Southwest.[25]

His work around labor inequality in the United States is what eventually brought Galarza to Washington, DC. He began working with labor organizer Luisa Moreno at the Pan American Union (now known as the Organization of American States) in the mid-1930s.[26] In 1936, he and his wife moved to Washington, DC, where he began his job at the Pan American Union as a research associate in education. Galarza quickly climbed the ranks to become the organization's first director of the Division of Labor and Social Information.

In his role at the Pan American Union, Galarza was part of a growing diplomatic class in Washington, DC. Having emerged from World War II as a world superpower, the international profile of the capital had grown, and many international and domestic people of color were settling in the District.[27] The growing international population, as much as it chafed against the rules of Jim Crow, would ultimately find a settled place within this racial system.

Jim Crow in Washington, DC

In the 1940s, despite the increasingly urban and cosmopolitan nature of Washington, DC, the city was deeply entrenched in Jim Crow segregation.[28] Like the rest of the South, Black Washingtonians faced Jim Crow limitations about where they could live, work, and play.[29] A National Capital Housing official explained that, in the 1940s, "segregation [was] the accepted pattern of the community."[30] The *Norfolk Journal and Guide* pointed to the injustice of having Jim Crow in the nation's capital, ostensibly a beacon for democracy: "It is a galling and widely-known fact," the article read, "that in this city where is located the head of the government of the United States of America, the vaunted greatest democracy on earth, the evils of segregation are just about as foul in their existence as they are in the backwards regions of the Mississippi Delta."[31] Comparing Washington, DC, to what many at the time saw as "the most Southern place on Earth"[32] was more than rhetorical flair.

The segregation in Washington, DC, was deeply engrained and had profound consequences for Black residents of the city.[33] In 1948, 30 percent of the city was Black, yet 70 percent of low-income housing was occupied by Black residents. Black Washingtonians represented 60 percent of tuberculosis deaths, Black babies born in 1946 were almost twice as likely to die as white babies, and Black mothers were six times more likely to die than white mothers.[34] Jim Crow in the District, as in the rest of the South, was quite literally killing its Black residents. The *Washington Star* newspaper noted that "the Confederacy, which was never able to capture Washington during the course of [the Civil] war, now holds it as a helpless pawn."[35]

Inequality became even more entrenched in the Washington metropolitan area in the 1940s as a result of the confluence of the influx of southern African Americans fleeing the Deep South in the Great Migration and white families moving to the District's newly established suburbs in Virginia and Maryland. The federally financed expansion of the suburbs was foreclosed to African Americans who were restricted from living in these neighborhoods through practices of redlining and racially restrictive covenants.[36] This influx of Black migrants concurrent with white flight meant that desperately needed tax revenue was evacuating the city at the same time that large numbers of Black residents were settling in. As a result, white schools were sparsely attended, while Black public schools were often overcrowded.[37]

The post–World War II era also signaled a decline in status for Black Washingtonians and the further entrenchment of segregation in everyday life. The small civil rights gains made during the war were systematically rolled back as troops began returning home. Stores that had begun serving Black customers during the war were pressured to return to segregated service. In 1945, the DC Board of Recreation reinforced its commitment to segregation policy in public recreational facilities.[38] The Fair Employment Practices Committee was shuttered in 1946 after segregationists successfully campaigned against the organization.

Latino people, therefore, began to arrive in the District at a time when Black and white Washingtonians were locked in a struggle to define the future of race there. The 1930s and 1940s were a time of robust political activism for the Black freedom struggle in Washington, DC.[39] Nationally, World War II was a critical turning point as activists used the war as a way to demonstrate on an international scale the hypocrisy of fighting fascism abroad and preserving Jim Crow at home.[40] Indeed, activists waged a Double V campaign hoping to achieve the twin victories of defeating fascism abroad and Jim Crow at home.[41]

Latino People under Jim Crow's Washington, DC

The Galarzas were not the only Latino people in Washington, DC, at the time, and these communities continued to grow in the nation's capital in the postwar era. The District represents a special case of southern urbanism that offers important insight into Latino racial formations in the Jim Crow era. As the United States' presence on the international stage grew in the wake of World War II, Washington, DC, became home to several new embassies and international organizations.

Because so much of the District's Latino community was affiliated with the foreign service, embassies became important social hubs for Latino people. Ramberto Toruella recalled that "the only Latinos in this town were embassy personnel, the support staff of the embassy. So we grew up with all the embassies."[42] When any Latin American embassy would throw a party, many local Latino people would flock to attend. Toruella's comments suggest that both embassy personnel and support staff were drawn into the orbit of these gatherings, indicating that even if there were not deep cross-class relationships, there were moments of identification among Latino people across class.

A diverse cross section of migrants accounted for the District's earliest Latino community, and the social scene reflected that diversity. Gatherings included fundraisers such as one in Fairmount Heights, Maryland, that featured performances of Mexican, Dominican, and Cuban dances and booths staffed by various Latin American members of the community.[43] Other celebrations marked important dates like the celebration of the Dominican Republic's Independence Day, which included a full guest list from the United States, Dominican Republic, Peru, Mexico, Cuba, and Puerto Rico.[44]

Class likely played a role in why so many Latin Americans were able to access elite and segregated spaces. This, after all, was a particular kind of migration that drew economic and intellectual elites from Latin America and across the United States. However, when it came to questions of racial segregation, non-Black Latino people across the class spectrum were categorized as white. Among those categorized as white were the working-class Latin Americans who found jobs as support staff in embassies and in the homes of elite Latin Americans. This included Providencia Marquez, twenty-four, who was born in Puerto Rico and worked as a secretary at the Pan American Union. She lived with her sister, Elizabeth, who worked as a secretary at the Embassy of Paraguay.[45] Judiline Iglesias, twenty-eight, and her sister also came from Puerto Rico to work as secretaries at the Pan American Union.[46] It also included Mexican-born Francisco Ledesma who worked as a "servant/footman" at the Peruvian embassy and lived with two European immigrant women who also worked at the Peruvian embassy as a tutor/governess and a cook.[47]

Black Latino people more often forged community with African Americans as a product of both the rich African American community and life in Washington, DC, and the exclusion they faced.[48] When Evelio Grillo, a Black Cuban boy from Tampa, Florida, moved to Washington, DC, he attended "colored" schools. He also reveled in the opportunity he found in the city to immerse himself in the Black community. Unlike Tampa where his Cubanness and Blackness produced internal and external conflict for the young Grillo, in the District, he was, as he described it, "free to be unambiguously Black."[49]

Washington, DC's African American community was also a culturally vibrant and politically powerful community that many Black Latino people were excited to join. As sociologist Ginetta Candelario describes of Dominicans' identification with the District's African American community in the 1940s, "In Washington D.C. there was and continues to be a structural incentive to Black self-identification."[50] The same influx of southern Black migrants and the exodus of white people to the suburbs that produced overcrowding in the schools also meant that African Americans maintained a numerical majority in the city and, therefore, were able to mobilize and win some political power. They held, for example, many local positions of power, and several Black institutions, like Dunbar High School and Howard University, were producing the next generation of the Black elite. For this reason, Candelario argues, Dominicans in Washington, DC, identified as Black nearly twice as often as Dominicans in New York.[51] A fusion of racial exclusion because of their Blackness and the exciting dynamism of the District's African American community drew Black Latino people to identify as Black.

Remaking Race: The Galarzas in Washington, DC

Throughout this time period, Washington, DC, and much of the US South lacked a coherent or consistent racialization of non-Black Latino people. As a result, Latino people experienced both increased access to white spaces and individual moments of exclusion and discrimination. Jim Crow also operated on myriad levels, so although non-Black Latino people may have been permitted access to white schools and white neighborhoods, they also were denied access by individual hotel clerks, restaurant managers, and neighbors who served as agents of Jim Crow.

In Washington, DC, non-Black Latino people were often able to find a home in whiteness, but they did at times face prejudice. A *Chicago Defender* report on the mistreatment of foreign dignitaries recounted the story of a "distinguished Bolivian educator who was invited to Washington by the State department on a good-will tour." However, because the man was "an Indian and dark of skin," the journalist continued, "our Bolivian educator should have been informed that our brand of good-will stops at the restaurant door or the hotel clerk's office in Washington." Unaware of this, the Bolivian educator had attempted to eat at a DC restaurant where he was refused service. The report also details the story of an "influential Puerto Rican Senator" whose visits to Washington had to be carefully choreographed by his host, a resident commissioner in the District, who struggled to find a place for him to stay. "On one visit [he stayed with] a private family in Alexandria. On another, a Puerto Rican Newspaperman took him into his home. On a third, the Commissioner asked the Senator to sleep on the couch in his office."[52]

Elizabeth "Betita" Martínez faced similarly paradoxical forms of inclusion and exclusion in Washington, DC. Born in the District in 1925, she remembered what she called the "bizarre" context of Washington, DC, which had, at the time, Betita recalled "about 20 Mexicans [in] it, maybe 25 [and] no Mexican restaurant." Her father was a dark-skinned Mexican man, and like the Bolivian official, he also faced Jim Crow exclusion. During a trip downtown when a young Martínez and her father attempted to sit in the front of the bus, they were sent past rows of empty seats to the back of the bus in accordance with Jim Crow segregation. When Mártinez asked her father why they were unable to sit in the front, he quickly hushed her, "I'll tell you later, I'll tell you later."[53]

Her story, along with the story of the Bolivian official, demonstrated that color played an important part in shaping Latino people's acceptance into certain social institutions. When telling the story, Mártinez emphasized her father's dark skin as the cause for this Jim Crow treatment. Additionally, the Bolivian official was singled out as being "of dark skin." These moments of color-based exclusion, while certainly painful, were rare and were often resolved through diplomatic ends.

However, even Betita, who was lighter skinned than her father, remembered feeling different. "People would sort of look at me," she remembered. Students in her elementary school class asked, "Are you Hawaiian or something?" and Betita responded, "No I'm Mexican," which was met with confusion. In another story, she recalled how the little white girl next door was forbidden to play with her because she was Mexican.[54]

Betita's story, however, demonstrated the conflicted forms of whiteness Latino people could experience in Washington, DC. Many of Betita's stories of social exclusion occurred in white spaces. Betita attended all-white schools from kindergarten through college. The little girl who lived next door was white, because Betita's family lived in an all-white neighborhood. Although some of Betita's stories point to her racial difference from her white peers, they also position her firmly within white Jim Crow institutions that were tightly policed through school segregation and racially restrictive covenants. Karla Galarza endured similar forms of social exclusion, and, like Mártinez, was still able to attend white schools.

The two young women also shared a relatively elite background. The schools they attended, the neighborhoods they lived in, and the education they both received belied a level of class privilege that was not representative of the majority of Latino people in the United States at this time. However, as previously noted, class alone cannot adequately explain the way non-Black Latino people were able to navigate southern racial systems. The totality of Jim Crow meant that working-class and elite Latino people alike interfaced with questions of racial sorting, and they shared, across class divisions, the experience of provisional whiteness.

Like Betita, Karla Galarza, despite her access to provisional whiteness, understood how racial prejudice functioned. Karla's daughter, Lori Pepe, recalled that Karla had grown up hearing stories from Ernesto about the ways Mexican people were taken advantage of through labor exploitation. Karla learned from Ernesto that it was important to "stand up for yourself as a human being and for everybody else."[55] At this time Ernesto Galarza was an established leader in the movement for racial and labor justice. Her identity, then, was likely influenced by her father's commitment to combatting anti-Latino racism and broader commitments to social justice.

For Galarza, the treatment of braceros, those workers from Mexico who came on temporary work visas as part of a wartime labor program, was a stark example of the regimes of racialized labor that targeted Mexicans and Mexican Americans.[56] Galarza's work, his politics, and his increasingly public persona suggested that he saw himself as in struggle with working-class Mexican Americans. During the 1930s and 1940s in the West and Southwest, as other historians have noted, racial solidarity was growing along with some of the earliest expressions of what would become Chicano nationalism.[57] Galarza was influential in the nascent Chicano organizations, suggesting his racial politics were aligned with other Mexican Americans who saw racism (alongside imperialism and capitalism) as an oppressive force that needed to be dismantled. However, when he first arrived in Washington, DC, he found his Mexicanness meant something different from what it did in California.

Karla and Betita's families shared another important distinction—both sets of parents had entered into interracial marriages between Latino men and white women. It is significant that non-Black Latino people were marrying white southerners without the pushback one might have expected given the resistance to interracial marriages between Mexican and white couples elsewhere in the country.[58] In Washington, DC, white people's fears of interracial sex were evident at a public hearing about integrating the District's recreational facilities. Gordon M. Atherholt, president of the Northwest Citizen's Council, testified that "members of the Negro race" had "a high prevalence of tubercular and social [venereal] diseases." As a result, "The joint use of facilities . . . would present a potent factor for the spread" of these conditions. One DC resident at the same forum, Mrs. Werner M. Moore, worried that intermingling in recreational spaces could lead to interracial sex and "the tragedy of mongrel children."[59] Despite the feverish anxieties about miscegenation, evidence suggests that Latino people occupied racially marked places within southern white families (both in the District and elsewhere in the region).[60]

The ability of Latino and white people to marry was not a result of the former's ability to "pass" as white. For example, Texas-born Florentino Samarripa, age thirty-two, was marked in the census as "Mexican," while his wife,

Catherine Samarripa, age twenty and born in Maryland, was marked as "white." The couple had two children, Consuelo and Rudolph, who were marked as "Mexican." For at least one census taker, Mexican and white were not synonymous. Unlike other Latino people who were marked as white, the Samarripas were treated as an interracial couple, and as a result, the race of their children followed rules of hypodescent. Florentino, who worked a white-collar job for an oil-refining company and lived with his white wife in a white neighborhood, found that his racial difference was passed down to his children. By categorizing the family this way, the census taker built into the official record a personal vision of the boundaries of racial difference and interracial marriage.[61]

Thus, despite the repressive and exacting miscegenation laws applied to African Americans, non-Black Latino intermarriage with whites represented a fairly common phenomenon under Jim Crow. In historian Julie Weise's analysis of marriage patterns of Mexican and Mexican American men in New Orleans, she found that by 1930, 41 percent of Mexican and Mexican American men had US-born white wives and 17 percent of Mexican and Mexican American women had US-born white husbands.[62] A broader look at the 1940 census suggests that Weise's findings apply to many states in the South.

Racial categorizations, as the census records in Washington, DC, show, were often insufficient to capture the Latino population. For example, Arnoldo Gutierrez, a Nicaragua-born crew chief for the US Army Air Corps, was marked as "Nicaraguan and white," and his wife Victoria, a white woman born in Georgia, was marked as "white."[63] Their daughter Rumalda, seventeen, who was born in Georgia, was marked as "Nicaraguan and white." Both their second daughter, Leonor, fifteen, and their son, Arnoldo V, thirteen, were initially marked as "white," but then "white" was crossed out. Their youngest son, Ajenor, nine, was marked as "Nicaraguan."[64] Notably, "Nicaraguan" has never been a racial categorization for the census.

The census taker who categorized this family produced four different racial categorizations within one family. The additions, revisions, and erasures necessary to place the Gutierrez family illustrate that, for this census taker, race was a slippery category that required careful mediation. However, even if the racial markers on the census seem to suggest that Latino people were pushing at the boundaries of Jim Crow, the ability of Arnoldo and Victoria to be able to marry and live together in a white neighborhood suggests that Arnoldo's racial difference, in fact, could be managed by Jim Crow.

This seeming paradox of exclusion and inclusion meant that non-Black Latino people experienced a provisional whiteness in Washington, DC, and much of the South. The ability of many non-Black Latino people to evade Jim Crow treatment demonstrates the capaciousness of Jim Crow. The same Latino people who would have likely been barred from "white" entrances in California and Texas were able to find relative freedom in the Jim Crow racial order. A diverse group of people could seemingly access key benefits of whiteness without being seen as fully white. That flexibility did not extend to Black Latino people or to African Americans.

In contrast, Black Latino people had different experiences of the District's Jim Crow order. Fatima Cortez was born in 1945 in Washington Heights, New York. She attended school with a diverse cross section of New York's upper middle class, including two light-skinned Dominican girls (the goddaughters of a member of the family of Dominican dictator Rafael Trujillo), a Korean girl, and a Filipina girl. Cortez was Afro-Puerto Rican. When her high school took a trip to Washington, DC, she was barred from attending because she could not stay in the all-white hotel the school had selected. Even in her racially diverse group, Cortez's Blackness prevented her from staying in the hotel. Cortez was destroyed. When her mother spoke to her about the incident, she lamented, "That's just how white people are." But "they're [the other students] not white," Cortez responded. "Well," her mother said, "that's how they're considered."[65]

Washington, DC's Black Latino communities developed strategies for navigating Jim Crow. Ramberto Toruella, a Black Dominican growing up in the District in the 1940s, recalled that his mother would caution him and his sister to "never speak English in public. Always speak Spanish." When they went to a restaurant that did not serve the "colored" population, the family would speak Spanish at which time the waitress would realize, as Toruella put it, "Oh, they're not colored; they're foreigners. You can feed them."[66] This treatment was not reserved to Black Latino people, and other Black visitors tried to use their foreign status to gain access to white spaces. When four students from the British West Indies sat at a DC lunch counter, the waitress informed them they "would have to stand to be served." However, once they produced their British diplomatic passes, the waitress apologized, remarking she did not realize they were "not niggers."[67] The story of these students demonstrates how foreignness could offer, at times, some protection from segregation.

Other non-Black Latino people also used Spanish as a way to move through Jim Crow. Rather than trying to hide their racial difference, some Latino people actively invoked their difference as a form of protection. When a Spanish woman living in Washington, DC, was hosting the daughter of the minister of education from a Central American republic, she was faced with a challenging situation when her visitor wanted to see the film *Great Expectations*. However, as this Spanish host was certainly aware, movie theaters in Washington, DC, were segregated. To avoid a thorny situation, the Spanish host and her friends did not tell the visitor about the practice of segregation, and "when the party approached the box office, everybody talked loudly in Spanish. The strategy work [sic]." In this case, the Spanish woman, rather than attempting to "pass," exaggerated and amplified her difference through the invocation of Spanish. It is not clear if the Spanish host feared being Jim Crowed because of the arrival of her Central American guest or if that was a concern she navigated daily. Perhaps it was the display of foreignness that protected her and her guests, or perhaps something particular about speaking Spanish worked as a buffer.[68]

Black Latino people and visitors of African descent, however, had a much more difficult time ameliorated only as a result of a concerted campaign on the part of the federal government to manage relations with foreign powers. Many US diplomats and politicians were particularly concerned about how Jim Crow tarnished the nation's image as a beacon of freedom and democracy on the international stage, and repeated incidents with foreign diplomats facing Jim Crow only exacerbated this image problem. This was especially problematic as diplomats traveled down Interstate 95 from the United Nations in New York to the nation's capital, which took them through Maryland and Virginia. Discrimination was so common and egregious that the State Department launched the Route 40 campaign, which was designed to aid desegregation efforts in Maryland to make passage of foreign dignitaries easier.[69] Additionally, as early as 1945, the State Department encouraged all foreign visitors to advise them of upcoming trips to circumvent this type of treatment.[70]

Despite these campaigns, many Black diplomats continued to suffer harsh discrimination in Washington, DC. Housing, for example, proved especially challenging for African diplomats. State Department official Pedro Sanjuan noted that, unlike African diplomats, Latin American, Asian, and European diplomats were able to find apartments in some of the nicest areas of Washington, DC, "without great difficulty."[71] Similar to the Galarza family, non-Black diplomats were able to find housing throughout the District without the challenges Black Latino and other Black people faced.

Karla Galarza and the DC School System

Schools were critical institutions in the preservation and reproduction of Jim Crow segregation. As such, the Galarza family's decision about Karla's schooling is significant. When the Galarzas moved to the outskirts of northwest DC in 1936, they came face to face with the question of their position in Jim Crow segregation. On arrival, Karla enrolled in grade 7A at MacFarland Junior High School, a white school.[72] A year later, in September 1937, the Galarza family moved to Arlington, Virginia, a suburb of Washington, DC, and Karla again enrolled in white schools, first at Washington and Lee High School and later at Thomas Jefferson High School.[73] DC schools were racially segregated, as were those in Virginia, and, with the exception of the Margaret Murray Washington Vocational School, all of the schools Karla attended while living in the DC area were exclusively for white students. The fact that Karla did not face any resistance to her attendance in Virginia schools is striking given the white residents of the state were so staunchly opposed to integration that, in an act of "massive resistance," the state of Virginia shut down its entire public school system rather than adhere to the call for integration by *Brown v. Board of Education* (1954).[74]

Karla's attendance in white schools was not the only marker of the Galarzas' increased entrée into whiteness. They also lived in a segregated white part of northern Virginia. These racially exclusive enclaves were a far cry from the working-class Sacramento neighborhood where Ernesto Galarza grew up.[75] The Galarza family was making a home in some of the most tightly regulated segregated spaces in the Washington metropolitan area: schools and neighborhoods. The Galarzas, therefore, were embedded in and benefiting from southern white supremacy. This did not mean they were unambiguously welcomed into all spaces. It did mean, however, they were able to profit from and be protected by southern whiteness.

Karla's experience in DC schools, along with the stories of other Latino people in the area, even before her time at the Margaret Murray Washington Vocational School, show how the presence of non-Black Latino people were not disruptive to the functioning of Jim Crow or the racial-binary thinking that structured Washington, DC, in the 1940s. Educational institutions were particularly important sites of inclusion because, as historian Jennifer Ritterhouse argues, ideas about racial hierarchy solidified for southern youth during their high school years. It was a time when young southerners came into their own both as sexual beings and also as autonomous participants in the Jim Crow order.[76] This fusion of increased racial awareness and emergent sexuality made high schools particularly important battlegrounds for white southerners fearful that the "key to the schoolhouse door," as the southern saying went, "would unlock the key to the bedroom door."[77] The inclusion of Latino people in this tightly protected Jim Crow institution likely had echo effects for the future of these Latino students and their ability to navigate white society in their adult years.

Galarza's attendance in these schools, however, was not without precedent in the US South. Weise describes the story of the Landrove family in Mississippi who successfully convinced Governor Theodore Bilbo in 1931 to allow their daughter to attend a white school. The Landroves did so by appealing to the Mexican consulate, who, in turn, invoked the Good Neighbor Policy rather than trying to claim legal or biological whiteness as a way to gain the students access to white schools.[78] The Landrove case shows that as early as the 1930s, Mexicans were able to successfully access white privileges without rejecting their Mexicanness.

Other cases hinged on whether Latino students had any "negro blood." In an earlier 1916 case, Mexican families had successfully lobbied to have their children attend white schools in Cheneyville, Louisiana. One school board member led the charge against these students, arguing they should be excluded because they had "negro blood." Ultimately, school officials opted to allow students to attend the white school. They did not, however, acknowledge that these students were white. Instead, what was referred to by school officials as their mestizo identity was noted but acceptable so long as they were clearly not of African descent. The Cheneyville case centered on whether the students were Black; their Latinidad, however, was not a cause for concern. In this case, Latino people were again accepted as Latino under the condition that they were not Black.[79]

In the Washington, DC, area, most non-Black Latino students were accepted into white high schools and colleges. A survey of yearbooks for local colleges and universities found a handful of Latino students at many schools.[80] They maintained small numbers but were a consistent presence through the District and the surrounding metropolitan areas. Their acceptance into these schools, however, did not prevent Latino students from being marked as racially different. Their stories suggest that their inclusion in these institutions was not predicated on their ability to "pass" but rather that their racial difference could be contained in "whiteness."

Latino students were targets of racism in the form of jokes about accents and the deployment of racial tropes to describe Latino coeds.[81] Venezuelan student Francisco Gonzalez, for example, was admired in his senior yearbook for his "Latin American intensity."[82] Medical student Luis Felipe Gonzalez was described as "Speedie . . . from South of the border way." Gonzalez was actually from Puerto Rico, but this reference to Speedy Gonzales, a cartoon associated with Mexicanness, did not seem to bother his classmates. They went on to describe the teasing Gonzalez faced, writing that "his Spanish interpretation of English and his squat physique have been the target of friendly jocularity."[83] One of Gonzalez's classmates, Carlos Vicens, was described as "probably the most subdued and least emotional of our Latin American colleagues."[84] Each of these descriptions referenced a damaging racial trope. Although these students were admitted and were successful in these white schools, they were marked in important ways as "other."

Accents were another recurring topic in yearbook quotes. Both from Puerto Rico, Manuel Rafael Fossas had "a sousand and one weemen"[85] written in his yearbook and Robert Hess was teased for his pronunciation of "Meestair Foley."[86] Like the racial tropes, these jokes marginalized and undermined these students' intelligence and capacity.[87] These same accents, however, made it possible for some Latino people to attend movies or be served at restaurants because of their foreignness. Accents, and language, would continue to serve as a double-edged sword for inclusion and exclusion in the story of Latino communities in the South.

Despite being marginalized, many of these students became leaders in their school communities. Many, like Beatriz Bolivar, who was described as a "dark beauty," served as class presidents and members of the student council.[88] Others participated in honorary and social fraternities and sororities—institutions designed to consolidate and protect racial and class hierarchy. These students were also overrepresented in international clubs and Pan American clubs.[89] The clubs were largely funded by government and foundation monies and were nestled between the fading era of the Good Neighbor Policy and the emergent years of the Cold War, when Latin America became an important geographical locale in the fight against communism.

Black Latino people also faced exclusion in schools as a result of their difference from the District's African American population. Juana Campos remembered attending a Black school in Washington, DC, with four other Dominicans only to find that they were teased for speaking Spanish.[90] Evelio Grillo, who migrated to Washington, DC, from Tampa in the late 1920s, also recalled that his use of Spanish "made [him] a strange one" in Paul Dunbar High School despite the presence of children of diplomats.[91] However, despite his Cuban heritage, Grillo was, as he put it, "considered simply a Black boy."[92]

Schools, like housing, were one of the key sites of Karla Galarza's initial inclusion into her provisional whiteness and were spaces where the rules of Jim

Crow segregation sorted Black and non-Black Latino people. Grillo attended Paul Dunbar High School, which served the District's long-standing elite African American community and helped him go on to attend Xavier University, a Louisiana university that served the Black community. At Dunbar, Grillo attended classes with members of the middle- and upper-class African American community from the District along with the children of diplomats from Caribbean families.[93] Although Dunbar High School was a shining accomplishment in the eyes of many of the District's Black elite, the pressures from growing school populations as a result of the Great Migration were starting to put Black public schools in an increasingly dire situation.[94]

"Not a Negro": The Expulsion of Karla Galarza

For Karla Galarza and her family, these segregated spaces became home. Between 1936 and 1947, the Galarza family lived in Washington, DC, but continued to travel back and forth to California. Ernesto was involved in organizing farmworkers, primarily Mexican and Mexican American, to form unions and strike for better wages and work conditions.[95] In 1947, toward the end of his time in the District, Ernesto was working in his capacity as an organizer for the Pan American Union to develop a booklet that "told the story of America." It was designed to aid new immigrants in becoming "better acquainted with one another's customs, habits and modes of dress."[96] While meeting with people he hoped would assist him in this project, he was introduced to Cordelia Wharton who taught dressmaking at the Margaret Murray Washington Vocational School.[97]

At the same time, Karla, who had since graduated from high school, became increasingly interested in fashion and design and began to research DC design schools. After meticulous research, she decided that the course with Cordelia Wharton best prepared her for a career in fashion. As an aspiring fashion designer, Karla had strong opinions about who could best prepare her for the fashion world. Cordelia Wharton's credentials were impeccable: she had studied design in both New York and Paris.[98] Wharton's course focused more on the creative aspects of design, whereas the course at Burdick Vocational High School (the white vocational school) focused on more technical aspects of dressmaking.[99] Years later, Karla's daughter, Lori Pepe, maintained that it was Karla's fierce drive to get the best education in design possible that led her to enroll at Margaret Murray Washington, the "colored" vocational school in the District.[100]

On February 3, 1947, twenty-two-year-old Karla Rosel Galarza enrolled at the Margaret Murray Washington Vocational School, but her stay would prove to be short-lived. One month into her attendance at the school, Assistant Superintendent Dr. Garnet C. Wilkinson requested that Karla voluntarily withdraw and enroll instead at the white vocational school. During their March 10, 1947, meeting, Wilkinson informed Karla that, in his assessment, she was white and, as a result, not "entitled to attend" the Margaret Murray Washington Vocational School.[101]

Wilkinson's decision to remove Karla was connected to his beliefs about race and education. As the assistant superintendent, he was a leading voice in increasing funds for Black vocational training, including adding a nursing program to the Margaret Murray Washington Vocational School. He was also a steadfast supporter of segregation in the schools. One Black newspaper referred to him as "a staunch defender of the status quo." Wilkinson felt that segregation offered unique benefits to Black students in the DC school system. Therefore, his claim that Karla was "not entitled" to or did not have the "privilege" of attending Margaret Murray Washington may have signaled his deeply held belief that separate education offered an opportunity for Black students to thrive.[102]

After being confronted by Wilkinson and asked to leave, Karla, with the support of her family, declared she would not leave voluntarily. Karla, after all, had attended the Margaret Murray Washington Vocational School for a month without incident before Wilkinson intervened, and she had grown close with her teachers and classmates during this time. As a result of Karla's refusal to leave the school voluntarily, the school board met on April 2, 1947, to make a decision regarding her attendance. The white superintendent of all DC schools, Hobart M. Corning, submitted a report to the board that outlined his case for removing Karla from Margaret Murray Washington. He opened the report by noting that a "question has arisen to her racial status."[103]

Karla's previous attendance in white schools in the area also served as evidence for the Board of Education that she was improperly attending Margaret Murray Washington. Corning argued that Karla, because of her prior attendance at white schools in the area, was "not entitled" to attend Margaret Murray Washington. The schools she attended "do not admit Negroes as students," and her attendance, Corning went on, "indicates that she is not a Negro."[104] Seemingly following W. E. B. Du Bois's observation that to be Black is to be Jim Crowed, the fact that she attended white schools was damning evidence that she was not Black.[105] According to Corning, Karla did not have to be white to be excluded from Margaret Murray Washington, rather she had to be proven "not a Negro." Her absence of Blackness, as opposed to a racial claim that she was white, caused her removal.

It was clear to the DC school board that Karla was not Black, but they avoided affirmatively declaring her as white and sought to limit the scope of their classification. A "question ha[d] arisen to her racial status," and it was the job of the school board to settle whether she belonged in a "colored" school.[106] The school board report on Karla's case read: "The Superintendent is of the opinion that Miss Karla Rosel Galarza is a white person within the meaning of the Rules and Regulations of the Board of Education requiring separate school for white children and for colored children . . . and that she should be so classified for purposes of school attendance." Elsewhere in the decision, he wrote that the school board found "that Miss Karla Rosel Galarza, for the purposes of school classification, is a white person, and she is therefore so classified for school attendance." These are the only two times Karla was referred to as "white." In the rest of the report, she is referred to as "not a Negro."[107] Her presumed "Mexicanness" is not discussed at all. The DC school board report was careful in its articulation of Karla's race. They made clear that she was "white" as a result of a set of administrative realities rather than of a claim about her biological or cultural ties to whiteness.

When the DC school board met to adjudicate Karla's case on April 2, 1947, the decision to exclude Karla was made by the nine-member school board that included votes from the three Black members of the board. John H. Wilson, an attorney and one of the Black members of the committee, made the motion for the adoption of the report. Mrs. Velma Williams, a native of Mississippi, voted to support the motion, adding that it was "because of the existing [segregation] law" that she voted favorably. "However," she continued, "I regret deeply that in this democracy of ours there has to be a separation of education."[108] The third Black member, attorney George E. C. Hayes, who was former president of the local National Association for the Advancement of Colored People (NAACP), lamented that "we as a board are obligated to determine whether children are white or colored. I realize it is the law but I am voting against my personal feelings."[109] Hayes conceded that part of the work of the committee was not just enforcing commonsense racial segregation but actually producing racial knowledge through the classification of Karla Galarza. On April 2, 1947, Karla Galarza was officially barred from attending Margaret Murray Washington Vocational School as a result of her status as "not a Negro."

Corning defended the school board's ability to adjudicate Karla's race for the purposes of school attendance by citing a 1910 decision of the Washington,

DC, appellate court, *Wall v. Oyster.* In 1909, Isabel Wall enrolled in Brookland White School in Washington, DC. However, shortly after her enrollment, she was ordered by the principal to leave the school because she was decided to be a "colored child." Conceding that she was one-sixteenth Black, Wall's attorney argued that "she [was] a white child in personal appearance, and is so treated and recognized by her neighbors and friends." The school board argued that Wall was Black because one of her grandparents had been buried in the "colored section of Arlington cemetery." The judge in the case agreed that Isabel Wall was not discernibly Black. He wrote, "There was to be observed of the child no physical characteristic which afforded ocular evidence suggestive of aught but the Caucasian." However, he went on, "Her father, while of light complexion, presents to the eye racial characteristics which identify him of negro blood; her mother, formerly wife to a Mongolian, is taken to be white."[110] Race, in this case, was in the eye of the beholder.

Ultimately, the judge ruled that Wall was, in fact, "colored" not because of the visual evidence he felt that her father offered, but instead because she was at least one-sixteenth Black. More important, he also ruled that the school board was within its rights to define children racially for the purposes of school segregation. *Wall* affirmed the "one-drop rule," ensuring that the presence of any amount of Blackness was enough to preclude whiteness. As a result, *Wall* empowered the superintendent and the school board to classify Karla and exclude her from the Margaret Murray Washington Vocational School for being not-Black.[111]

Many would interpret the votes of the three Black members as a capitulation to the Jim Crow order, but they also may have been safeguarding the precious few resources available for Black children's education. In 1947, the year that Karla was removed from Margaret Murray Washington Vocational School, the DC school system spent $120.52 per Black child compared with $160.21 per white child. Moreover, the white junior high schools had 1,851 unused spaces while the Black schools were accommodating 2,234 more pupils than they had space for.[112] Most Black schools were working far beyond their intended capacity, and, therefore, some may have been protecting resources by maintaining segregated facilities.

Schools, because they were such important institutions in Jim Crow, also helped fuel the DC civil rights activity in the 1940s. Fighting against racially restrictive covenants and school segregation, Black activists saw these institutions as key to toppling Jim Crow in the nation's capital. This included *Carr v. Corning* (1947), a case brought on behalf of Marguerite Carr, an African American student at Browne Junior High School. Marguerite's parents sued after being blocked from enrolling their daughter in a white school. Browne Junior High, the "colored" school Marguerite was assigned to, was overcrowded and underfunded. Browne Junior High School was designed to educate 783 students, and by 1947, it was at more than double its capacity, with 1,727 students. This overcrowding had led to the practice of "part-time" schooling, in which Black students attended classes in shifts to alleviate the overcrowded classrooms. As a result, they received less instructional hours than their white counterparts who were attending school full time and had a surplus of space.[113] As the *Carr* suit worked its way through the court system, parents formed the "Browne Parent Group for Equality of Educational Opportunities," which took on more direct-action approaches to challenge the school board. On December 3, 1947, parents withheld their children from school in a strike to protest, among other things, the practice of "part-time" schooling.[114] The *Carr* case was ultimately unsuccessful, and DC courts upheld Jim Crow segregation once again.

Karla's challenge, which overlapped with the *Carr* case, also suggests that she and her father had activist motivations. In addition to the *Carr* case, the District's Black activist community was growing a collection of high-profile cases challenging segregation.[115] Among those were campaigns led by African American women for voting and citizenship rights, the sit-in movement emerging out of Howard University, and a series of cases challenging segregation in DC public schools.[116] Therefore, in 1947 Washington, DC, Karla's case was a part of a growing wave of antisegregation activism. The media coverage even linked Karla's case with the *Carr* case as twin efforts to challenge the Jim Crow DC school system.[117] Because of the growing movement in Washington, DC, Karla's case received media attention as a symbol of the swelling tide of antisegregation activism in the District and the Southeast writ large. As soon as the vote was final, the Galarza case began to receive national media attention.

The reaction in the Black press to the school board decision also suggests that Galarza's case was seen, by some, as part of a campaign against Jim Crow in DC. Focusing on the votes of the Black members of the school board, the Black media represented this case as an important example of the failures of Black leadership. On April 19, 1947, two weeks after the school board made the decision to exclude Karla, *Pittsburgh Courier* columnist Horace Cayton wrote a scathing critique of the school board and focused on the Black participants who upheld this decision. "Just how could Brother Hayes," Cayton questioned, "in these circumstances, have considered it more important to uphold his oath of office which, according to his interpretation, meant the perpetuation, continuation and protection of segregated institutions than to uphold his manhood and dignity as a human being?" Because of this political apathy, Cayton wondered whether the case demonstrated the limited impact of the struggles to get Black officials elected. "Of course," he wrote, "we work hard to get Negroes on various boards and should continue to do so. But once they are there, and especially when they act as representatives of the Negro group, we've got to 'learn 'em' when to resign, when decency, integrity, and manhood are more important than keeping a job."[118]

Many in the Black press saw the three Black council members' votes to remove Karla as a violation of the growing activist focus on school desegregation. In the *Baltimore Afro-American* Harry Keelan wrote that as a thank-you for "upholding their way of life, the grateful white Americans of the District of Columbia should give these three colored board members . . . each a large, red bandanna handkerchief, with three kyah-kyah-kyah's delivered in the best Hattie McDaniel style!"[119] To Cayton and Keelan, Karla Galarza's case, although not a typical desegregation case, still represented an opportunity to fight Jim Crow. Therefore, the failure of the board members to keep Karla Galarza in Margaret Murray Washington Vocational School represented the further entrenchment of white supremacy and Jim Crow.

Other organizations also weighed in, recognizing Karla's case as a potentially significant point in the District's fight against segregation. On June 14, 1947, the Washington, DC, chapter of the Unitarian Fellowship for Social Justice urged the board to reconsider Karla's case and to "strive toward a more integrated school system in Washington's public schools." Less than a month later, on July 1, the American Federation of Teachers, Local 27 wrote a letter in support of Karla. They protested not just Karla's exclusion but also other discriminatory practices in the DC school system that had led to the *Carr* case.[120]

In response to Karla's exclusion, Ernesto Galarza fired a letter back to the school board in support of his daughter and protesting the expulsion. In the letter he made two arguments: (1) that Karla's exclusion was unjust because the two courses were inexorably different and therefore Karla was being prevented from taking a course that she should have access to, and (2) that segregation in the District was unconstitutional and robbing his daughter of a proper education.

First, Galarza argued that a comparable course "is offered in no other school in the city." The course at Burdick, called "Trade Dressmaking," focused on preparing students for positions in "the production and commerce of the trade." However, Karla wanted to take the course at Margaret Murray Washington called "Dress Designing and Costume Making," which focused on "creative design, construction and art skills."[121] At the invitation of the school board, Karla and her father visited both schools, talked to the principals, and read the courses of study, which only confirmed Karla's initial assessment of the courses as fundamentally different.[122] This emphasis on course content, although it may have reflected an earnest frustration felt by Karla, also set the foundation for their argument that the District's segregated schools were not producing the "separate but equal" that was promised. If the courses were as different as Karla suggested and the white vocational school did not offer an equivalent, this case could, theoretically, demonstrate the failures of "separate but equal."[123]

Ernesto Galarza's letter then turned to the larger question of segregation. He noted that Wilkinson suggested to him and Karla that she must withdraw "because Washington is a southern city." However, this practice of segregation, he argued, was depriving his daughter of "equal protection under the law," and, he went on, "it would take . . . a decision of the Supreme Court to persuade me that I am legally in error." Galarza took aim at the historic practice of segregation in the city that was denying his daughter a much sought-after opportunity to work with an expert costume and dress designer.[124]

In his response to the school board, Galarza was sparing in his mention of the question of Karla's race. He did address, however, the suspicion of his family's racial history that emerged during the Board of Education's investigation. He wrote to the school board, "I must leave on record my surprise and my deep regret that school officials have made public statements concerning their investigation of the racial status of my daughter and family." Galarza continued, "I happen to be a Mexican by birth. At one point, apparently the school officials considered the possibility of assimilating Karla's presumed Mexican ancestry to the Negro race, under an old ruling of the United States Bureau of the Census."[125] Galarza's mention of his own Mexican ancestry is the only mention of Mexicanness in any of the proceedings—if it came up in the investigation by the school board, it was not present in the final report.

Galarza went on to object to the investigation into Karla's racial background. Galarza continued, "I recognize that those officials were bound to study carefully every aspect of so important a matter; but that the privacy of our family should have been needlessly invaded is preliminary and finally irrelevant inquiries is to be greatly regretted."[126] Perhaps Galarza's frustration with the violation of his privacy stemmed from a desire to keep Karla's adopted status private. Perhaps it was dissatisfaction with Karla potentially being categorized as "Negro." Either way, the question of race was never a "private" one. Galarza's letter was noted at the school board's next meeting, but it was not read into the record and did not make it into the meeting discussion. Despite the Galarza family's objections, the school board saw the case as resolved.

The archive tells us very little about the inner life of the Galarza family at this time. In fact, even in such a robust collection of archival material, there are very few references to Karla's case. As a result, the archive does not tell us the personal reasons why Karla and Ernesto Galarza waged this campaign.[127] Years later Karla's daughter, Lori Pepe, insisted that it was an effort to receive the best possible training that drove Karla and her father's fight. However, their case was also unfolding amid several other attacks on DC school segregation.[128] Ernesto Galarza claimed that it was foremost about his daughter's access to classes and only secondarily about segregation as an institution.

There are many potential readings of the Galarza family's intentions in pursuing Karla's case. One is that they saw it as potentially bolstering the growing number of cases challenging school segregation. Another is a sense of entitlement to the resources and classes that Karla desired. Because of Galarza's own activism and the mounting civil rights challenges in the DC school system, it is unlikely that this action was taken on without some consideration for the potential consequences for those engaged in fights against segregation. Regardless of the Galarza family's intent, the case became embedded in the growing national discourse about race and education.

The Galarza Case in the Media

Karla's case garnered national attention that cut across Black and white press outlets. The media coverage exposed a critical tension in the case—Karla's race. Although Karla was white, the coverage of her case suggests ambiguity in how the media understood her racially. Journalists varied in how they identified Karla's race, which had important political consequences for the definition of the case. Newspapers sometimes referred to her as white and other times as Mexican. More specifically, white newspapers identified Karla as white, whereas nearly half of the Black newspapers refer to Karla as Mexican or Spanish.

The white newspapers reported the case as a white girl being barred from a Black school. The *Toledo Blade* referred to Karla as a "pretty, 22-year-old white girl," the *Times-Picayune* chronicled "a white girl ousted from a Negro public school," and the *Sunday Oregonian* introduced Karla as a "white girl" and the "daughter of former educational adviser to the Pan-American union."[129] For the

white media, this was an interesting story of a reversal of the traditional narrative of desegregation: a white girl was trying to attend a Black school. Karla's
race, however, warranted no further discussion.

There was almost no coverage of the case in Spanish-language newspapers.
The exception was *La Prensa* (San Antonio), which ran an article titled "Una
joven de raza blanca insiste en estudiar junto con los negros" (Young white
woman insists on studying with Negroes).[130] Like the white newspapers, they
categorized Karla as "white" but made little other mention of her race or the
oddity of the race reversal at the center of a desegregation case.

The Black press also used Karla's case to critique Jim Crow in Washington, DC. However, unlike the white press, they referred to Karla as "Spanish-
American," "Latin American," "Mexican-American," and "Senorita" [sic]. One
of the effects of racializing Karla in the Black press was that it pointed out
the absurdity of Jim Crow segregation. Karla, a supposed non-white girl who
elsewhere in the country would have faced educational segregation, was being
kicked out of a Black school. In doing so, they dramatized the irrationality of a
system that purported to sort the world into a necessary binary.

For example, Black journalists undercut the supposed logic of Jim Crow by
highlighting the process of Karla's classification as white. One writer for the
Baltimore Afro-American used the heading "Classified as White" when writing
about Superintendent Corning's decision to remove Karla.[131] To this journalist,
Karla's story was not about a white girl, but instead a girl who got to be classified
as such. The emphasis on classification highlighted the mediation necessary to
sort a diverse population into a racial binary.

Another journalist, "Mr. Treadmill," in the *Chicago Defender*'s column "Adventures in Race Relations," emphasized the school board's decision to classify
Karla as white. He wrote that "the Spanish-American girl Karla Galarza who
attends the 'colored' Margaret Murray Washington Vocational School has been
declared 'white,' as we indicated here she would be."[132] This "Spanish-American"
girl had to be declared white rather than her being innately white. Many saw
Karla's whiteness as part of a commonsense racial classification necessitated
by Jim Crow, but this writer pointed to the mediation and decision making required to declare Karla white. That a "Spanish-American" girl was being shoe-
horned into a Jim Crow system made clear that DC schools were, as he saw it,
"segregated not by law but based on tradition and custom." Some of Treadmill's interpretation can likely be attributed to his location in Chicago. While
Karla was being classified as white in Washington, DC, those living in Chicago

at that same time were likely witnessing the destruction of robust Mexican American communities as a result of Great Depression–era repatriation and deportation.[133]

Another writer for the *Baltimore Afro-American* highlighted the difference between Karla and many other Latino people throughout the United States. He described Karla's background in the following way: "Although Miss Galarza's parents are Mexican, they were living in the United States before her birth, her father (an educational adviser of the Pan-American Union) being a graduate of both Stanford and Columbia Universities."[134] The writer's elaboration on Karla's presumed citizenship status based on her birth in the United States and Ernesto Galarza's educational pedigree evidenced the important role class played in shaping Karla's racialization.

Karla, her family, and many of the Latino people in Washington, DC, benefited from protected forms of citizenship that made them less vulnerable to state violence. However, their citizenship alone does not explain their broad acceptance in the District given that Mexican Americans who were citizens of the United States faced discrimination and, in the case of the Great Depression, deportation. That is to say, citizenship did not always provide protection, but in Karla's case, as the *Baltimore Afro-American* writer pointed out, it supported her racial ascendancy.

Other writers focused on Karla's supposed foreignness to critique Jim Crow in the United States. Harry Keelan, in his "Voice in the Wilderness" column in the *Baltimore Afro-American*, referred to Karla as "Senorita Karla Rosel Galarza" [*sic*]. Karla, a "young Latin-American," Keelan wrote, was being excluded by the "Nazi travesty" that was the DC public schools. He added that Karla's admirable protest originated from the "real education" she received "in the schools of her own country." As a result of this education, presumably in Mexico, "she could not accept, [the] primitive reasoning, and appealed to the Board of Education."[135] However, Karla was not educated in Mexico. Karla was actually educated in Washington, DC, and Northern Virginia schools for middle school and part of high school and completed her high school degree in Sacramento, California. If Keelan assumed that Karla's seemingly progressive racial politics grew out of Mexico, he was mistaken.

The Black media highlighted Karla's racial difference to critique the absurdity of Jim Crow. This young woman, who was by all accounts presumed to be non-white, had been thrust out of a "colored" school and forced into a white one. By narrating the process of racial classification and reclassification of Karla, the

Black media demonstrated the racial heterogeneity of whiteness—calling into question the claims underlying the imagined purity of whiteness in Jim Crow.

This rhetoric, designed to critique Jim Crow's logical fallacies, also points to Jim Crow's capaciousness. Whiteness, under Jim Crow, was fluid enough to hold Karla's presumed racial difference, so long as she was decidedly not Black. As the Black press highlighted, a supposed non-white girl was being designated administratively as white to protect the system of segregation. Non-Black Latino people like Karla could be absorbed into parts of whiteness if it was in service of Jim Crow's ultimate goal—maintaining white supremacy through Black subjugation.

Karla's story received press coverage from across the country, and her high-profile father made the case even more interesting. Even though her case was an oddity, some wondered if it would be worth pursuing in the courts. The press coverage drew the attention of activists across the country who were in the process of building a set of integration cases that would overturn "separate but equal" in 1954.

The Legal Limits of the Galarza Case

When the DC Board of Education made their final decision to expel Karla from Margaret Murray Washington, she and her father vowed in a public statement to take "what legal redress we have."[136] The school tried to assuage the Galarza family by offering to hire Wharton as an extracurricular tutor for Karla, however, the Galarzas were unmoved and continued with action to bring her case to court.[137]

Even before Galarza reached out to lawyers, the NAACP picked up on the case from news coverage. Only a week after the school board's decision, the NAACP began discussing the case. On April 9, 1947, Robert L. Carter, the assistant special counsel to the NAACP's Legal Defense and Educational Fund, wrote to Charles Houston about the case to see if the NAACP had any plans to pursue it in court. Houston, a native of Washington, DC, a Harvard Law School graduate, and vice dean of Howard Law School, wrote back to Carter that he agreed that the NAACP should "handle [Galarza's case] from the outset."[138]

Houston's interest signaled that Karla Galarza's case was being discussed by some of the most important leaders in the legal fight against segregation. In the 1930s, Houston became special counsel to the NAACP, and in the 1940s, he was one of the legal strategists behind the cases leading up to *Brown v. Board of*

Education (1954). Houston was eager to add Karla's case to the growing list of school desegregation cases being waged by the NAACP.

Despite the NAACP's early interest, the American Civil Liberties Union (ACLU) became the lead counsel for the case, with the NAACP playing a supporting role. Robert Carter, writing to ACLU lawyer H. A. Robinson, said that the "[NAACP] and the ACLU, as you probably know, work together in this field and Miss Galarza and her parents apparently preferred that the ACLU represent her in this suit. We are cooperating with the ACLU, however, in all phases of this matter."[139] When acting director of the ACLU, Clifford Forester, wrote to Charles Houston about the case, he thanked him for assistance with the work and clarified that "from a practical point of view, I should think it would be preferable if your name did not appear as counsel at this stage."[140] Both the ACLU and the NAACP spent the summer studying the case and considering what form their legal challenge could take.

One pressing concern was that the case could potentially negate arguments that segregation inherently disadvantaged Black people. ACLU lawyer Jonathan Bingham wrote that "under any equal protection theory such a discrimination against whites could be pointed to for the purpose of proving the equality of a segregated system." If Karla won, segregation advocates could argue that inequality was equal under segregation and that Black and white people both dealt with the challenges of a necessary social system. That dangerous line of thinking had already begun to get some traction in the wake of Karla's case. In a letter written by the American Federation of Teachers, Local 27 in support of Karla's claim, they stated that "in plain English, both racial groups are discriminated against, under the present system."[141] While the American Federation of Teachers was writing this as a critique of segregation, this "equal inequality under segregation" flew in the face of the NAACP's legal strategy, which emphasized that Black people were uniquely disadvantaged in segregated institutions.[142]

In addition to these concerns, the NAACP and ACLU felt this case was not representative and, therefore, did not offer an opportunity to establish case law that could aid in the legal fight to end segregation. Clifford Forster wrote that "it was also our conclusion that your daughter's case was really a freak because of its discrimination against whites, and that it would have no general application." In another letter, Marian Wynn Perry, the assistant special counsel of the NAACP Legal Defense and Educational Fund, wrote of Karla's case that "this case is not anything except a 'fluke' and should not be one which we expend a great deal of energy."[143]

Therefore, on January 20, 1948, Clifford Forester wrote to Ernesto Galarza to let him know that the ACLU would not be taking his daughter's case to court. Galarza replied two days later writing that "the decision of the ACLU on our case is naturally very disappointing."[144] As a result, the strange case of Karla Galarza's segregated education received no further attention from these organizations. Unimpeded by this setback, Karla went on to attend the Fashion Institute of Design in New York, worked in a fashion house, and eventually had her own label where she designed suits and coats.[145]

Although the Galarza case did not continue to make national news and ultimately was not one of the cases that helped overturn segregation in education, it unearths a great deal about how race operated in the South during the 1940s. The stories of Ernesto and Karla Galarza show that in a city that was governed by Jim Crow, non-Black Latino people found relative freedom in a racially restrictive order. Although Latino people may not have always been seen as "fully white," their Latinidad did not prevent them from getting the most important protections of whiteness: access to white schools, access to white neighborhoods, and freedom from white violence. Education and homeownership, critical tools in the construction of wealth and security, were available to non-Black Latino people in Washington, DC, during a time when those same benefits were being withheld from Latino people in the West and Southwest. Many of the non-Black Latino people in Washington, DC, were elite like Karla's family, but these protections cut across class lines. Southern Latino people did not have to be white to receive these protections, as Karla shows us: they simply had to be "not a Negro." That was enough to preserve their provisional whiteness.

These experiences suggest that Jim Crow was capacious enough to incorporate the presence of these groups that were neither white nor Black. A diverse group of people could be categorized as "white"—even in a moment of growing concern on the part of many white southerners about the urgency of preserving racial segregation. However, the racial mobility reflected in these histories was not present for African Americans or Black immigrants to the region.[146] The flexibility of Jim Crow, therefore, had boundaries defined by Blackness. In this way, the same system that could bend to incorporate Latino people retained structural integrity by maintaining Blackness as the "other" against which these new groups were measured.

Racial difference and even racial diversity permeated southern white communities and institutions as Jim Crow mutated and adapted to new populations. Southern white views of Latino people could simultaneously incorporate their racial differences, while fiercely guarding against Black equality. It was not racial difference, as such, that drove the need for school segregation, anti-miscegenation laws, and racially restrictive covenants. Instead, it was a set of regional ideas about Blackness that could incorporate difference so long as it was not Black.

Importantly, the stories of Latino people suggest that their presence was not disruptive to Jim Crow. Jim Crow was a mechanism used primarily to preserve anti-Blackness and to sort Latino people according to their distance or proximity to Blackness. The presence of Latino people, however, was not a challenge to institutionalized segregation. Instead, the Latino world of Washington, DC, mirrored the non-Latino world: it was separate, unequal, and organized around Blackness. This did not mean that non-Black Latino people did not encounter moments of discrimination, confusion, or dissonance in the Jim Crow South. Instead, it suggests that being white was not a prerequisite to inclusion in "white" Jim Crow spaces, but being not-Black was.

Led by Black southerners, challenges to Jim Crow continued to mount in the postwar years throughout the South. As a result, white southerners doubled down on preserving the sanctity of segregation. Some white southerners fought violently against the attacks on white supremacy, while others sought ways to escape into new kinds of white supremacist fantasies. Mexico, and illusions about Mexicanness, became one place for this kind of escape.

Many Americans, including those in the South, were beginning to use their postwar affluence to travel outside of the United States. Some headed south of the border to Mexico. For those southern travelers unable to afford a trip to Mexico, southern roadside attractions were becoming places they could fantasize about these exotic locales far away from the growing US civil rights struggle.

■ ■ ■ ■ ■ ■ ■ ■ ■ ■ ■ ■ ■ ■ ■

CHAPTER TWO

Pedro Goes to Confederateland

Playing Mexican at South of the Border, 1945–1965

R esting right at the border between North and South Carolina, the Mexican-themed rest stop, South of the Border, was an iconic fixture in 1950s and 1960s US roadside culture. Even today, drivers on Interstate 95 (I-95) traveling 100 miles north or south of Dillon, South Carolina, are well acquainted with the South of the Border billboards that crowd the sides of the highway. On one of the more famous signs, Pedro, the mascot of the road stop, beckons drivers to visit South of the Border with the promise "You Never Sausage a Place" and "Everyone's a Weiner at South of the Border." A cartoon figure of a short, rotund, dark-skinned Mexican man, Pedro appears on each of these billboards promising the best in leisure and consumption—plenty of stores in which to buy "Mexican" wares, restaurants that serve both Mexican and more traditional "American" bar food, and a hotel for travel-weary drivers. At its pinnacle in the 1950s and 1960s, South of the Border was one of the most popular stops for travelers on the newly built I-95. Perfectly positioned as a halfway point between New England and the booming tourist destination of Florida, South of the Border became a memorable roadway stop for many US travelers and a place where both tourists and locals came together to make new meanings of race and region.

Opened by Alan Schafer in 1949 as a beer depot, South of the Border rapidly expanded over the 1950s. Over these years, Schafer added a motel, several restaurants, souvenir shops, and amusement park attractions. It was also during these years that Schafer gave the rest stop its "Mexican" theme. Restaurants were covered with sombreros, serapes were available for purchase at all of the gift shops, and promotional materials were filled with puns referencing the Mexican theme. The built environment also began to reflect this theme: cartoonish statues of the rest stop's mascot, Pedro, began to pop up throughout the road stop, southwestern architecture littered the roadside, and a massive seventy-seven-ton and several-stories-tall neon statue of Pedro loomed over

South of the Border entrance sign in the image of Pedro. Courtesy Carolina Studio, Photograph Collection, South Caroliniana Library, University of South Carolina, Columbia.

the rest stop and the highway. The rest stop eventually became home to "Confederateland," a roadside attraction that fused South of the Border's "Mexican" theme with the swelling "Lost Cause" ideology that was formed in response to growing civil rights protest.[1]

South of the Border emerged in the 1950s and Confederateland was constructed in 1961. Before this, the 1940 census reported that there were only nineteen Mexican-born people living in all of South Carolina. The previous 1930 census found only nine. Although there were isolated examples of seasonal Mexican laborers, in both North and South Carolina, like many states in the US South, a consistent migration or Latino community formation did not occur until after the 1970s.[2] Thus, South of the Border becomes even more significant in light of the apparent absence of Latino people in the nearby areas. For North and South Carolinians and for its myriad visitors, the tourist destination offered one of the only available images of Latino people—that is, a stereotypical visage that stood alone because of the absence of local Latino people.

As was the case with genuine Latino people living in places like Washington, DC, imagined Latino people did not disrupt Jim Crow or the white supremacist structure that undergirded it. Elsewhere in this book, I talk about the way Jim Crow physically sorted Latino people; in this chapter, I examine how Latino people were sorted in the field of imagination and play. South of the Border shows how ideas about Latino people were used to reinforce Jim Crow segregation in the civil rights era. Fantasized Mexicanness became an escape for those white southerners in the midst of a civil rights revolution and, therefore, reinforced rather than unsettled southern ideas about race and power.

South of the Border also exemplifies how Latino racial formations can be produced in the absence of actual Latino people. The performances at South of the Border did not require a population of Latino people to retain their significance. Racial ideas that had formed largely in the West and Southwest were repurposed with regional sensibilities in the US South. Therefore, South of the Border is a case study in the racial antecedent to the xenophobia that would accompany the post-1970s large-scale migration of Mexicans, Mexican Americans, and Central Americans to the Carolinas.

Little is known about the racial scripts that predated the arrival of Latino people and how they overlapped and departed from other racial discourses formed in Jim Crow. At South of the Border, white fantasies about Latino people in the US South oscillated between seeing Mexicans as perpetually foreign and seeing them as intimately domestic. Pedro, portrayed as both the ultimate "racial other" and the mirror image of white southerners, was as at home in a sombrero as he was in a Confederate uniform. Like in Washington, DC, local white people were making choices that situated, in this case admittedly fictitious, Latino people into their racial order. In the process, Alan Schafer, and the visitors at South of the Border, did not simply consume national ideas about race and Mexicanness; they also generated new racial ideologies that were regionally specific. Just as Karla Galarza could be both Mexican and provisionally white, Pedro could be both Mexican and southern.[3]

Even before the large-scale migration of Latinos to the "nuevo South," white locals and visitors to South of the Border in the 1950s and 1960s were developing and transforming racial scripts about Mexicanness. For example, being able to "play Mexican" by dressing up and affecting a mock accent was one of the necessary pleasures of visiting South of the Border.[4] At South of the Border, most of the staff wore "Mexican"-themed costumes and patrons were encouraged to do the same. Visitors delighted in the opportunity to ornament themselves with serapes and sombreros and document their time at South of the Border with photographs of this racial dress-up.[5]

As with actual Latino people who were enrolled into Jim Crow as provisionally white, imagined Latino people like Pedro at South of the Border became weapons for white southerners to reassert their power and identity. It is impossible to disentangle the rise of South of the Border from the rise of the civil rights movement and the emergent backlash politics. As the civil rights movement reconfigured everyday life in the South, South of the Border became a place for white southerners to reclaim the white supremacy they feared losing.[6] Because southern racial identity was deeply connected to the structure of Jim Crow, threats to this system became threats to the fundamental meaning of "whiteness." White southerners and visitors of the rest stop used what I call "playing Mexican" as a way to moderate the rapidly changing postwar South.[7]

Over time, South of the Border evolved from a roadside attraction that traded in white fantasies of tropicality to a site that also contained more regional brands of white supremacy like "Confederateland." Throughout, Alan Schafer, white locals, and white tourists played with and redefined race in ways that served local needs. In a moment and a region where life was so clearly defined in Black and white, South of the Border shows how some white southerners imagined Mexicans, a population that was neither white nor Black. South of the Border, therefore, not only received national narratives about race but also produced new ideas about Mexicanness and whiteness that were distinctly southern. It was a place where circulating ideas about race and region collided and produced alchemic racial formations in the process.

History of South of the Border

South of the Border's origins can be traced to the border between North and South Carolina. In 1949, as part of a protemperance movement, Robeson County, North Carolina, on the border of North and South Carolina, passed a local option ordinance that outlawed the sale of beer. Other counties in the area followed suit creating a "dry" community surrounding Alan Schafer's nascent alcohol distribution company: Schafer Distributing Company. Schafer responded by purchasing three acres of red clay in Dillon, South Carolina, just south of the North Carolina border. His property sat on the South Carolina side of the US-301 highway where he built an eighteen-by-thirty-six-foot building where he sold beer to South and North Carolina residents seeking alcohol outside of their newly dry towns. He named it "South of the Border Depot," referencing the building's strategic placement just south of the North Carolina border.

The initial border, between North and South Carolina would prove politically relevant over the lifetime of South of the Border. South Carolina's more relaxed regulations on things like alcohol and fireworks turned the rest stop into a site for locals on either side of the Carolina border to access restricted items. To deflect criticism from the anti-alcohol religiously conservative community, Schafer took the advice of then South Carolina governor Strom Thurmond and, in 1954, added a ten-seat grill and renamed the business "South of the Border Drive-In" at which point it took on its Mexican theme.[8]

The year the rest stop took on its Mexican theme proved to be an auspicious one for the history of race in the United States. That year saw the successful end to "separate but equal" schooling in *Brown v. Board of Education* (1954) and the onset of what was called "Operation Wetback," a mass deportation effort led by the federal government. Signs of progress and retrenchment, respectively, these two moments set the context for Schafer's decision to invest in a racialized fantasy of Mexicans. He was likely informed by both the growing anxiety on the part of many southerners about their changing way of life with the end of segregated schooling and national ideas circulating about Mexicans and their so-called illegality.

Schafer's South of the Border was also rooted in the changing political economy of the South in the 1950s and 1960s. In the postwar years, the South saw the expansion of tourism as a result of the growing highway system and postwar prosperity for some and the turn away from agriculture and investment in new industries. In the late 1950s, tourism had become an increasingly vital part of the South's economy, so much so that tourism's economic impact surpassed that of agriculture in several states. Regional tourism boomed after World War II when postwar affluence made leisure travel more accessible.[9] As highways and interstates snaked across the country, entrepreneurs and local governments capitalized on the nation's fantasies of the South and built up a regional roadside culture that highlighted the history and culture of the area.[10] Schafer was particularly well positioned at an exit for both Route 301 and I-95—one of the most traveled north–south interstates.

South of the Border was also perched between Dillon County, South Carolina, and Robeson County, North Carolina. Dillon was a largely rural community that was almost evenly split between Black and white residents, with a slightly larger white population. Robeson, South of the Border's direct neighbor to the north, was one of the largest counties in North Carolina and home to a

Aerial view of South of the Border, postcard. Courtesy Postcard Collection, South Caroliniana Library, University of South Carolina, Columbia.

large Lumbee Indian community.[11] In 1960, Robeson County was almost evenly
split with white, Black, and Indian residents. This even split produced tripar-
tite segregation in Robeson County during the Jim Crow era. Most churches,
schools, restaurants, and businesses were segregated three ways—something
possible only with a sizable Lumbee community to populate those institutions.[12]

Unlike Latino populations in this period, the Lumbee posed a significant
complication to the Black/white binary.[13] The local Lumbee population, somewhat like Latino people elsewhere in the South, occupied an "in-between"
space. They were racially non-white but retained some protections from Jim
Crow that were unavailable to African Americans. However, unlike Latino
people, racial categorization of the Lumbee had important consequences for
the struggle for tribal recognition and sought-after federal funds. Oscillating
between "white" and "colored," the Lumbee actively worked to create a third
racial category separate from white or Black as a way to make their claim for
tribal recognition. The presence of a large Lumbee community also meant that
most locals understood that racial differences could exist beyond just Black and
white. Pedro and the Mexican theme at South of the Border would represent its
own kind of interstitial racial formation.[14]

South of the Border's over-the-top expressions of racial difference also may have been part of Schafer's effort to manage his own marginalization as a Jew in the 1950s Carolinas. Grandson of Abraham Schafer, one of the first Jews to move to Dillon, Alan Schafer was active in the small local Jewish community. The Jewish population in Dillon and neighboring counties was always small, with Dillon's Jewish population peaking at eighty-four people in 1930. In the mid-twentieth century, many Jews throughout the United States struggled against anti-Semitism to make a space for themselves in whiteness. Southern Jews conformed to social mores even more than their counterparts elsewhere in the United States. However, rather than gaining access to whiteness, Jews were frequently alienated by white southerners who felt that, as historian Eric Goldstein writes, "by casting Jews out of the pale of whiteness . . . they were reinforcing, purifying, and removing the troubling ambiguity from their own racial identity."[15] Schafer may have used the racial overtones of South of the Border and Pedro as a way to lessen his perceived difference—a strategy employed by many white ethnics throughout the twentieth century.[16] That is to say, Schafer's religious and ethnic difference was minimized when he stood in the shadow of Pedro.

The regional investment in tourism came from a concerted campaign led by business owners in the Carolinas and local and state governments to use tourism as a way to stimulate the economy. Although this offered business owners huge opportunities because of a growing investment in infrastructure and advertising, it also meant that those on the increasingly crowded roadside were all jockeying for tourist attention.[17] To draw tourists, many roadside attractions in the region chose to emphasize their connection to America's romanticized ideas about a southern pastoral era filled with moonlight and magnolias. Schafer chose to focus on another site of American fantasies: Mexico.[18]

Making South of the Border Tropical

As South of the Border grew, so too did the Mexican theme. By 1954, some of the key elements of South of the Border's Mexican theme were in place. To target families traveling the I-95 corridor, Schafer built a Disney-style compound that sprawled across both sides of the highway creating a world unto itself. The addition of the motel made South of the Border a tourist destination, rather than a quick stop for travelers merely passing through. South of the Border continued to expand to include several bars, including one with a patio shaded by the giant brim of the roof shaped like an enormous sombrero. Another restaurant, called the Hot Tamale, sold American roadside fare like chili dogs as well as more thematic foods like "Mexi-Burgers." Pedro's Coffee Casa was a large drive-up coffee shop and restaurant that had an adobe thatched roof and rounded arches to mirror the architecture of the Southwest. The size of South of the Border meant that visitors could have an immersive experience. With a motel, swimming pools, golf, activities for the kids, and several restaurants, those visiting South of the Border had little reason to leave the fantasy world Schafer had created.[19]

The Mexican theme quickly took hold and saturated the whole rest stop. Scattered throughout the compound were statues of the rest stop's mascot, Pedro. These statues, all slightly larger than life size, had the same wide-open smile, moustache, sombrero, serape, and sandals. The mold of each statue remained the same with the coloring of both Pedro's clothing and skin changing slightly in each.[20] At the core of the compound was the main building that housed the Mexico Shop gift shop and the Fiesta Room. Both of these buildings sat in the shadow of the several-stories-tall metal statue of Pedro that weighed seventy-seven tons, required an eighteen-foot-deep support in the ground, and contained four miles of wiring to power its neon glow. Referred to by employees as the "big fella," the colossal sombrero-wearing Pedro loomed above the entire compound.[21]

Schafer never explicitly outlined why he chose to make this rest stop "Mexican," but several factors likely contributed to this decision. One potential origin for the Mexican theme was the 1939 Gene Autry song "South of the Border," which grew in popularity throughout World War II. Before this popular song, the phrase "South of the Border" largely referred to the geographic location of Mexico and Latin America. However, after the song's release, the phrase became linked specifically with cultural tropes about "old Mexico." In the song, he laments having to leave a woman he meets in Mexico whom Autry describes as a "picture in old Spanish lace."[22] Other popular films and television series like Zorro created the world of "old Mexico," a place with corrupt Mexican officials, dangerous bandits, and beautiful mestiza women in need of saving.

The Mexican theme was also certainly inspired by the growth of tourist travel to Mexican border towns in the postwar years.[23] In 1946, nearly 245,000 US tourists were heading to Mexico, and by 1953, Mexico was the most common travel locale for US tourists. Similar to the South, many in the United States saw Mexico, and Latin America more broadly, as a premodern world of leisure. The domestic sale of commodities like tequila only deepened these associations

Pedro statue, South of the Border.
Courtesy John Margolies Road-
side America Photograph Archive
(1972–2008), Library of Congress,
Prints and Photographs Division,
Washington, DC.

as advertisers for tequila used the imagined linkages between Mexicanness, alcohol, and civilizational backwardness as a way to promote their products.[24] This narrative of civilizational backwardness was operating at many registers by legitimizing both forms of vice and pleasure as well as larger geopolitical moves on the part of the United States.[25] Moreover, the image of Mexico many in the United States held bore a striking resemblance to narratives in the US North about the rural South as a place untouched by industry or civilization.[26]

Latin America also served as a place for US tourists to escape the sexual confines of Cold War domesticity and indulge in cheap sex, casinos, and alcohol. Historian Catherine Cocks has written about the interest from US tourists in "tropical" spaces. Tropical locales shared certain kinds of landscapes and social organization, or as Cocks quotes, "waving palms, slothful negroes, odd tropical fruits, and early venturings on the part of buccaneers from Spain." Tropicality, Cocks argues, was not necessarily a categorization of a set of geographic spaces but rather a network of ideas created by tourists, travel writers, boosters, and diarists in the nineteenth and twentieth centuries.[27] These ideas, South of the

Women lounging by the South of the Border pool, postcard. Courtesy Postcard Collection, South Caroliniana Library, University of South Carolina, Columbia.

Border shows, could be imported to regions and areas that were not traditionally seen as "tropical."[28]

Schafer, in his construction of South of the Border, created one of these tropical spaces in South Carolina. His rest stop was full of lush palmetto trees, spaces to swim and tan, and some light encouragement to participate in the excessive sexuality of tropical spaces. Postcards from South of the Border advertised that just a stone's throw from the highway, visitors could enjoy perfectly manicured golf courses, gleaming pools, and rich Mexican food. One postcard featured several bikini-clad women draped around a turquoise pool with a several-stories-tall sombrero looming overhead. Towering over the American flag in the corner of the photo, the panoptic sombrero, along with the palmetto trees lining the pool, brought the tropicality of the place into focus.[29]

Several promotional materials included mentions of sexuality as an important draw for visitors to the rest stop. The back of one postcard featured the customary "Pedro speak" advertising South of the Border's golf course: "Pedro got all kinds of year 'round' sports for ever'bodee . . . golf, swimming, tennis, shuffle-board, ping-pong, honeymooning. Y'all come!" Schafer sought to corner the honeymooners' market by making clear that South of the Border was a place a new couple could let loose. Highlighting the new motel rooms, South of the Border advertised its "20 Honeymoon Suites (Heir Conditioned!) Motel." In a March 1965 letter written to South of the Border from visitors, Mr. and Mrs. "R. H. K., Jr." the couple exclaimed "the bed (round!) was out of this world." If their night at South of the Border resulted in a boy, they wrote, "I am sure his name will be Pedro." In the middle of one of the most religiously conservative areas of the country, Schafer created a tropical space that embraced rather than restricted sexuality. However, Schafer toed a delicate line in these advertisements: maintaining the desire for sexual transgression but in the context of a heterosexual marriage.[30]

Some of Schafer's discussions of sex were less subtle. One of his billboards included a giant three-dimensional firework in the shape of a barely veiled phallus. The text of the billboard read: "Pedro's Fireworks (Does Yours?)." In 1958, the South of the Border gift shop, the Mexico Shop, included an adult section that featured the sign "Men Only—Ladies Keep Out." Separated from the rest of the Mexico Shop by a beaded curtain, this adults-only section included racy magazines, pin-ups, and cigars. Eventually it would become a standalone "Pedro's Dirty Old Man Shop."[31] These references to sex, while certainly intended to be cheeky, were more transgressive when situated in the religious and socially conservative milieu of late-1950s South Carolina.

In spite of these strictures, Schafer made South of the Border somewhere that tourists and locals alike could escape the restrictive sexual and moral codes of the Cold War era. This even included dancing at "Pedro's DISCOTHEQUE!" which was "open til 1AM in the Top O' the Sombrero building."[32] Schafer imported key features of tropical destinations to create a world of leisure where white visitors could find an escape on the side of the highway. In short, Schafer made South Carolina tropical.[33]

South of the Border advertised itself as a place where several overlapping vices could flourish. Mimicking the looser moral codes that those in the United States believed they would find in Latin America, Schafer highlighted the vices like sex, dancing, and excessive consumption that visitors could find at South of the Border. For those travelers unable to afford to fly to Mexico or the Caribbean, South of the Border offered a place to engage in the transgressive activities imagined to be reserved for those spaces.

A necessary feature of tropical spaces was an encounter with racial difference. Tropicality, Cocks argues, "became a critical element in the consolidation of racial difference." Tropical spaces, it was argued, "produced dark-skinned, lazy, passionate people and temperate zones pale-skinned, hard-working, cool-headed ones." To enjoy the pleasures of tropicality did not necessarily require a direct encounter with tropical people, but the specter of their presence was important for white people to feel they could act differently. The creation of Pedro as a central feature of South of the Border represented Schafer's effort at creating a (two-dimensional) embodiment of racial otherness.[34]

Importantly, the tropicality of South of the Border gestured to a kind of racial difference that originated outside of the United States and therefore was not tainted by the very present concerns of civil rights activism occurring all around South of the Border. Although the racial scripts surrounding South of the Border's Mexican theme certainly echoed those about Black people and hypersexuality, they were situated in a foreign place where that racial difference posed little threat to the daily lives of white southerners. It was important, then, that South of the Border and Pedro circulated in racial ideas about Mexicanness as distinct from Blackness.

The Creation of Pedro

The Mexican theme at South of the Border was not complete without Pedro. Although some of the earliest billboards advertising South of the Border included only a sombrero and serape in the corner as a gesture to the Mexican theme, they quickly moved to highlight Pedro as the rest stop's mascot. Rather than an amorphous Mexican "theme," Pedro emerged as a critical (and fantastical) interlocutor for South of the Border's visitors. Short, round, dark-skinned, mustachioed, widely grinning, and always donning a serape and sombrero, Pedro was the perfect fantasy of racial difference for South of the Border's visitors.

There are several stories of how Pedro came to be the mascot at South of the Border. In one of Pedro's many origin stories, Alan Schafer traveled to Mexico to build import connections for his beer distribution company where he met two Mexican men who he recruited to work at South of the Border. Upon his return, Schafer successfully acquired US visas for the men, who then worked at South of the Border as bellboys for many years. Although their actual names are unknown, staff and guests "started calling them Pedro and Pancho, and eventually just Pedro."[35]

The story seemed to be more than apocryphal. When Schafer was on trial for voter fraud in 1982, his lawyer retold the story of Pedro and Pancho as evidence of Schafer's generosity. Additionally, scholar Nicole King found further evidence of this story when she interviewed Shirley Jones, who began working at South of the Border in 1965. Jones confirmed the story, explaining that Pedro "worked over at the motel when [she] started." If the story was true, then

Pedro and Pancho, like Karla Galarza and her family, were another example of the many small Latino migrations to the Southeast that were managed by Jim Crow.[36]

In another related origin story, the Pedro character emerged from the first nickname guests gave to motel workers, regardless of the race of the workers. By the 1970s, the South of the Border staff would include many Lumbee Indians from nearby Robeson County who were also referred to as "Pedros."[37] In fact, South of the Border advertised open positions, writing, "We need Pedros (bell hops)," demonstrating that the practice of calling employees "Pedros" stretched beyond the potentially darker-skinned Lumbee employees.[38] Instead, it was common practice to refer to all bell hops as "Pedros." In this story, Pedro was not drawn from specific Mexican people but rather a collective fantasy enacted by South of the Border's visitors.

Perhaps partly inspired by these visitors, Schafer claimed in another interview that the origin of "Pedro" grew out of customers' repeated question, "Where's the Mexican guy that runs this place?" The question is revealing in two ways. First, it demonstrates that Schafer's decision to add the character of Pedro had more to do with meeting the needs of his customers' fantasies than with naming two workers at the rest stop. Second, it shows that visitors at South of the Border sought engagement with racial difference when they visited. In fact, according to Schafer's sister, Evelyn Hechtkopf, people would mistake local Lumbee Indians or even dark-skinned Jews like herself for Mexicans. "People would go up to them [the Lumbee]," Hechtkopf recalled, "and think that they're Spanish. They will come up and think we know Spanish. They'll see dark people and think that they speak Spanish." Customers' continued search for racial difference at South of the Border brings to the fore Schafer's success in fostering tropicality at his rest stop. Pedro, real or imagined, was important for fulfilling the desires of visitors for encounters with racial others.[39]

It is not clear if Pedro emerged from real people, the imagination of Schafer, or the longings of visitors. Regardless of his origin, he quickly took on a cartoonish image more characteristic of the era. Speedy Gonzales made his first appearance in 1953 and got his own show in 1955. *The Cisco Kid*, which ran from 1950 to 1956, featured Pancho, and in 1959, José Jiménez was launched to national fame on the *Steve Allen Show*. The links between José Jiménez and Pedro are particularly striking. Jiménez was created for the *Steve Allen Show* by Bill Dana, a Hungarian Jew born William Szathmary. The character was famous for his accent and his inversion of the letter *h* for *j*. "You" became "ju," "yes" became "jes," and in a skit featuring Jiménez as Santa, "ho, ho, ho" became "jo, jo, jo." The character propelled Dana's career, helping garner him Grammy Award nominations, a television series, and a performance as Jiménez at President John F. Kennedy's Inauguration Ball. José Jiménez and Pedro represented characters drawn from the same patchwork of racial ideology—both were designed by Jewish men and shared thick accents and darkened faces.[40]

Although Pedro emerged out of a different history and was doing different cultural work from blackface minstrelsy, the linkages are hard to ignore.[41] In the 1950s, as blackface grew increasingly controversial and unpopular, Pedro's perpetually wide grin, oversize mustache, and sombrero easily evoked the wide-lipped, ear-to-ear smile of most blackface minstrels. Like blackface, Pedro was a product of white fantasies, and there was both a complicated identification with and a violent distancing from the subject of imitation.[42] Unlike blackface, however, the production of Pedro was not serving as the cultural foundation for Jim Crow and other forms of racial violence. He was therefore connected to, but distinct from, these other anti-Black forms of culture.

A critical part of the creation of the Pedro character was his accent—which mirrored that of José Jiménez.[43] His heavily accented speech, only expressed through South of the Border's promotional materials, was always spelled out phonetically to dramatize the broken English. For example, when Pedro is quoted in South of the Border's advertisements, the word "big" is replaced with "beeg," "the" with "zee," and "business" with "beezness." An advertisement for the newly renovated Sombrero House read, "AMIGOS! pedro at long las' haz feenesh heez $100,000 kitchen renovation—and NOW eez ready to cater your NEXT PARTY!"[44] The emphasis on his accent used humor as a way to mark Pedro as racially non-white.

However, the same humor that animated characters like Pedro and Jose Jiménez affected how actual Latino people were being racialized. Historian Adrian Burgos notes, for example, that Latino baseball players were often misquoted or had their accents exaggerated in the press as a way to racialize them as non-white. In one case, a 1957 edition of *Sporting News* quoted Miguel Angel González, a coach for the St. Louis Cardinals, saying, "No need to tole someboddy else how to run heez beez-ness." His speech mirrored much of the same exaggerated accent for which Pedro was famous.

Baseball players were not alone; other Latino stars faced similar treatment in the media. Estelita Rodriguez, a Cuban singer and dancer described by one paper as a "Black-haired Cuban, tiny and fiery," was quoted complaining, "Everyones treat me like a keed." Elsewhere in the story the accent appears, including her saying things like "I theenk" and "heem."[45] More than simply poking fun,

Burgos argues, this press coverage contributed to the "intellectual disenfranchisement" of these players, reinforcing popular perceptions of Latino people as "exotic, inarticulate, and unintelligent."[46] What may have seemed like an innocent joke at the expense of fictional characters like Pedro and Jose Jiménez, was helping undergird the systematic racism faced by Latino people in this era.

Characters like José Jiménez fit what media studies scholar Charles Ramírez Berg has called the "male buffoon"—one of several archetypes of Latino people in film and television.[47] The male buffoon was simpleminded, struggled with standard English, and was overly emotional. Pedro's English was often broken to the point of illegibility, and his childlike humor and liberal deployment of all-capitalized writing evidenced his crude emotionality. The construction of Pedro drew on these racial ideologies that were formed largely in the West and Southwest but would later take on southern expressions. His broken English would be accented with southern speech patterns, and his simplemindedness was often juxtaposed against the even greater foolishness of Yankees.[48]

The emergence of the male buffoon was a counterpoint to more insidious racial ideologies of the time. South of the Border's heyday in the 1950s overlapped with the mass deportation campaign known as "Operation Wetback." This campaign to deport unauthorized migrants drawn to the United States, in part, by the Bracero Program resulted in the apprehension of more than 800,000 Mexican migrants between 1953 and 1955. Traditional sites of Mexican settlement like California, Texas, and Illinois were particularly hard-hit by these deportations. The cultural effects of the campaign were felt by Mexicans and Mexican Americans accused of being "wetbacks." Accused of stealing jobs and draining precious welfare resources, the "wetback" figure was reviled by white and Mexican American alike.[49]

The constellation of racist ideologies that formed Pedro were particularly salient in the West and Southwest of the United States. The history of conquest and large Mexican and Mexican American populations in those regions meant that these Latino archetypes carried different weight in the West and Southwest where policing brownness was an important feature of white supremacy.[50] The Southeast, however, would not see these racial tropes weaponized to deport Latino people until much later.

This did not mean, however, that the South was insulated from national discourses about Mexicans. Southern news coverage of Latino cultural production mimicked some of these tropes. For example, the *Jackson Sun*'s coverage of the performance "Romance of Old Mexico" noted how the lead, Senorita Rubio [*sic*], was able to draw on her "Incan ancestry, which dates back to about the year

1100 AD," to strengthen the "authentic and historical" Mexican review.[51] North Carolina coverage of "Fiesta Mexicana" emphasized connections to "ancient Aztecs and Mayans" and celebrated the show's ability to be "alternately exotic and subtle as the program dictates."[52] Setting aside the fact that the Inca Empire had no presence in Mexico, these events emphasized the exotic pleasures of Mexico that were coded as both Indigenous and premodern.[53]

The Mexico Shop and the other satellite gift shops, which were marquee features at South of the Border, also traded on these ideas of premodern Mexico. One billboard referencing the famous gift shop at South of the Border featured a large elephant and the text, "Fill up yo' trunque weeth pedro's junque." The shops sold a mix of "authentic" Mexican goods and pieces of memorabilia that prominently featured Pedro's image. This included an array of Pedro dolls, dishtowels, plates, keychains, t-shirts, and ashtrays.

The same whimsy that defined the consumption characteristic of South of the Border's many gift shops also contained racist and violent undertones. Scholar Steven Dubin has written about the power of items like these in the South to extend social control and racial hierarchy. Focusing primarily on images of Black servitude drawn from blackface minstrelsy that circulated in the South during the Jim Crow era, Dubin argues that "Blacks and other minority groups" have been "kept in symbolic servitude by the repetition of particular images in mass-produced items." Dubin's analysis extends beyond the use of Black imagery in the US South to consider the way a diverse cross section of non-white communities were commodified through the use of these objects. These objects helped define who was outside of the social boundaries of whiteness and, as a result, produced solidarities among white consumers.[54]

The consumption of Pedro paraphernalia, while emerging from a different history than the blackface-inspired products examined by Dubin, circulated in overlapping ways that produced social solidarity among white visitors at South of the Border. Using, for example, an ashtray with Pedro's sleeping figure in the center melded the humorous content and violent components of these "totem-like" products. Their functional use, literally putting cigarettes out on the figure of Pedro, Dubin would argue of similar objects in his article "Symbolic Slavery," "transmit[ted] a message of violence which is activated through employment of force on a minor scale." At the intersection of humor and violence, objects bearing Pedro's image linked their white consumers. This expanded beyond the consumption of Pedro into racial play, and visitors would also find social solidarity in embodying these images by "playing Mexican."

Playing Mexican

Pedro initially became famous for his "Mexi-speak" on the hundreds of bill-boards that crowded the highways for nearly 100 miles north and south of South of the Border. One famous billboard featuring Pedro with a large ape, read, "NO MONKEY BUSINESS! Joost Yankee Panky!" Another featured a hand of playing cards and the writing, "BEEG DEAL." One of the billboards was entirely upside down with the writing "Too Moch Tequila?" This selection demonstrates that even if these expressions were not linked with Mexico, Pedro's mimicry of a "Mexican" accent connected these disparate ideas.[55]

South of the Border's influence continued to grow locally, expanding the power of its racial logic. In August 1961, Alan Schafer began running a weekly column called "Borderlines" in the local newspaper, the *Dillon Herald*. It was primarily a recurring advertisement for the rest stop, but it also featured up-dates on prominent visitors to South of the Border, welcomes to new hires, and best wishes for departing employees. The addition of a weekly column also signaled the growing power of the rest stop in the Dillon community. Much of the column was written in the "Mexi-speak" for which Pedro became famous. The explanation of the new column read: "Thees South of the Border, she grow an' grow & grow.... So beeg pedro hisself have hard time keep opp weeth every-theeng goin' on.... So theenk maybe have regular place een papaire write down all about South of the Bordaire. Thees way pedro & all hees frans also keep opp, maybe out see for self."[56] The "Borderlines" column eventually became a bit more readable, but its thickly accented prose remained a consistent feature of the publication.

Pedro was the perpetual narrator of South of the Border's promotional materials, and his accented and broken English matched his swarthy, musta-chioed embodiment. When the "Borderlines" column celebrated its 143rd week of publication, the announcement read: "pedro happee to announce, these ees hees WAN HUNDRED FORTEE THIRD anniversary . . . been printing pedro's Bor-daire Lines for 143 weeks. . . . You like, no?" His broken dialect was mimicked in all of South of the Border's advertisements and in the weekly "Borderlines." The authors of the column followed the protocol established in South of the Border promotional materials by never capitalizing Pedro's name, quite literally representing his inferior status.[57]

Although South of the Border has been famous for its history as part of roadside culture, it was also a particularly influential institution in Dillon and

Sombrero Room, South of the Border, postcard. Courtesy Carolina Studio Photograph Collection, South Caroliniana Library, University of South Carolina, Columbia.

neighboring counties. As economic engines, South of the Border and Schafer's beer distribution company were among the area's biggest employers. South of the Border was also a space where people celebrated events, hosted business meetings and conferences, had family outings, and even went on honeymoons. In February 1965, the Dillon High School International Relations Club went to South of the Border to "partake of Mexican food and 'culture.'" They ate in the Fiesta Room, a cafeteria-style diner with the ceiling covered in sombreros. Writing to Pedro after their visit, they thanked him for his "help een study(ing) Latin countries."[58] In addition to serving the local community as a hub for so-cial life, the Dillon High School International Relations Club's decision to visit South of the Border as a way to engage in Mexican culture suggests some locals saw it as a site of authentic Mexicanness. South of the Border's racial discourse, therefore, was perhaps more powerful for locals than visitors because the social and cultural worlds of Dillonites were entangled with the rest stop.[59]

One way that South of the Border visitors engaged with the racial milieu of the space was to "play Mexican." To play Mexican was to dress up in Mexican costumes and mimic a Mexican accent as part of the performance. The pho-tographic archive of South of the Border includes several family photos from white visitors who dressed up in "traditional" Mexican costumes to match their exotic new setting.[60] Women wore billowing skirts decorated in large

Tourists at South of the Border with burros. Courtesy Carolina Studio Photograph Collection, South Caroliniana Library, University of South Carolina, Columbia.

embroidered flowers in the style of many traditional Mexican garments. Men wore ponchos, serapes, and the omnipresent sombrero. Children were carefully posed next to burros in images framed by blooming palmetto trees.[61] In one photograph, a white family posed men in sombreros seated on the ground with their heads bowed so they appeared to be sleeping. In this image, the racial play was not just sartorial. Mimicking Pedro's typical sleeping pose, these white families personified racist narratives of Mexicans as drunk and lazy.[62] The performance of these racist images was key to the (re)production of whiteness and white identity for South of the Border's visitors.

The phrase "playing Mexican" draws on Philip Deloria's concept of "playing Indian." In his book *Playing Indian* (1999), he argues that white people "played Indian" as a way to negotiate anxieties associated with modernization in the twentieth century. This play included dressing up in costumes, participating in powwows, and becoming dedicated hobbyists interested in researching and reproducing Indian traditions. He argues white Americans' fixation on Native Americans came from the feelings of dislocation produced by the brutalities of

Tourists at South of the Border gift shop. Courtesy Carolina Studio Photograph Collection, South Caroliniana Library, University of South Carolina, Columbia.

World War II and the modernizing world around them. Native Americans, as they imagined them, represented a simpler, premodern time.[63]

Given that South of the Border rose to prominence in the postwar years, its visitors also were likely affected by this disruption in sense of self. This was even more extreme for local white Carolinians who were experiencing the challenges to the system of Jim Crow laws in the US South. Black Carolinians, along with Black southerners across the region, were also waging a war against white supremacy in all its forms. In the summer of 1955, fifty-seven Black adults signed a petition demanding an end to segregation in the Orangeburg, South Carolina, public schools—an area less than two hours south of Dillon. The local White Citizens' Council published the petition in the white-owned newspaper along with the names of the signers—exposing the Black signers to white vigilante violence.[64] In response to this publication, Black residents in nearby Clarendon County organized a boycott of Citizens' Council–owned businesses, which grew when the NAACP threw its support behind the movement.[65] Orangeburg was not alone, and civil rights activity on both sides of the Carolina border was escalating throughout this period.[66]

It was in this context that South of the Border visitors dressed up and "played Mexican." Being able to "play Mexican" gave some white visitors a place to find pleasure and also navigate the changing landscape of the second half of the twentieth century. With their growing fear that whiteness might be dislocated from its meaning, playing Mexican allowed them to play with racial hierarchy even in the absence of actual Mexicans to challenge this type of cultural violence.

The tourist fascination with Cherokee culture and the popularity of "chiefing" suggests that "playing Indian" could serve as more than a metaphor in an analysis of southern roadside culture.[67] Nearby Cherokee populations also exploited the expanding roadside culture and the desire of white tourists to play with race on the roadside. In the 1940s, Cherokee men set up teepees near roadside souvenir shops and donned the headdresses of the Plains Indians to draw in tourists who would pay to have their photo taken together. This practice came to be known as "chiefing." When some "chiefs" attempted to wear traditional Cherokee buckskins, rather than the culturally mismatched Plains Indian headdresses, they found tourists were less responsive. Henry Lambert, a "chief" from the region, said of the choice to wear attire not traditional to the Cherokee tribe, "If you are going into show business, dress for it." Tourists sought interactions with Native Americans that affirmed their narrow racial fantasies. Therefore, the roadside was a place where white tourists looked to play with ideas about race and difference.[68]

Because of the large Lumbee population in nearby Robeson County, imagined "Indianness" circulated quite differently than fantasies of "Mexicanness." In the 1950s and 1960s in Robeson County, Indianness was a category that was being actively contested through struggle, and, therefore, "playing Indian" may not have provided the escapism from a changing world that many white southerners longed for in these racial performances. To "play Mexican," however, did not invoke these embattled questions of tribal sovereignty. Lacking a local Mexican population, "playing Mexican" allowed participants to evade questions being raised by American Indian, as well as African American, movements for social justice.

Visitors were not the only ones who dressed up in Mexican costume. They were likely taking their cues from the staff who were dressed in similar garb. A photo of South of the Border staff shows that sombreros and serapes were typical for the men, while women wore white shirts and skirts with ruffled layers and flowers that most closely mirrored a flamenco outfit. However, the same photograph shows that among the staff, segregated by race in the image, only white workers wore Mexican-themed costumes. The Black staff all wore simple kitchen uniforms.[69]

The difference in costumes also suggested a division of labor at the rest stop that placed white employees in front-of-house positions and Black employees in the kitchen and behind the scenes. The most immediate implication of this is material. Black employees held jobs that traditionally paid less and were likely unable to work in front-of-house positions because their race would disrupt the fantasy of South of the Border.

In the image of the segregated staff, we see that Black labor was a part of the functioning of South of the Border, and therefore white visitors likely interacted with Black staff during their visit. Despite all the racial play at South of the Border, it was a place structured by Jim Crow, and staff were separated by race both in the way they appeared (costumed versus noncostumed) and the labor they did. One might wonder why Black staff were even included in the image if they were not part of the fantasy. However, an important part of the fantasy was racial play with the safety of Blackness and whiteness preserved as distinct poles. It was, in fact, this marked difference that made it possible for white visitors to play with brownness.

Similarly, Deloria found that white people believed that "playing Indian" should be reserved for white people. The policing of Blackness in spaces of racial play, he argues, was necessary because he writes, "In the absence of firm lines around Blackness and redness the very notion of being white became unstable." As in the case of "playing Indian," lines around whiteness, brownness, and Blackness needed to be tightly ordered. Only white people could transgress and play Mexican. Aside from the staff, nothing in the archive shows Black visitors at South of the Border in the 1950s and 1960s, much less Black visitors dressing up as Mexican.[70]

Despite the lack of archival evidence, Schafer claimed on multiple occasions that South of the Border had been integrated since its founding. As he put it to a *Washington Post* journalist: "We were the first major motel/restaurant south of Washington who from the start always had an open-door policy—first come, first served. And also we checked only the color of their money, not their skins."[71] However, there is no indication in the ads run by Schafer that it was integrated, and South of the Border is not found in the 1950 or 1960 editions of the *Green Book*, an African American travel guide that designated places where

Black travelers could eat and stay on the roadside without facing Jim Crow.[72] Moreover, given the proliferation of the Klan in the area and the violent battles fought over integration, it seems unlikely South of the Border could succeed while openly defying the Jim Crow order.[73]

No evidence indicates that South of the Border welcomed Black patrons, but it did seem to serve local Lumbee Indians. Karen Blu in her study of the Lumbee found that "Indians frequently proclaimed, whether correctly or not, 'You can get anything there.'" During the dry years in Robeson County, Blu writes, "Indians seeking to purchase any [illegal items] often drove to [South of the Border], where they could be also entertained by the passing parade of, to them, strange people with strange ways." The Lumbee, like many Latino people elsewhere in the South, occupied a complex racial position between the poles of white and Black. They were able to access this space that seemingly prohibited Black patrons, and yet the presence of the Lumbee at South of the Border did not necessarily mean that Schafer and other white locals were welcoming to the local Indian community.[74]

Lumbee Indians were targets of Klan intimidation and violence, were excluded from many spaces, and, in the case of South of the Border, were ridiculed on the billboards. One of the billboards advertising South of the Border's motel read: "Don't be a lost injun! Get a reservation."[75] It also featured Pedro dressed up in a cartoonish image of a Native American wielding a knife and making smoke signals.[76] Pedro, the billboard showed, could also "play Indian." In this billboard, the Lumbee were given a similar treatment as Pedro—flattened and made easily consumable by white visitors.[77] Billboards, however, were not the only way South of the Border communicated ideas about race.

Part of playing Mexican was the mock Pedro accent, which allowed the pleasures of racial play to extend far beyond the limits of South of the Border. One of the many ways that visitors were encouraged to play Mexican was through the mimicry of Pedro's accent. In the weekly column "Borderlines," there was a section for "LOVE LETTERS to pedro," where tourists who had visited South of the Border could write to reflect on what a good time they had and practice their Pedro accents. "Senor y Senora [sic] RB" wrote to Pedro after they had visited South of the Border when traveling from Charlottesville, Virginia, to Florida to reach their ultimate destination, Rancagua, Chile. They split their letter into two parts—one in English and the other in "Pedro speak." They began by complimenting Pedro on the "pretty original thing [he has] going" at South of the Border and concluded with their imitation of Pedro, writing, "pedro theenk eet prettee Chillee here, too, Amigo!" Another letter read: "pedro, Mi Amigo:

Averytheeng, she more Hokey-Dokey. She muy Bueno . . . from Senor y Senora [sic] WRH and Family." The letters in this column were largely addressed to Pedro rather than Schafer or the other South of the Border employees. However, it was Schafer who was the author of Pedro's accent and the creator of Pedro's world.

Along with the gifts and trinkets they purchased, many enjoyed using Pedro's "Mexi-speak" while reflecting on their time at South of the Border. In one of the "Guest Check Comments" left by visitors at South of the Border, a guest wrote: "Thee sees wan fine place, amigo! I'm happy I stopped Sous of these Border—Si!"[78] The interaction with Pedro, even if only imagined, was clearly significant for white visitors. By writing these letters, visitors carried with them, beyond the confines of the rest stop, the pleasures of playing Mexican.

South of the Border's advertising also invited white visitors into this racial fantasy. Advertising invited white visitors to imagine themselves as Latino. For example, one postcard read, "Sommtheeng for every Juan to do! (Juanitas, too!)."[79] The postcard hails visitors at South of the Border, the vast majority of whom were white, to imagine themselves as Latino or as Juans and Juanitas. These advertisements gestured to the fantasies of racial play at South of the Border. The choice to dress up and mimic Pedro's fictional accent were all ways that Schafer created a world in which visitors could play with the boundaries of their own racial identity.

South of the Border not only was steeped in this rhetoric of civilizational backwardness, exoticism, and authenticity; it also reshaped these tropes. For example, the accent mimicked by visitors and South of the Border promotional materials paralleled some of the national styles of "Mexi-speak," like those used by José Jimenez and Speedy Gonzales, but Pedro was not simply an amalgam of these images. Taking it far beyond the consumption of national tropes, visitors were encouraged to embody and perform these tropes. In the process of this performance, ideas about Mexicanness were transformed. At South of the Border, Schafer and visitors infused these symbols of Mexicanness with southern ways of speaking and southern iconography.[80]

Making Pedro Southern at Confederateland

Pedro's Mexicanness was often embedded with southernness. For example, Pedro's voice in the weekly column "Borderlines" often moved between a "Mexican" and southern accent. When reporting on one of the workers, Senora [sic] Rosali Phillips's recent move to a neighboring town, "Borderlines" offered their best wishes: "Hope y'all lak yo' new home, Rosie." On the back of a previously mentioned postcard advertising South of Border, it read, "pedro got all kinds of year 'roun' sports. . . . Y'all come!" The "Borderlines" column welcomed new employees to South of the Border writing, "Welcome to the BORDER, y'all!" Pedro's famous Mexi-speak frequently slipped into, and at times was nearly identical to, a southern accent.[81]

The particular brand of southernness Pedro performed was often "Confederate." In the South of the Border menus and billboards, Pedro offered food that was "Confederate Cooking!! (Yankee Style)," and in his newspaper columns he used southern phraseology. The gesture to "Yankee Style" might indicate he was trying to split the difference and speak to his two audiences: tourists and locals. The back of one postcard offered "World famous Mexican-Confederate Cuisine in pedro's Sombrero Room."[82] In one advertisement, South of the Border promoted "Pedro's SPESHUL THEES WEEK: CONFEDERATE FRIED CHICKEN complete with all the trimmins' and REBEL FLAG." Here the Southern accent, "the trimmins'," and "Mexi-Speak," "speeshul," are seamlessly blended in Pedro's voice.[83]

Schafer's South of the Border was not entirely alone in the southeastern Mexican food market.[84] However, by fusing southern and Mexican imagery, Schafer departed from other Mexican restaurants in the Southeast that focused on their authentic Mexican food as their major selling point. Places like Casa Montez in Arkansas advertised itself as "Home of authentic Mexican food," El Patio in Louisiana offered "only genuine 'south of the border' dishes," and the Plaza Café, also in Louisiana, invited diners to "Enjoy Mexican food just as they serve in Old Mexico."[85] Schafer instead used "authenticity" sparingly and emphasized the fusion of Mexican and Confederate cuisines. This divergence from the advertising strategies used by other Mexican restaurants was seen both in the foods offered and the advertisements for South of the Border. Moreover, although other Mexican restaurants amplified their "foreignness" as a way to legitimize their authenticity, Schafer kept South of the Border both foreign and local as he injected southern loyalty into the rest stop.

The embrace of a Confederate Pedro also meant mocking Yankees as a way to further establish South of the Border's southern bona fides. Another billboard from the early 1960s read, "Pedro never shot a Yankee . . . (but maybe robbed a few?)." In a reversal of the carpetbagger story, Pedro, in this advertisement, was a southerner able to outwit northern "Yankees."[86] In a "Borderlines" column, Schafer wrote that a member of the New York Stock Exchange was interested in investing in a proposed horse-racing track. However, he wrote, "Pedro moch flattered, bott prefer to keep these a Local Community Project . . . jus' need YANQUIS to help PAY FOR EET!"[87] Yankees were always the punchline in these jokes. Alan Schafer imbued the rest stop with a tropical ethos but made sure to keep it rooted in its southern context. South of the Border's advertisements used accented southern prose, the Confederacy was celebrated, and Yankees were ridiculed.

The southern theme at South of the Border took its fullest form when Alan Schafer opened Confederateland within the rest stop. The family-friendly theme park included a Confederate Train that weaved through the Haunted Swamp, Tobacco Road, Buffalo Billage, Peacock Alley, and Cactus Mountain before turning into Pedroville Station. Schafer also opened a Confederateland Golf Course and Pedro's Plantation.[88] The centerpiece of the new site was Fort Pedro, a log cabin that operated as a "museum and Confederate souvenir bazaar." As evidenced by the names of several sites at Confederateland, Pedro was an integral part of Schafer's newest invention. Pedro played his part promoting the new attraction as he did for South of the Border; however, this time he was wearing a Confederate uniform.[89] In another form of provisional whiteness, Pedro's appeal was drawn both from his foreignness and his role as a symbol of local white nostalgia for the Confederacy.

The opening of Confederateland, like the rest of South of the Border, was a spectacle. On August 28, 1961, Schafer welcomed an estimated 6,000 people to South of the Border's newest attraction.[90] "This is Confederateland," he began, "and most of us here are Confederates. But if you should see any Yankees wandering around don't treat them too rough. Somebody's got to pay for all of this!"[91] Photos of the opening show several white men dressed in Confederate uniforms and Dillon High School's majorettes in form-fitting jumpers decorated with the stars and bars of the Confederate flag. Another image shows a group of visitors milling outside Fort Pedro with the South of the Border sombrero sign in the background. In this second image, the omnipresent Mexicanness collides with the opening of Confederateland. Rather than separate this new attraction from the Mexican theme, Schafer chose to let the two intermingle.[92]

The construction of Confederateland was part of a larger regional investment in Lost Cause narratives in which Confederate soldiers were defenders of their southern way of life against vindictive Yankees who used their deep pockets to crush the Confederate army in a particularly brutal and inhumane fashion. This reimagining of the Civil War tried to legitimize the southern war

Confederateland opening. Courtesy Carolina Studio Photograph Collection, South Caroliniana Library, University of South Carolina, Columbia.

effort both in terms of the valor of the soldiers and the righteousness of their cause. To commemorate the event, Schafer had constructed the Confederate Star Tower, which soared ninety-six feet over Confederateland and rotated day and night. Dedicated to "the noble men of the Confederacy who gave their lives and fortunes for a cause they believed right," the tower, along with Confederateland, stood as a memorial to the Lost Cause.[93]

Additionally, one of the floats at Confederateland's opening featured an image of a soldier giving another soldier water with the following inscription: "Sgt. Richard Kirkland of Camden Giving Wounded Enemy Water."[94] Images like these focused on the nobility of Confederate soldiers in the face of Yankee belligerence. In addition to recasting Confederates as victims of Yankee aggression, these discourses reimagined slavery as a benign, and even benevolent, institution. The Lost Cause narratives took many forms, including films like *The Birth of a Nation* (1915), the formation of groups like the United Daughters of the Confederacy, and monuments to the Confederacy, which began to appear across the South many years after the war was over.

The Confederate theme was always serving two constituencies—north-erners fascinated by the South and southerners anxious about their changing region. Like other fixtures in southern roadside culture, South of the Border played an important role in perpetuating Lost Cause fantasies and shoring up regional and racial identity during the civil rights movement. South of the Bor-der stood alongside Confederama, Lookout Mountain, and other "southern" or Confederate-themed road stops, as sites for the consolidation of white southern identity as Black protest threatened to reconfigure race in the region.[95]

The creation of these Lost Cause monuments, of which Confederateland was a part, helped inscribe onto the southern landscape a commitment to white supremacy that was under attack in the civil rights era. The construction of monuments to the Confederacy peaked in 1910, during what has been called the nadir of race relations, and had a resurgence between 1954 and 1968, some of the most active years of the civil rights movement.[96] Confederateland, con-structed in 1961, fits squarely into this period when southern communities began to build monuments to the Lost Cause as a way to defend against the victories of the civil rights movement. Schafer's choice, therefore, to highlight a mythic Confederate past, was saturated with his contemporary concerns about race and region.[97]

Lost Cause fantasies were so intoxicating in part because of the growing civil rights movement throughout the region. Confederateland, and South of the Border more broadly, was about escaping Black protest and reveling instead in doctored memories of Black servility. This included confining Black employees to the back of the restaurant and enforcing uniforms that cordoned them off from Pedro's world.

Additionally, the creation of Pedro's Plantation at Confederateland helped re-imagine a southern world free of the brutality of slavery at the same time it was deifying slavery's defenders. Visitors at Pedro's Plantation were invited to "pick tobacco, cotton, or taste a bit of sugarcane."[98] With the creation of Pedro's Plan-tation, Schafer envisioned Pedro not just as part of the Confederateland milieu but also as a plantation owner. By retooling the Pedro figure as the owner of enslaved peoples, his space in a provisional whiteness was secured. Certainly, Pedro remained the caricature of Mexicanness he had always been—but his injection into the history of the slave south also gave him a claim to a vexed kind of whiteness.

At Pedro's Plantation, Schafer refashioned the plantation landscape of dom-ination and control as one of leisure and play. Like the racial dress-up and the letter writing in Pedro's accent, Pedro's Plantation actively engaged visitors in the production of South of the Border's racial world. Schafer allowed white visitors to play with the types of labor done by enslaved people. In this way, South of the Border, and more specifically Confederateland, helped white visitors imagine a pre–Civil War South free of the violence of slavery and a contemporary southern moment free of the growing demands made by African Americans. Playing Mexican allowed visitors to lessen their growing anxiety of the changing postwar world. Pedro's Plantation allowed them to assuage their anxieties about the past.

Pedro's presence at Confederateland enforced, rather than destabilized, the racial binary in the South. By enlisting Pedro into the extension of Lost Cause ideology, Schafer demonstrated that Mexicanness could be used in service of white supremacy. While everything about Pedro seemingly chafed against a racial-binary system—his cartoonish visage clearly displayed how white southerners viewed Mexicans as "different"—he also became a tool in the fight to preserve white supremacy and segregation in the South. His image, his humor, and his difference were all part of what made him a compelling Lost Cause figurehead to usher visitors through the rest stop.

White southerners used racial play to manage these fears, and they also engaged in more direct forms of violence to maintain racial hierarchy. During the 1940s, white South Carolinians launched a vicious campaign against African Americans, which included violent and often deadly acts of white supremacy in an effort to exert social control. In 1957, James "Catfish" Cole led a Klan revival in both North and South Carolina. Cole, along with his fellow Klan members, terrorized local Black communities targeting activists and their families with violent intimidation. However, in one of Cole's most famous defeats, he led a group of Klan members to Robeson County to threaten the Lumbee population. As Cole began his speech, the lights were shot out and the rally was attacked by a group of local Indians, including Cherokee, Siouan, Lumbee, and Tuscarora community members. Cole and his fellow Klansmen were chased into the nearby swamps.[99]

For Dillonites, the civil rights movement was not happening somewhere else. The same white locals who were visiting the Fiesta Room at South of the Border after a long day of work were finding their world under attack. On February 1, 1960, a year and a half before the opening of Confederateland, four Black students from North Carolina A&T sat in at a Woolworth's in Greensboro, North Carolina, only two hours north of South of the Border. By October 1960, four national chains gave in to protestor demands and announced they would integrate 150 stores in 112 cities. Resulting in more than 3,600 arrests, the sit-in movement included more than 70,000 participants in 100 cities.[100] White southerners, and white Carolinians in particular, were witnessing a watershed moment in the evolution of race in their communities.

Black protest was, therefore, the unnamed backdrop of the founding of Confederateland. Pedro, despite all of his blatant racialization, was most importantly not Black and thus could extend the fantasies of white visitors searching for Lost Cause nostalgia and tropical pleasure. The integration of Pedro into a Confederate world, his southern accent, and his embrace of southern foodways suggest that southerners were imagining a Mexicanness that was not necessarily mutually exclusive with southernness. Mexicanness could mean something new at Confederateland, and in the figure of Pedro, some southerners could reconcile the paradox of his perpetual foreignness alongside his southernness and regional loyalty.[101]

Playing White

The escapism of South of the Border and Confederateland gains new meaning in light of these historical realities. Racial play was likely a way for white people to make meaning of the quickly shifting racial terrain. The loss of Jim Crow seemingly made the meaning of both whiteness and Blackness uncertain. As many in the nation dealt with the feeling of a loss of identity, white southerners experienced that acutely as they feared the racial order they held dear had begun to unravel.[102]

Schafer's choice to make this new attraction "Confederate," rather than another southern formation (e.g., "redneck" or "hillbilly"), animated a regional white supremacist politic within the rest stop. Constructing Confederateland at South of the Border imbued the existing white supremacist sensibilities of the rest stop with regional flavor. As such, the site was not only a place where white people fantasized about Mexicanness; it was also a place where they recast the meaning of southern whiteness. By Confederateland's 1961 opening, the United States had seen several important civil rights victories. Lost Cause monuments, like Confederateland, began popping up as symbolic and cultural bulwarks against civil rights progress.[103]

The construction of Confederateland threw South of the Border directly into a heated civil rights battle when Schafer invited the South Carolina Confederate War Centennial Commission (SCCWCC, originally named the South Carolina War Between the States Centennial Commission) to help open the new attraction. This controversial group had seceded from national centennial efforts after refusing to hold meetings in an integrated space. The highly contested conflict over Civil War commemoration, in which Confederateland was situated, became yet another battleground for southerners to fight against the advances of the civil rights movement. How the country remembered the war struck at the core of the, then contemporary, battle for civil rights. A 1960 editorial from the Black newspaper the *Atlanta Daily World* said of the struggle, "The South may have lost the war, but it is sure going to win the centennial." [104] In the midst of this, Schafer chose to invite to the opening of Confederateland members of the SCCWCC. The controversy worked its way to the national stage when President John F. Kennedy was forced to wade in to the fray and denounce the SCCWCC. The SCCWCC, then, was a group that had gained national fame as defenders of segregation and fierce protectors of the Lost Cause fantasies of the Civil War.[105]

South of the Border may have been defensive against the changing racial order, but Confederateland was on the offensive—producing and cementing Lost Cause narratives that recast the South as victims of northern aggression. At the opening, "pedro's special guests" included SCCWCC President John May who, in his "Confederate grays," gave a welcome speech. "All of this vast and beautiful development, and this Confederateland designed to foster and preserve the traditions we southerners hold dear," he began, "are the realization of the dream of Alan Schafer, who had the courage and the talent to make his dream come true."[106] The invitation of May and the SCCWCC aligned Schafer and Confederateland with a reactionary brand of white supremacy.

The opening not only imported controversial secessionist figures but also featured several local leaders. Among those in attendance included Dillon's mayor, Rudolph Jones, and the entire city council, which postponed its normal Monday night meeting to attend the opening.[107] The inaugural event at Confederateland was both a pageant designed to lure visitors from out of town and a local celebration of a new Dillon landmark. Confederateland, like South of the Border, despite its appeal to tourists, remained a profoundly local institution that was important in the racial imaginations of local Dillonites and nearby North and South Carolinians.

Images from the opening of Confederateland show that, in addition to Schafer and May, several other men wore Confederate uniforms.[108] This use of the uniform is significant. It echoed the white families at the same rest stop who wore sombreros and serapes in another form of racial play. The same way that the sombrero and the serape linked white patrons in their performance of racial difference, the Confederate uniform produced its own form of racial unification across a diverse subset of white people. It linked, for example, John May, a white South Carolina segregationist, with Alan Schafer, a Jewish entrepreneur.

This connection is significant given the marginal place of Jews in the South during this period. Southern Jews were excluded from social clubs, accused of being communists and agitating for civil rights, and subject to a marked increase in antisemitism during the years after *Brown v. Board of Education* (1954). This antisemitism was often deadly and included several attacks on southern synagogues, including the bombing of Temple Beth-El in Charlotte, North Carolina, on November 11, 1957. Four months later, Temple Emanuel in Gastonia was attacked as well, saved only by a faulty fuse attached to thirty sticks of dynamite. Gastonia and Charlotte were each less than three hours away from Dillon, South Carolina. Given the heightened antisemitism of the time, Schafer's decision to put on a Confederate uniform served as its own kind of dual racial play and act of self-preservation.[109]

The Confederate uniform could seemingly erase ethnic difference and allow Schafer to perform a whiteness from which he was often excluded. In an article announcing the opening of Confederateland, Schafer confidently posed in his Confederate grays. In the photo, Schafer has his leg propped up on the side of one of the two cannons protecting Fort Pedro. He is staring into the distance surveying what had developed into a multiacre roadside compound that showed no signs of slowing expansion. In the background, the Confederate star loomed above him with a giant mushroom cloud behind in the sky. The mushroom cloud, which had been superimposed by the photographer, brought a modern mark of warfare to this historic commemoration. The image, which appeared on the cover of the *Dillon Herald*, cast Schafer as a military leader— a nostalgic Confederate symbol of noble male virility. Schafer, who was likely involved in the staging of this photograph, was performing his whiteness to the Dillon community.[110]

Despite, or perhaps because of, the tentative place of Jews in the South, Alan Schafer's choice to don a Confederate uniform contained deeper meaning about race and racial play. Schafer, as a Jewish man who owned a bawdy rest stop in conservative South Carolina, found a way to connect with his southern white peers. It was through the anti-Blackness baked into the Confederate nostalgia and the engagement with fantasies of Mexicanness that Schafer was able to play white in his own way.

The overlapping and interwoven layers of racial play at South of the Border evidence the complexity of racial ideology in a region largely considered Black

"Kunnel Pedro," *Dillon (SC) Herald*, August 23, 1961. Courtesy South Caroliniana Library, University of South Carolina, Columbia.

and white. The caption underneath the front-page image of Schafer leaning on the cannon referred to Schafer as "Kunnel Pedro." This was not the only place he was given the moniker of colonel, or "Kunnel." Another image of Schafer in Confederate regalia, this time in front of Fort Pedro, included the caption: "KUNNEL PEDRO, Suh, resplendent in Confederate uniform."[111] Schafer being coined Kunnel Pedro, rather than a marker of racial difference, was further evidence of his whiteness.

Kunnel Pedro represented many of the overlapping racial performances at South of the Border. On the one hand, it was Schafer, a Jewish man, performing a brand of southern whiteness from which his religion precluded him. On the other, it was "Pedro" in a Confederate uniform, confirming the links between Mexicanness and southern whiteness and Pedro's provisional whiteness. Ultimately, it was Schafer posing as Pedro—connecting the two performances. After all, Schafer was the brainchild and author of much of South of the Border's advertising and promotional materials.

At the heart of it, Schafer was Pedro. He created this character and embodied him as he wrote the weekly "Borderlines" in Pedro's voice and created Pedro's world at South of the Border. The two were impossibly intertwined such that it was not clear where Schafer ended and Pedro began. The Mexican who ran this place, Kunnel Pedro, the one whom so many visitors sought out, was the fusion of Pedro and Schafer. White, Mexican, and Southern, Kunnel Pedro represented a southern Latino racial formation that linked fantasies of Mexicanness to southern white supremacy.

This southern Latino racial formation reinforced, rather than unsettled, strict separation between Blackness and non-Blackness. Pedro's inclusion in Confederateland showed that he could be embraced in a context in which some of the most straightforward efforts to preserve segregation continued. Pedro, and South of the Border's broader Mexican theme, was easily mobilized in service of anti-Blackness and white supremacy.

It was in the "tropical" spaces at South of the Border that these varied forms of racial play could flourish. Designed to capture both local and tourist visitors, South of the Border was a space where visitors were reimagining what it meant to be white in the era of the civil rights movement. As meanings of race evolved in the 1950s and 1960s, South of the Border changed as well. It made Mexicanness southern, and it became a staging ground for new types of racial consolidation. For locals, this meant fusing national and regional ideas about race to create a Mexican mascot who was also southern. For others, it meant "playing white" to mask ethnic difference and defend their provisional position in the category of whiteness. Decades before the beginning of large-scale migration of Latino people to the US South, Schafer, local Dillonites, and tourists were negotiating how Mexicanness and southernness intersected.

Although contemporary southern sensibilities about Mexicanness and Latinoness are different than they were in the 1960s, South of the Border remains largely unchanged. What Alan Schafer opened as a beer depot in 1949 stands today as one of the most well-known rest stops on the eastern seaboard. Today, its clientele is more local. Travelers headed from Maine to Miami rely primarily on air travel, leaving South of the Border to locals on their way south to Myrtle Beach or north to Virginia Beach. The rest stop endures as a beacon of racist fantasies of Mexicans and Latino people. Pedro is little changed in South of the Border's advertising or in the aging statues that litter the area. Gift shops are still brimming with trinkets covered in Pedro's image and the sombrero-heavy décor remains.

However, these visitors will not have exactly the same experience as Schafer's original customers in the 1950s and 1960s. Most prominently, Confederateland was eventually consolidated into "Fort Pedro," a Confederate museum and souvenir shop. Though Fort Pedro has since been shuttered, as late as 1986 it was grossing more than $3 million a year.[112] Despite its absence, the echoes of Confederateland remain throughout the rest stop. Confederate paraphernalia, both kitsch and commemorative, is available in most of the gift shops along-side "authentic" Mexican crafts, dream catchers and other "Native" crafts, and souvenirs with Pedro's enduring image. South of the Border, therefore, remains at the crossroads of several racial fantasies about Mexicanness, southern white-ness, and Indigeneity in this contemporary moment.[113]

In 2002, South of the Border produced a brochure titled "Pedro Presents South of the Border Award Weening Billboards," which included another ori-gin story of Pedro and South of the Border. This "heestory" began in 1950 when "pedro" (uncapitalized throughout) was "hitch-hiking down US 301, on his way back to Mexico" and got lost. In search of food, Pedro arrived in Hamer, South Carolina (an unincorporated community in Dillon County), and managed to "scrounge some bread and cheese" before returning to the road to resume hitch-hiking. At the roadside, a "Hungry Yankee" offered him five dollars for the sandwich that cost only a nickel in bread and cheese. Pedro, a hopeful entre-preneur, began by selling his "sanweech" for five dollars. When no one stopped, he reduced the price to fifty cents, and as a result, "Business Boomed!" Pedro sent for "hees" brother "pancho" to help staff his roadside "sanweech" stop. The story takes a tragic turn when, in the "Mad Rush" for sanweeches, "pancho was run over by a New York Cab Driver who had no insurance." Pedro moved away from the roadside for safety and installed signs for visibility and subsequently "leev happily Ever Seence!"[114]

The story of the "sanweech" casts Pedro both as a savvy trickster who has capitalized on Yankee ignorance, and a blundering fool unable to return to Mexico without getting lost and nearly dying. Additionally, by employing "Yankees" as the gullible consumers willing to pay such a large markup for a simple sandwich, the story conveys, with little subtlety, the abiding regional allegiances of the rest stop. Note, for example, that the motorist who killed Pedro's brother was a driver from New York. The death of Pancho both pokes fun at northern drivers and renders Mexican life expendable. The story of Pan-cho is even more disturbing in light of one of Schafer's earlier explanations that the character "pedro" emerged out of two workers, Pedro and Pancho, who eventually visitors simply called Pedro. The erasure of these real men's individ-uality and history by the guests is depicted as a death in this retelling.

This contemporary origin story is much more folktale than the other stories articulated by Schafer and South of the Border workers. Importantly, however, it reveals the persistent role of region in shaping Mexicanness at South of the Border. Published in 2002, the story was composed after some of the first waves of Latino migration to the South had already begun. Although the origin places Pedro on a quest to get "back to Mexico," he makes his home in South Carolina where he can capitalize on spendthrift Yankees. Pedro's southernness lingers in a moment when "southern" and "Latino" were incongruous for many.

South of the Border captures a forgotten moment in the history of southern racial ideology. Over the past two decades, the proliferation of draconian anti-immigration legislation throughout the South has been driven by growing nativism and white supremacy. Today, white southerners' views of Latino people are based on xenophobia that relies less on images of exoticness and tropicality and more on criminality and illegality. Pedro represented some of the most insidious forms of racial myopia, but he also held the potential for many southerners to see themselves reflected in his regional sensibilities. Pedro's southernness illustrates the importance of region in the formation of racial ideology.

Identifying Pedro's southernness is not an effort to recuperate a usable past of white southern fealty to Latino people. Rather, unearthing the regional nature of racial scripts helps us better understand the ever changing nature of white supremacy and its relationship to fantasies about Latino people. Racist tropes from the West and Southwest influenced southern racial discourse about Latino people, while white southerners also broke away from those narratives to produce new racial meanings that recruited Pedro into Lost Cause ideology. In the case of Pedro and South of the Border, white southerners reveled in the consumption of some of the most damaging racial discourses about Latino people and also produced new racial scripts that were regionally distinct.

Latino people, however, were not simply imagined by southerners in the civil rights era. At the same time that white southerners were using fantasies about Latino people to protect themselves from the growing civil rights movement, actual Latino people were actively participating in the movement to end southern Jim Crow. Their stories show what happened when southern fantasies about Latino people collided with reality.

■ ■ ■ ■ ■ ■ ■ ■ ■ ■ ■ ■ ■ ■ ■

CHAPTER THREE

Black, White, and Tan

Latinos, the Student Nonviolent
Coordinating Committee, and the
Civil Rights Movement, 1960–1970

After returning from a full day of canvassing for voter registration in the hot Mississippi sun, Luis Zapata, along with a Black Student Nonviolent Coordinating Committee (SNCC) organizer, suddenly found himself stranded at three in the morning with a flat tire on an unlit road in the Mississippi Delta. It was the early 1960s and, as Zapata described it, "a flat tire on a country road, being a known SNCC worker, was not a healthy thing to do." More than unhealthy, being caught without transportation late at night was a potential death sentence. In the midst of the fear and panic ensuing from the discovery that the car did not have a jack, a man drove up and offered to repair the tire, someone Zapata immediately identified as Mexican. After changing the tire, the man turned to Zapata and said, "If you see me in town, if you ever see me, you don't know me." Zapata understood the warning. Reflecting on the experience, he said, "'Cause his kids got to go to the white school and he wasn't about to lose that privilege, because there weren't enough Latinos for them to know."[1] Certainly, as the previous chapters have shown, "that privilege," as Zapata describes it, was a part of this man's reticence. However, the fear of being caught helping two interracial civil rights activists was another likely motivator for this man's insistence that Zapata not identify him again.

While white southerners in places like Dillon, South Carolina, were reimagining a Latinidad that could work alongside white supremacy, Black southerners and the Latino people who joined the civil rights movement were crafting their own notions of race. If fantasies of Mexicanness offered some white southerners in Dillon a reprieve from the growing energy of the civil rights movement, actual Mexican Americans were traveling to the South to fuel the fight against Jim Crow. Luis Zapata and the handful of other Latino organizers in SNCC who traveled from across the country to participate in the southern civil rights movement were also experiencing southern Jim Crow for the first time.

Using the stories of these activists as a way to think about race in the 1960s South, this chapter juxtaposes the stories of Black and non-Black Latino activists to demonstrate the importance of Blackness in structuring race among Latino people in the South. It traces how these activists moved through the Deep South during the civil rights era and how they struggled to reconcile their own racial identification with the way Black and white southerners understood their race. Additionally, it traces SNCC's evolving ideas about interracial organizing through the lens of its Latino organizers and, in the process, uncovers new dimensions about race, Latino people, and southern social movements during this time.

The stories of these SNCC workers are the first historical accounts of Latino people organizing in the southeastern civil rights movement.[2] Scholars have documented the coalitional politics of SNCC and how the organization built cross-racial linkages with Latino communities in the West and Southwest, but they have not yet attended to the experience of Latino people within the organization.[3] Existing literature on SNCC has largely focused on Black and white participants, and to the extent that it has focused on racial formation, it has been fixated on those two categories. However, SNCC's embedded beliefs about the categories of "white" and "Black" became clear when Latino members collided with the group's budding Black Power politics. As the group became more committed to various strands of Black Power (especially as it had shifted in the mid to late 1960s), many moved away from the commitment to interracial organizing and instead turned to building African diasporic power. In the process, non-Black Latino people discovered that, regardless of their self-identification as Mexican American or Chicano, their non-Blackness became the crucial barrier for their involvement in the organization. Their stories offer a window to understand how one Black-led southern civil rights organization conceptualized Latino activists and Latinos more broadly in this period.

Few sources capture how African American southerners viewed Latino people at this time. Therefore, SNCC volunteers, staff members, and local people, the majority of whom were southern and whose ideological center was located in the South, offer a distinct opportunity to see what Black southerners thought about Latino people in the civil rights era. Following SNCC's views on the racial position of Latino people in the organization over the course of the

1960s demonstrates the power of region in shaping ideas about race, and more specifically, how Black southerners reconciled Latino racial difference while also acknowledging the structuring role Blackness played in southern racial systems.

The South, therefore, becomes a powerful vantage point from which to consider the successes and limitations of organizing between Black people and non-Black Latino people.[4] SNCC's history, in particular, offers insights into the opportunities and challenges posed by these cross-racial alliances. As SNCC's racial ideology changed over the 1960s, the status of Latino members in the group changed as well. This evolution occurred at the same time as what would come to be known as the Chicano movement was growing in the West and Southwest. Chicano, an identifier that emerged from progressive Mexican American social movements, represented a turn toward cultural nationalism and ushered in a new era in Mexican American identity. However, even as the Chicano movement began to swell, many in SNCC understood Latinidad through the lens of US southeastern racial systems. As a result, non-Black Latinos occupied a fraught and eventually contested space in the civil rights organization.

Turning to the civil rights era extends a major thread of this book by examining how the southern racial system morphed to incorporate Latino people during a time that it was violently defining the boundaries of white and Black. Rather than the clearly demarcated boundaries between Black and white that segregationists claimed were at the heart of the southern way of life, racial boundaries were porous and flexible. Whiteness opened to incorporate, if provisionally, non-Black Latino activists. However, the rigid borders around Blackness meant that Black Latino people experienced none of the provisional whiteness of their non-Black peers. As in earlier periods, Black Latino people were experiencing the effects of Jim Crow in the civil rights–era South.

Juxtaposing the story of Fatima Cortez, a Black Puerto Rican woman who traveled South to organize with the Congress of Racial Equality (CORE), with those of the non-Black Latino people in SNCC, lays bare the logic at the heart of the southern racial system at this time. Indeed, while some people suggest that Latino people "complicate" or require us to think "beyond" the Black/white binary, the stories of these activists suggest that, in this time and place, that binary looked more like a Black/not-Black binary. That is to say one's distance from or proximity to Blackness was far more important than one's actual "whiteness." While all the activists discussed in this chapter were "Latino," Cortez's Blackness set her apart in many ways. Her non-Black Latino peers were not necessarily seen as "white," but their non-Blackness enabled them to assimilate—even if they were still seen by many as foreign.

This racial context was embedded in the ideology of SNCC and other southern civil rights organizations. Additionally, the racial milieu shaped how Latino activists, traveling from across the country, were received by the Black and white southerners they organized alongside. The provisional whiteness of non-Black Latino people would both make them powerful forces as organizers in the US South and eventually subject them to suspicion and distrust as Black nationalist ideology reconfigured the racial politics of civil rights organizations like SNCC. In the eyes of SNCC workers, the same provisional whiteness that had given non-Black Latino people the ability to benefit from Jim Crow, made them ill-equipped to lead the movement to end it. These Latino activists became uneasy allies for the southern Black communities fighting to end a racial system from which non-Black Latino people had spent decades benefiting.

Coming to SNCC

In the postwar years, the South was not alone in its growing movements against racism; it was, however, an incubator for some of the most radical movements against racial discrimination in the United States. In the 1950s, it was home to several of the most prominent attacks on Jim Crow, including the Montgomery bus boycotts; the Little Rock Nine's integration of Central High School; and on February 1, 1960, the Woolworth sit-ins in Greensboro, North Carolina, that would lead to sit-ins across the US South. Two months after the sit-in movement began, a group of young people, along with movement leaders Ella Baker and Dr. Martin Luther King Jr., sent a call to fifty-six schools and fifty-eight southern communities inviting young people to gather Easter weekend of 1960 at Baker's alma mater, Shaw University in Raleigh, North Carolina.[5] There, among the 126 student delegates who attended, they formed what became the youth-led vanguard of the civil rights movement: SNCC. This organization harnessed the power of the sit-in movement and brought together young people ready to engage in the direct-action techniques other civil rights groups had hesitated to use.[6]

It quickly became clear that this movement was "larger than a hamburger or even a giant-sized coke," as Ella Baker put it, and the energy behind desegregating lunch counters began to take root in community organizing efforts.[7] After North Carolina, SNCC established its first foothold in the Mississippi Delta. Bob Moses, an organizer Baker sent to find communities willing to partner with SNCC, traveled south and found welcome support from Amzie Moore and a growing group of Black activists fighting for voter registration in the Mississippi Delta. This partnership would prove one of the most enduring relationships among civil rights organizations as SNCC organizers traveled to Mississippi to partner with local people already doing voter registration work on the ground.

SNCC had begun as a youth-led movement, but its arrival in Mississippi ushered in the merging of two radical traditions—those of the student movement in the South and local people like Moore who saw the potential in SNCC to work alongside their communities in the fight for racial justice. From then on, the Mississippi Delta would remain a key organizing and ideological hub for SNCC. Although SNCC was engaged in the "spade work," as Charles Payne puts it, of building a grassroots movement in the Delta, they were also part of a network of civil rights organizations who were seeking to capture the attention of the national media as a way to recruit funds and volunteers to the South.[8]

Among those volunteers recruited were a group of Latino people who were drawn south to fight Jim Crow. Elizabeth "Betita" Mártinez, Maria Varela, Luis Zapata, and Fatima Cortez, like many young people in the United States, felt called south during the civil rights movement, and this call was driven in part by an identification with the racism Black people were facing there. Mártinez, introduced in chapter 1, experienced the unstable whiteness of many Latino people in Washington, DC. She lived in white neighborhoods and attended white schools, but she also felt the sting of exclusion when a neighborhood child was told she could not play with Mártinez because she was Mexican.[9] In her discussion of the decision to join SNCC, she described these moments of exclusion and discrimination as one way in to her understanding of the brutality of Jim Crow for southern Black people.[10]

Maria Varela also chose to work with SNCC, in part, because of the anti-Mexican racism that permeated her early life. Born in 1940 to a chemical engineer father who had immigrated from Mexico and an Irish mother, Maria Varela grew up in several cities throughout the East and Midwest. Her family came to the United States after fleeing the Mexican Revolution and settled in San Antonio, Texas. With no clear end to the revolution in sight, Varela's grandfather moved the family to New Jersey to escape the virulent anti-Mexican sentiment in San Antonio. The anti-Mexican racism left a mark on the family, and after they arrived in New Jersey, her grandfather forbade the use of Spanish in the house. This decision to expunge Spanish was, in part, to prepare them for school where immigrant children were routinely punished for speaking

Maria Varela. © La Raza Staff. From the La Raza Photograph Collection. Courtesy of the UCLA Chicano Studies Research Center, University of California, Los Angeles.

Spanish in the classroom. However, it also served the goal of helping assimilate the grandchildren into a society that subjugated those who were seen as "different."[11]

These early experiences of racism, coupled with her growing commitment to, and connections with, social justice movements, brought Varela to SNCC. Varela attended Alverno College, a Catholic women's college in Milwaukee, where she became more deeply involved with the Young Christian Students (YCS), a progressive Catholic training program. Describing the goals of the organization, Varela wrote: "We were shaped by liberation theology, which holds that as Christians our vocation is to be actively engaged in dismantling racism, economic injustice, antidemocratic forces, and unjust war."[12] After she graduated, Varela attended the yearly YCS convention where she met the founders of the newly formed organization, Students for a Democratic Society (SDS). Late in 1961, Varela met with SDS founders Al Haber and Tom Hayden in New York to discuss potential alliances with SDS and ecumenical organizations. As her involvement with SDS grew, Varela was still a full-time organizer for YCS. She was paid seven dollars a week to travel across the Midwest and East to recruit students to join YCS and to participate in the southern Freedom Rides. However, it was through SDS that Varela met Sandra Cason Hayden, known by those in the movement as Casey Hayden. Varela's growing relationship with Hayden and work recruiting volunteers for the Freedom Rides eventually brought her to an impasse. As Varela explained, "How could I, a YCS staff member, continue to exhort students to support fellow students in the South if I refused to go?" In the summer of 1963, Varela reconciled this internal conflict by boarding a bus to Georgia with plans to work with Casey Hayden in the Atlanta headquarters.[13]

Luis Zapata, screenshot from videorecorded oral history interview by Emilye Crosby, June 27, 2013. Courtesy Civil Rights History Project collection (AFC 2010/039), American Folklife Center, Library of Congress, Washington, DC.

Another Latino activist who worked in the South with SNCC was Luis Zapata. Like many Mexican Americans in California in the postwar years, Zapata witnessed both anti-Mexican racism and the early coalescence of Mexican American social movements against racial inequality. Luis Zapata was born in December 1944 in Southern California, and he grew up in the politically conservative Orange County community. Zapata's paternal grandparents were born in Mexico and immigrated to California where Zapata's father, George, was born. In middle and high school, having a Mexican father and an Anglo mother "caused problems" for Zapata, and he was attacked more than once by white children because of his parents' interracial marriage.[14]

Zapata's experience was not isolated. California had long been a site of anti-Mexican and Mexican American racism and flourishing Mexican and Mexican American communities. California was, for example, the site of the famous Zoot Suit Riots in 1943 during which white US service members, off-duty police officers, and civilians attacked primarily Latino and Black youths in Los Angeles. Many public schools segregated Mexican-origin children, and residential neighborhoods were similarly segregated and faced hyperpolicing. Labor conditions for the agricultural jobs held by many Latino workers were brutal, and those working outside of the fields faced discrimination in the workforce.[15] Zapata, for example, worked throughout his teen years as a dishwasher, short-order cook, and farmhand.[16]

By the 1960s, California, and the West more broadly, was home to a growing momentum of resistance. As was the case in the South, returning GIs from World War II provided renewed fuel to the growing Mexican American movements in California. The World War II generation of Mexican Americans joined civil rights organizations in record numbers during this period, many of which were concentrated in California and Texas. By the 1960s, Luis Zapata's California was filled with the energy of these movements coupled with the rising farmworkers movement and nascent Chicano organizing.[17]

As a college student, Zapata found his way to the California's Latino-led organizing after facing exclusion in other social justice movements.[18] In 1961, Zapata enrolled at San Jose State College where he encountered active political movements, including the precursors to the Free Speech movement at the University of California, Berkeley, and anti–Vietnam War protests. Within campus organizing, he felt stymied by racism. He said, "Even in political groups I remember being in a group and it was about 20 of us sitting there, mostly guys; they would ignore any Latino speaking, the same way they ignore someone who was Black, you would suggest something and it wasn't until an Anglo said it that it was good enough."[19] Despite the radicalization of youth happening across the nation, Zapata felt frustrated with his college classmates because of the apathy they demonstrated toward the struggle led by farmworkers. Zapata found that few of the politically engaged students flocked to the United Farmworkers (UFW), which was in its early stages of development. In contrast, and likely as a result of his race and his previous agricultural work, Zapata was drawn to the UFW, helping organize the strawberry boycott and later the nationwide Delano grape boycott.[20]

Zapata's work with the UFW would eventually be the catalyst for his traveling South to organize with SNCC. In 1962, Cesar Chavez, one of the leaders of the UFW, came to a collection of UFW organizers and relayed a message from SNCC and the Council of Federated Organizations (COFO) in Mississippi. SNCC and COFO were assisting local people in the Delta to start the Mississippi Freedom Labor Union (MFLU), a union of sharecroppers, and they were looking for support. They wanted "someone who knows something about unions," and, as Zapata put it, "we were experts in unions."[21] Zapata was the only one to heed the call, and so in the winter of 1962, he dropped out of San Jose State and drove a car donated to SNCC from California to Cleveland, Mississippi, to help organize with the MFLU.

Black/Not-Black: Being Latino in SNCC

These Latino activists who became involved in the civil rights movement were driven in part by an identification with the violence and injustice faced by Black southerners. They had shared experiences of segregation and exclusion and felt that fighting Jim Crow was a way to attack the larger system of racial injustice. However, the Latino activists were surprised not to find the anti-Mexican racism they knew elsewhere in the country in the Deep South. Their early time in SNCC was spent navigating their new racial status—trying to decipher how they fit into the Jim Crow system. Zapata described his arrival in the South saying, "It was like going to another country."[22]

Throughout his three and a half years organizing with SNCC and the MFLU, Zapata would make his home in the Mississippi Delta, where he organized in sometimes unconventional ways. Like many SNCC organizers, Zapata woke up before sunrise to try to reach the agricultural workers before they went to the fields. He was working to get them both registered to vote and invested in the union effort. Then he would go to the fields, where he used his understanding of agricultural work from his time in California to labor alongside potential union members and voters. After working, Zapata often headed to the local Black bar. For most activists, their evenings were spent at church in mass meetings, but Zapata was never drawn to church and instead saw the bar as a potential space for growing the movement. "I can drink, and I can dance," he laughed, recalling the nights he shared beers with local people who would become union members.[23]

Zapata was not the first non-Black Latino person to socialize in Black bars. Less than two decades earlier, Mexican bracero migrants, who were guest workers in the United States as part of a wartime effort to deal with labor shortages, were spending time in Arkansas bars with fellow agricultural workers after being excluded from white leisure spaces. As historian Julie Weise demonstrates, it was by leveraging the power of the Mexican state that the braceros were able to fight their classification as "colored" and gain important protections from Jim Crow. By appealing to the southern Mexican consulate, braceros successfully convinced the Mexican state to threaten to withhold future braceros from Arkansas if they did not remove "No Mexicans Allowed" signs from local businesses. Although their story suggests that non-Black Latinos in the mid-1940s South did not always receive a warm welcome, it also shows that their non-Blackness could serve as a bulwark against the worst of Jim Crow.[24] Perhaps, in part, as a result of this history, Zapata was decidedly racialized as not "colored" for the purposes of Jim Crow categorization.

Nowhere was Zapata's non-Blackness clearer than in his interactions with the police. After a Jackson, Mississippi, march that resulted in hundreds of arrests was broken up by police, it became clearer to Zapata where he stood in the eyes of the law. Because the number of protestors that were arrested far exceeded the prison capacity, the police commandeered a local armory where they held the protestors for about a week. In this large warehouse, lines were drawn to separate men and women and to separate white people from Black people. Zapata was segregated in the white section until he was sent to solitary for, as he put it, "causing trouble." Zapata said, "The cops thought I was white because I'm light-skinned enough." His distance from Blackness, then, was garnering him more than access to better seating or accommodations; it was shielding him during some of the most potentially dangerous encounters with white violence.[25]

Maria Varela's time in the South would be similarly shaped by both her Latinidad and her non-Blackness. After arriving in Atlanta to work with Casey Hayden, Varela was quickly transferred to Selma, Alabama, to work on the Selma literacy project because of an extreme shortage of organizers in the field. In Selma, Varela had her first opportunity to work "undercover." Unexpectedly thrust into the Deep South, Varela battled fears of violence and being "discovered" as a civil rights worker. Describing the experience, she said, "I was doing as I was told, I was not supposed to go to the SNCC Office, and I didn't want to, I was scared to death of going."[26] Even if she was passing as white, she was still at risk of being discovered as a civil rights movement worker. Her fears were obviously not misplaced. In the summer of 1964, three civil rights workers, James Early Chaney, Andrew Goodman, and Michael Schwerner, two of whom were white, were abducted by members of the Ku Klux Klan and members of the local police department and brutally murdered. These killings made it clear that even white civil rights activists had much to fear.

Varela lived in an all-white community in Selma, and she worked in the St. Elizabeth parish in an all-Black community. She believed that her presence as a light-skinned woman was largely accepted because of the history of missionary workers at the parish. Slipping under the radar as a presumed missionary, Varela began to organize literacy projects with the goal of preparing Black southerners to register to vote. Varela had been living undercover in Selma for a year when a protest quickly ended the project. On July 3, 1964, the day after the passage of the 1964 Civil Rights Act, which outlawed segregation in public accommodations, an integrated group of SNCC student activists went to a local Thirsty Boy ice cream parlor to celebrate. Instead of being served, they were arrested.[27] Without any other organizers available, Varela was forced to break her cover and travel to the jailhouse to bail out the workers. Describing the incident, Varela wrote: "Screwing up my courage, I put on my most feminine summer dress and went down to the jail. If I hadn't been so afraid, it would have been almost enjoyable to watch the expressions on the guards' faces as they tried to figure out who this light-skinned girl was and why she was there." It was at that point she had to openly identify for the first time as a civil rights worker, putting her life and livelihood at risk.[28] As with Luis Zapata, it was contact with police that further clarified her racial position in the South. After outing herself, she relocated to the Mississippi Delta, where she would spend her remaining years in SNCC.

Capitalizing on the selective ignorance of the majority of Mississippians, Varela described her survival strategy: attempt to go "unnoticed." Varela worked in Mississippi to create booklets to document successful organizing strategies, support many of SNCC's antipoverty campaigns, and photograph the struggle as it unfolded.[29] In the fall of 1966, while driving SNCC activists Willie Ricks and Stokely Carmichael to the Jackson airport, Varela's car broke down. The celebrity of her two passengers, combined with the violent tension of the Delta, meant it was a dangerous time to be civil rights activists or "outside agitators." Describing the scene, Varela wrote: "Ahead I noticed some young white men working on their cars at an otherwise closed gas station. I drove up and, putting on my best southern accent, breathlessly explained how I was 'just rushin' to pick mah Daddy up from the airport' and how he would be 'just so upset if ah didn't get back there on time.'" Again, Varela utilized her light skin and performed her vision of white womanhood to get her car fixed and get back on the road without incident. Enduring what she described as the "patronizing, knowing grins" of the men assisting her, Varela managed to escape unharmed and get Ricks and Carmichael, who had taken to walking on the highway to avoid being seen with Varela, to the airport in time for their flight.[30] We cannot know if these young white men saw Varela as white or Mexican. Either way, her presence in their car shop was not a violation of southern social mores. Varela's ability to work undercover in Selma, bail out SNCC workers, and get her car back on the road all demonstrated that in the early 1960s some Latino people used their racial privilege as the mechanism through which they could contribute to the movement.

Additionally, Varela's description of herself and her gender in these stories indicates that her time in the South had not changed her identification as Mexican American. In her retelling, her enactment of white womanhood is completely divorced from her sense of self. She recalls putting on her "most feminine summer dress," suggesting that, for her, performing race included a differently racialized gender presentation. She later described her "usual

SNCC guise" as "an unremarkable dress with 'going to church' shoes." Her reference to this outfit as a "guise" is telling. For Varela, both whiteness and white womanhood were performative categories that she used strategically for her safety and the advancement of the movement. Dresses, church shoes, and southern accents were symbols of a white southern belle, with whom Varela barely identified. Her mimicry of southern white womanhood pointed to the way Varela, as a Mexican American woman, conceptualized her gender differently from the white women surrounding her.

Varela's race and gender would again intersect in encounters with local Mississippians. When visiting a store in Jackson, Mississippi, a white man asked her "what she was." She responded that she was Mexican, which caused him to, as Varela said, "go on and on about señoritas and winking, to him it was like oh: sexual object."[31] The man's response was significant for two reasons; first, she did not meet the violent retribution often meted out for African Americans transgressing the color line. Second, this man's comment was also infused with racial scripts of Latinas as hypersexual. As was the case with South of the Border, national ideas about Mexicanness had traveled to, and had been repurposed, in the South. The anti-Latino images (including the hypersexual Latina) that underpinned a violent system of discrimination against Latino people outside the Southeast did not have the same power in this Jackson, Mississippi, store. This suggests that white southerners understood Mexicans as ethnically (and perhaps racially) different. Although at times Varela was legible as Mexican, she was able to move through white spaces safely because of her non-Blackness.

However, even as their race was an important asset for Latino SNCC workers to help with organizing, they remained adamant that they were not white. In her recounting, Varela never describes herself as "passing" for white. Instead, she calls herself "light-skinned." Her decision to not use the language of passing is important because white and Black locals did, at times, read Varela as Mexican.

To be Mexican and white was not incongruous in the Southeast as it was elsewhere in the country. Within SNCC, Varela remembered being marked as Mexican when a fellow SNCC organizer demanded that she "speak English" after she had pronounced her name with a Spanish accent. After that she went by "Mary" while in SNCC. Additionally, Varela also recalled that there was another Latina organizer in Laurel, Mississippi, but that she eventually left after growing frustrated with having to explain to fellow SNCC organizers that being Latino did not mean she was white.[32] At the same time Varela was singled out for being Mexican, another Latina resented being categorized as white. Confirming this woman's frustration, Varela remembered that for some SNCC activists "if you weren't Black you were white."[33] Elizabeth Mártinez remembered that she and Varela "tried to go around explaining 'Chicanos' to all the people who only knew Black and white. . . . [It] was understandable ignorance," she remembered, "but we had a hard time."[34]

Luis Zapata also chafed against those who might classify him as white. Zapata said that in SNCC "a lot of folks didn't know what to do with me, I wasn't an Anglo but I'm light skinned and certainly light enough to pass, but obviously wasn't and didn't act like the Anglos but I also didn't act like a [Black person]." Although his new racial status meant he was not subject to Jim Crow, Zapata was adamant that it "still didn't make me white. . . . They [just] didn't know what to do with me."[35] Zapata's history with racially motivated violence and exclusion from campus activism because he was Chicano made him spurn any identification with whiteness. However, regardless of his self-identification, Zapata's ability to escape the scrutiny and violence faced by his Black peers certainly enabled him to undertake more dangerous assignments with less fear.[36]

Zapata and Varela's insistence that they were not white likely emerged not only from their long-standing identities as Mexican Americans but also from the fact that in the South they were likely not "passing" as white. Instead, their classification as Mexican American or Latino would not have precluded them from many of the basic privileges of whiteness. As in the cases of Varela at the Mississippi store and Zapata with the flat tire, they were identified as Mexican. Therefore, to be given access to these spaces did not require a denial of their Latinidad. It did, however, require that they were not Black.

Those white southerners not involved in civil rights organizing also had expansive definitions of "whiteness," so long as that category was defined against a tightly controlled "Blackness." In September 1957, in Little Rock, Arkansas, a group of Black teenagers were attempting to change history by integrating Central High School. The resulting chaos, and ultimate federal military intervention, shook the South, as states feared that the time for "all deliberate speed" had arrived. When a white female student at Central High was interviewed, she suggested that the backlash resulted from two issues: first, the suddenness of the integration, and second, that the "Negros" were simply "too different." Black people, she argued, "never lived . . . close enough to us," and as a result white people "were just never around them really." However, she offered the following caveat to her white supremacist defense of segregation: "Well, I think like if a Spanish or Chinese person came here it wouldn't be hard to get along with them[;] it's just that the Negros are what you might say more different to us than a Spanish person might be." Her defense was that this desegregation fight was not about racism, as evidenced by her welcoming stance on "Spanish" and "Chinese" attendance in her school. Rather, it was simply that Black people were "more different."[37]

This young woman may have been acknowledging that there were, in fact, non-Black Latino people in many southern white schools.[38] This included people like Lila Quintero, an Argentinian girl who attended white schools in Alabama during the civil rights era. In her memoir and graphic novel, *Darkroom*, she wrote about her childhood angst trying to find a place in southern racial categories. In the novel she depicts her anxieties about racial classification in an illustration of a form that asks for her name, age, and race. "Let's see," she says in her thought bubble, "I'm certainly not a negro. That only leaves one choice. But I don't really *feel* white."[39] Lila felt that she fit into a small minority of the population, but when confronted with two options, she was decidedly "not a negro." Quintero's reflection on her childhood suggests that categorization was meditated rather than innate. Additionally, her story suggests that she may not have had a deeply held identification with whiteness but she had a clear understanding of herself as not Black.

Perhaps the strongest evidence for the power of Blackness in shaping the lives of southern Latinos is that of Black Latino people who organized with southern civil rights organizations. Fatima Cortez, a Puerto Rican woman, was born in 1945 in Washington Heights, New York. Cortez's mother was African American, and her father was, as she put it, "creative with his ancestry." He claimed that he was a "pure Castilian Spaniard," and it was not until later in life that she learned he was, in fact, Puerto Rican. With the support of her mother, Cortez became involved with her local CORE chapter. In 1964, when CORE and other civil rights organizations recruited college students to help with voter registration drives, at the age of eighteen, Fatima Cortez signed up to work in Louisiana.[40]

However, her trip to Louisiana was not the first time Cortez had ventured south of the Mason-Dixon Line. In 1955, when Cortez was nine, her maternal grandmother, who could pass as white, took her to visit family in Newport News, Virginia. Prior to this, Cortez had never really encountered Jim Crow segregation. Her family's class position meant that she could afford to circumvent some of the segregation Black people faced in the North. In an effort to assist Cortez in passing, her grandmother braided her hair as tightly as possible so it would look straight. "She capitalized on my Spanish and Native American background," Cortez remembered. "If I looked like that, I'd be ok." The

Pointe Coupee Parish, Louisiana. *From left*, activist Ernest Caulfield; volunteers Fatima Cortez and Sharon Burger; and activist Joseph Caulfield and his aunt, mother, father and activist Sargeant Caulfield, and neighbor. Photographer unknown, courtesy Civil Rights Movement Archive, Duke University Libraries, Durham, NC.

effort to make the young Black Latina Cortez pass as "Spanish" is telling of her grandmother's deft understanding of the southern racial hierarchy. Spanishness might allow Cortez freedom that her Blackness would otherwise prevent.[41]

Fatima's time in the South would mirror those of other Black Latino people. At the bus station, her grandmother, who could pass for white, left Cortez on the bus to get them some food. Cortez was warned not to get off the bus, but the urge to use the bathroom sent her in search of her grandmother. Her grandmother had gone to the white section of the restaurant to get food and was visibly dismayed when Cortez entered. "Oh my Jesus why did you come in here like this?" her grandmother lamented. Both Cortez and her grandmother were ushered to the "colored" dining room where two stools were cast against the harsh royal blue walls covered in grease. Cortez remembered this moment as her first "real acknowledgment that [she] was different." At this young age, the South was the place where Cortez learned about the cruelties of Jim Crow, while for non-Black Latinos, it was where they learned what it could mean to be free from that violence.[42]

Years later, on June 10, 1964, Fatima returned to the South, this time traveling to Baton Rouge, Louisiana, to work with CORE. Cortez remembered that she arrived in Louisiana in a "white linen dress in patent leather shoes . . . [and her] hair perfectly coifed." A former debutante, she was shocked to find the CORE workers dressed in their uniforms of coveralls and t-shirts.[43] Cortez spent her first two weeks battling the Louisiana humidity, keeping her hair in pink rollers throughout her nonviolence training before she gave up and embraced the CORE uniform. Along with other volunteers, she would wake up with the sun, spend all day going door to door registering people to vote, eat dinner when the sun set, and attend mass meetings at night. In Louisiana, Fatima went by "Cathy" and, despite identifying as "Spanish" at the time, was seen as "colored." "I was just colored," Cortez said, "and that was it."[44]

Being Black did not negate the significance of her Latino identity. Cortez remembered that when CORE workers would go dancing and a "piece of Latin music or one Tito Fuente song" came on, her peers would remark on her dancing: "Look at her[;] that's how those Puerto Ricans go." Cortez remarked, "They attributed my ability to dance salsa, or mambo or merengue to the fact that I was Puerto Rican."[45] These moments may have briefly highlighted Cortez's Latino identity, however, her position as a Black woman was never in question. For Cortez, and other Black Latino people in the South, being Latino may have mattered some of the time, but being Black mattered all of the time.

With white locals, too, Cortez enjoyed using her Latinidad to push at the boundaries of Jim Crow. When entering a segregated restaurant, Cortez would use her Spanish to defy white patrons and workers trying to restrict her to the "colored" section. "I could play around with folks a little," she said, because "I could speak a little Spanish. . . . They'd say, 'no you can't come in here,' and I'd go: 'qué no hablo ingles?' And they'd go: 'oh we've never had none of them here before, what are we gonna do about that?'" After an interaction like this, Cortez would usually leave because her limited Spanish would not allow her to hold a conversation, but it was just enough to, as she put it, "throw them off." As was the case in Washington, DC, when Latin American diplomats navigated Jim Crow, these moments highlighted how Latinidad, or more specifically the Spanish language, seemed to briefly confound Jim Crow's defenders. However, at the end of the day Cortez knew that regardless of her categorization as "Latino," or Puerto Rican, as she put it, "white people, they didn't care, I was colored."[46] Cortez's status as a Black Latina made clear that if race was complicated for some Latinos in the South, it was profoundly uncomplicated for those of African descent.

Certainly, her stories reveal that she could flirt with racial boundaries because of her ability to speak Spanish. However, in the most important day-to-day activities where she encountered Jim Crow, Fatima Cortez was Black. Cortez highlights how her Latino identity was erased in her revelation that, while in the South, she was "just colored." To the southerners she interacted with, her Puerto Ricanness was secondary to her Blackness. In Louisiana, with the exception of occasional moments when fellow organizers commented on her dancing, she felt her Latinoness shrink in importance.

By comparing Cortez with non-Black Latino activists, we can see that Jim Crow could incorporate a diverse group of non-Black people of color while also retaining rigid boundaries around Blackness. The racial mobility reflected in Varela's story and the stories of other non-Black Latino people was not available to African Americans or Black Latino people in the region. Black and non-Black Latino people, like their southern Black and white counterparts, lived separate and unequal lives on either side of the color line.

From Freedom Summer to Black Power

The same call to action that brought Fatima Cortez to Louisiana brought Elizabeth "Betita" Mártinez to Mississippi. In 1964, she was already active in the civil rights movement and was the head of SNCC's New York City office. However, when SNCC and other civil rights organizations made the call for activists to come to Mississippi for Freedom Summer, Mártinez quit her job in New York City and headed to Mississippi where she would work on a publication, *Letters from Mississippi*, which collected letters from Freedom Summer workers into a book that was sold to benefit SNCC's work.[47]

The call to participate in Freedom Summer came from several southern organizations inviting young people from across the United States to get involved with the civil rights movement by supporting voter registration efforts primarily in Mississippi.[48] The goal of Freedom Summer, from the perspective of SNCC, was twofold: first, to register Mississippians to vote, and second, to successfully challenge the Mississippi Democratic Party's position in the Democratic National Convention with their own third party, the Mississippi Freedom Democratic Party (MFDP). The result was a huge influx of young Black and white volunteers to the South, effectively altering the makeup of many of the southern civil rights organizations. Freedom Summer would add many new bodies to the movement, which both increased organizational capacity and caused growing friction among organizers that predated Freedom Summer.

The presence of white volunteers, although they undoubtedly helped expand SNCC's scope, also worried some in SNCC who felt they were not well trained

Elizabeth "Betita" Sutherland Mártinez. Courtesy Bob Fitch Photography Archive, Department of Special Collections, Stanford University Library.

in nonviolent organizing, not well equipped to work with local people, and not careful enough to avoid situations that might put them and other activists in harm's way. Luis Zapata recalled that people would "get upset with white volunteers, but less so with me."[49] Noting the tension, Zapata subtly distanced himself from the white organizers, who became the target of growing frustration. In their accounts of Freedom Summer, Maria Varela and Elizabeth Mártinez also discuss the "white volunteers" as a distinct group of which they were not a part.[50] Their distancing from white volunteers suggests that they saw themselves as ethnically, if also politically, distinct.

The fate of SNCC's future was, in many ways, tied up with what transpired next with the MFDP challenge in Atlantic City. In August 1964, the COFO, of which SNCC was a part, held a freedom ballot to demonstrate that, contrary to the perceptions of some white people, the low numbers of Black Mississippians registered to vote was not a function of political apathy but rather political repression.[51] After holding a "Freedom Ballot" in which Black Mississippians voted for their representatives, the MFDP traveled to Atlantic City to challenge the legitimacy of the Mississippi Delegation at the Democratic National Convention on the grounds that Mississippi's Black voters had been effectively blocked from the franchise. Led by Fannie Lou Hamer, Ella Baker, Bob Moses, and Aaron Henry, the activists spoke to the nation about the violence and political exclusion faced by Mississippi's Black community. President Lyndon B. Johnson, in an effort to create a compromise with the MFDP challengers, offered the delegation two "at-large" seats. Rather than accepting what they felt was a disingenuous and insufficient compromise, the group left Atlantic City feeling betrayed by the Democratic Party and white liberals.

The demise of the MFDP came at the end of Freedom Summer, creating a confluence of events that transformed SNCC. The MFDP's inability to get seated because of the betrayal by the Democratic Party made many Black activists wary of collaborating with white liberals. For SNCC, the MFDP rejection was a turning point in the organization's history. "Never again were we lulled into believing that our task was exposing injustices so that the 'good' people of America could eliminate them," recalled Cleveland Sellers, who would be elected as SNCC's program secretary in 1965. "After Atlantic City," he continued, "our struggle was not for civil rights, but for liberation."[52] SNCC organizers, especially those who were Black, were increasingly suspicious of interracial efforts that courted national attention and instead began to turn inward toward more local, and specifically southern Black, movements.

Concurrent with this nascent interest in Black nationalism, nearly 200 Freedom Summer volunteers, including eighty volunteers who remained with SNCC, decided to stay on past the summer and continue to work with the civil rights movement. Many of these volunteers were white and, in their decision to stay, they restructured the racial composition of SNCC and other civil rights organizations. The presence of so many white civil rights workers stoked fears that their participation would interfere with the development of the self-confidence of the local people. The growing question of white people's role in the movement came at the same time large numbers of white people entered the organization on a permanent basis. This set SNCC up for a collision still three years away.

In the post-MFDP era, SNCC's political program grew globally as it aligned itself with international social justice movements started by other people of color. Simultaneously, the political focus of many members of SNCC became more local, as organizers began to pour energy into all-Black movements in the rural South. Additionally, the years SNCC spent on the ground had demonstrated to many communities that these activists were committed to fighting for local change, even as SNCC organizers kept their eyes on the battles being waged at the national scale.

In November 1964, SNCC activists from across the country gathered in Waveland, Mississippi, to address some of the ideological and logistical challenges plaguing the organization. At Waveland, they dealt with some of the more mundane, although pressing, concerns about finances. Activists had not been paid, cars could not be filled up with gas, and the financial strain was only getting worse as the organization's reach continued to grow. They struggled over questions of how the leadership should be organized and if they should move from a decentralized to a more executive leadership structure. While James Forman proposed a more centralized executive structure, Maria Varela and Casey Hayden offered an alternative, which "suggested that local groups could decide themselves when to draw together to show collective strength." SNCC had rapidly grown over a short period of time, and this expansion was pushing at the limits of the organization's capacity.[53]

The logistical and ideological debates that first surfaced at Waveland would continue to haunt SNCC as the organization evolved after the loss of the MFDP challenge. At Waveland, they also began to ask questions about the role race would play in SNCC's future. Some pointed to the tension caused when white women organizers slept with Black men, the ultimate taboo in the South. Others feared that white activists playing too large a role in the organization's policy making would compromise the goals of the organization. It was here the group first debated SNCC becoming an all-Black organization. At Waveland, historian Wesley Hogan has argued, "Blacks were not asking whites to leave permanently, but rather to understand that they needed to talk alone among themselves." By the fall of 1964, the organization was already dealing with deep fractures in its vision. Despite division at the national and, in some cases, local level, SNCC continued to grow and challenge southern Jim Crow wherever it was found.[54]

At the same time that SNCC was shifting and organizing, the Latino members of the organization were trying to build linkages with the growing farmworker and Chicano movements in the West.[55] Taking advantage of SNCC's enlarged staff after Freedom Summer, some alliances began to form. Luis Zapata's recruitment from the National Farmworkers Association (NFWA, later the United Farmworkers or UFW) was an early sign of these kinds of collaborations, but they would deepen in the post–Freedom Summer years. SNCC's newspaper, *The Movement*, regularly reported on the growing labor and Chicano movements in California and held picket lines to support the Delano grape boycotts. SNCC even sent a field organizer to partner with the

UFW and started a San Francisco field office that was focused on farmworker struggles.[56]

Although SNCC's Latino activists experienced relative racial freedom in the South, all of the Latino organizers in SNCC remained keenly aware of the violent repression Latino people were facing elsewhere in the country. In the mid-1960s, SNCC's Latino activists began to build interpersonal and organizational relationships with Latino activists in the West, Southwest, and Latin America. Latino activists attempted to build and deepen the relationship between SNCC and the UFW and social movements in Latin America. Because of Elizabeth Mártinez's ties to the UFW and her ability to speak Spanish, she represented SNCC at the UFW's 1966 march to Sacramento. During her time in SNCC, Maria Varela carried information between the UFW in California and SNCC. Because SNCC organizers were in the planning stages of the MFLU, Varela created a "filmstrip in consultation with César Chavez and other worker leaders on how they organized the United Farm Workers Union in California."[57]

In the filmstrip, Varela's voice read a powerful script that drew direct parallels between farmworkers in California and the Mississippi Delta, while images of Delano Valley farmworkers rolled across the screen alongside those of Black farmworkers in the Delta. The filmstrip emphasized the racial and economic discrimination faced by Mexican and Mexican American farmworkers. "They call us boy," Varela read over the black-and-white images of Delano farmworkers. "We are not boys, we are men." Drawing again on the racialization of the laborers she continued, "They say we are poor because we are lazy and don't want to work." In perhaps the sharpest parallel drawn she continued, "Our work conditions are like slave conditions."[58]

The filmstrip was shown at meetings of Black farmworkers in the South and clearly had an impact. Varela recalled the reaction at a meeting of farmworkers who had been evicted from a plantation because of their involvement in the movement. One man who had spent his whole life working on a plantation in Tennessee and who had been evicted because of trying to register to vote, rose with tears in his eyes and said, "You don't know how it feels to know that we are not the only ones."[59] The filmstrip was particularly powerful as SNCC grew increasingly involved with local union efforts like the MFLU.

The participation of Maria Varela and Elizabeth Mártinez in these kinds of organizing efforts was also evidence of their identification with non-white Mexicanness or Latinidad. The filmstrip, for example, rehearsed some of the central ideas of what was becoming the Chicano movement. It told the story of the United States taking land that was formerly Mexico by "cheating, fighting, or killing." Varela's script exclaimed: "We were here before."[60] This story echoed the budding cultural nationalism of the Chicano movement that focused, in part, on shared ties to ancestral lands.[61]

These efforts also suggested an evolution in SNCC's ideas about how to best mobilize the efforts of Latino activists. Rather than leaning on their non-Blackness to aid in their ability to work in white spaces, they used their Latinidad to forge interracial alliances between SNCC and the UFW, among other organizations. In this way, these new alliances signaled that both the Latino members of SNCC and other SNCC members were starting to understand "Chicano" as a racially non-white category that could parallel the growing cultural nationalist beliefs in SNCC.

These changing ideas about Latino people also had to do with national shifts. The growing energy of the Chicano movement, the establishment of other civil rights organizations serving Latino communities across the country, and the passage of the Civil Rights Act of 1964 all meant that Latino voices calling for an end to racial discrimination were growing louder in this period. Although many of the national SNCC leaders in the late 1960s saw themselves as ideologically aligned with these domestic movements and the revolutionary movements in Latin America, this view manifested in few lasting links. Varela attributed the inability to maintain any serious cross-movement bonds to the small number of Mexicans, and more specifically Mexican men, in the organization.[62]

Ultimately, Varela and Mártinez's attempts to build a multiracial activist coalition faltered because race meant something different in the South than in the West. As articulated in the filmstrip, the alliance between the UFW and SNCC assumed a shared struggle against racism. Certainly, the violence that UFW organizers faced from local police officers and growers mirrored that of Black sharecroppers facing local sheriffs, police officers, and landowners. However, SNCC's rhetorical acknowledgment of a cross-racial, "third world" unity was limited in a region where non-Black Latino people simply did not face the same type of racism as Black people.

SNCC started to explore alliances with the growing decolonization movements in Africa, Latin America, and Asia. In 1964 and 1965 delegations of SNCC staff, with the financial support of performer Harry Belafonte, traveled to the newly formed African nation of Guinea. In 1965 SNCC staff members Bob and Dona Moses, as representatives of the organization, attended the meeting of the Organization of African Unity (OAU). SNCC also came out in opposition to the Vietnam War and supported decolonization struggles in Asia.[63] As 1966 began, SNCC's executive secretary, James Forman, wrote, "SNCC stood at the end of a period of internal crisis that had lasted less than a year and a half but had shaken the organization profoundly." The result of that crisis, he continued, was that "SNCC had clearly begun moving toward Black Power and the anti-imperialist position."[64] Forman's time as executive secretary reinforced the ties between SNCC and anticolonial leaders in Africa. Latino members of SNCC would find themselves caught in the middle of these ideological shifts toward Black Power and the third world. The evolving position of Latinos in SNCC revealed a great deal about SNCC's deeply held beliefs about race, Blackness, and Latinidad.

Despite SNCC's turn to the third world, Black SNCC members always saw themselves as being led by the Black community as evidenced by a conversation between SNCC's executive secretary James Forman and Maria Varela. Talking to Forman and others, Varela tried to contextualize the revolutionary movements in Latin America. Revolutionaries there, she argued, "had everything from Black blood to Dutch blood" and SNCC's inability to reckon with this fact would signal the closing of an opportunity to organize with "third world peoples." Varela recalled that Forman responded by saying, "[Blacks] should be in the leadership of this movement, of this worldwide global movement because we are the most oppressed."[65] In his eyes, and the eyes of many of those in SNCC, Black people across the globe needed to be the vanguard for revolutionary movements.

Many in SNCC saw their own struggles as running parallel to those of the Chicano movement but did not necessarily see the UFW and the Chicano movement's work as deeply penetrating their own. They could work in solidarity but not necessarily in coalition. SNCC's growing commitment to Black Power also put limits on how deep those coalitions could go. Additionally, in the wake of Freedom Summer and the challenges posed by interracial organizing, some organizers believed that the Southeast posed a unique set of challenges that demanded Black-led, and perhaps entirely Black, movements.[66]

At the same time, SNCC's activist vision was expanding to cover the entire globe, it simultaneously doubled down on southern rural organizing, what had long been the core of SNCC's mission. In the wake of the MFDP challenge, some in SNCC, having lost faith in the Democratic Party and white liberals more broadly, began to organize an all-Black third party in Lowndes County, Alabama. In 1966, SNCC activists, including the eventual leader of SNCC, Stokely Carmichael, began work to form what became known as the Lowndes

County Freedom Organization (LCFO). The party, whose symbol was a Black panther, marked a shift in SNCC's political efforts from the desire for liberal democratic inclusion evidenced in the MFDP challenge, to all-Black efforts for self-determination.[67] Formed a year before the Oakland-based Black Panther Party, the LCFO was more proof that the South had become an incubator for radical Black political movements.

The political ideologies behind these goals were as much a vestige of an engagement with C. L. R. James, Frantz Fanon, and Pan-African thinking as they were a product of homegrown movements for Black political power and Black self-determination. While organizing for the LCFO, SNCC members lived in Freedom Houses where SNCC organizer and field secretary Jennifer Lawson remembered "a lot of discussions about international issues and discussions . . . about what did Black Power mean." It was in these years that there was a growing awareness of, as Lawson put it, "the international scope of things."[68] This included reading and engaging the ideas of thinkers coming out of the Caribbean, Africa, Asia, and Latin America. "Everyone," SNCC organizer Karen Spellman remembered, "carried Fanon around [in their hip pocket]."[69]

The turn, then, back to southern rural organizing also pushed SNCC further in the direction of Black Power. Field secretary Charles McLaurin argued that "Black power wasn't new." For him, the work that had predated the explicit use of the term "Black Power" was as much a part of that ideology as what would come after. He continued, "We had been organizing all the time but we'd never told people about Black Power, we just talked about getting the right to vote . . . and doing things to improve the quality of life." As Karen Spellman explained, Black Power was about "controlling your own destiny, organizing, in your own community, becoming a united front, organizing for political power, [and] embracing the Black aesthetic."[70]

In January 1966, around the same time as the formation of the LCFO, the Atlanta Project was formed. This branch of SNCC, located in Atlanta, sought to add to the southern rural focus by including urban Black communities in SNCC's mission. The group had some uneven successes with their community organizing efforts. The primary contribution of this group, historian Clayborne Carson argues, was in "explicating the relationship between Black separatist principles and the southern Black struggle."[71] Those in the Atlanta Project were singularly focused on embedding principles of Black nationalism into SNCC's ideological frame. However, many of the original SNCC staff were critical of the Atlanta Project, arguing that they were more interested in cultural nationalism than community organizing. This tension between cultural nationalism and community organizing threatened, once again, to tear SNCC apart.[72]

The swelling tide of Black Power and cultural nationalism was being felt throughout the nation and, in SNCC, Latino members were feeling the change as well. On April 5, 1966, Mártinez penned a frustrated letter to the New York and Atlanta staff about her growing frustration with the organization. Having left Mississippi for New York City in January 1965, Mártinez had spent time working as an administrator in the New York City office. In her letter, she expressed annoyance at growing "Black hostility toward whites" in the organization. She clarified, however, that she was not resigning, simply stepping back in her role to work as a writer rather than an administrator. She cautioned that "some may interpret my actions as the result of hostility toward a non-Negro administrator," but that ultimately the decision was an effort to reduce her workload.[73]

Mártinez's description of herself as a "non-Negro" administrator is also striking. Having lived in Washington, DC, at the same time as Karla Galarza was kicked out of Margaret Murray Washington Vocational School for being "not a Negro," Mártinez's description seems intentional. Indeed, it seems she could read the shifting tides within SNCC, and despite her own identification as Mexican American or Chicana, her most important identity in the context of SNCC's changing racial politics was that of being not-Black. It was certainly possible that her desire to turn more fully to her writing may have explained her step back from the organization. However, it seems unlikely that her increasingly uncertain place in the organization as a non-Black staff member did not impact her decision to step back when she did.[74]

A major success for those trying to push SNCC toward Black nationalism was the election of Stokely Carmichael as SNCC's chair in May 1966. Stokely represented a sea change from the previous chair, John Lewis, who, to many, represented SNCC's initial vision of direct action and interracial organizing. The confluences of Black nationalism, southern Black Power, Nation of Islam, Black Marxism, and the success of the LCFO coalesced to create a growing desire for SNCC to be an organization dedicated less to interracial work and more to Black self-determination. As historian Barbara Ransby has written, "The goal of an interracial beloved community gave way to the call for Black power, which for some—not all—meant Black nationalism and racial separatism of some type."[75]

These twin commitments by SNCC—to third world movements and to Black self-determination—would prove hard to reconcile in the coming years. In 1965 and 1966, however, SNCC was struggling to resolve this growing desire for Black self-determination with their participation in rainbow coalitions that included Asian American, Latino, and Native American groups. These questions about race, coalition building, and leadership would come to a head in late 1966 when the group convened at Kingston Springs.

The Limits of Latinidad in SNCC

In May 1966 in Kingston Springs, Tennessee, SNCC, led by the group working out of the Atlanta Project, agreed that "white activists needed to organize in the white community" and that Black activists would organize in the Black community. The group maintained that white activists organizing in their communities could still work under the banner of SNCC.

Months later, in December 1966, the SNCC staff met again at the New York estate of Black entertainer Peg Leg Bates where the question of the role of white people in SNCC continued to vex the organization. "The two burning issues at the meeting," James Forman recalled, "were the objectives of SNCC and the role of whites in the organization," who at the time numbered about forty.[76] The debate about the role of white people in SNCC was put on the agenda for the morning of the first day—the debate lasted several days. On the final evening the debate continued to drag on until two in the morning. Most of the staff had gone to sleep but the remaining group called for a vote. The staff passed a resolution excluding white people by a vote of nineteen for, eighteen against, and twenty-four abstaining.[77] It was in these twilight hours that a minority of SNCC members officially decided to expel white staff from SNCC.

This expulsion was not unanimous and would continue to cause tension. Moreover, the expulsion has remained a thorny issue for historians and members alike.[78] James Forman, for example, was furious when he found out about the decision and stormed out of the meeting. Although certainly not all of the Black activists in SNCC agreed with the expulsion, the vast majority agreed that non-Black activists should have some type of modified status in the organization.[79]

As part of this decision, Maria Varela was expelled along with the only other Mexican American woman in SNCC at the time, Elizabeth Mártinez. Both women were surprised to find that they had been grouped with white activists. After all, they had spent their early life witnessing anti-Latino racism and their young adult life trying to bridge the southern civil rights movement with Latino social movements in the West. In a response to the expulsion, Mártinez wrote, "When I was a child, the girl next door wasn't allowed to play with me because I was a Mexican; remembering this and other experiences, something

seemed mixed up." Their classification as white seemed to confound these formative moments of racialization as well as both women's growing commitment
to discourses of racial pride flourishing among Chicanos in the US West and
Southwest.[80]

Zapata left SNCC before the battle over the role of white people in the movement took place, but both Mártinez and Varela were deeply affected by the
changing nature of SNCC. Writing many years later, Mártinez's memory was
increasingly focused on her identification as Chicana and the improper classification of her and Maria Varela as white during the expulsion. She wrote that
"as far as anyone seems to remember, we [Varela and herself] were classified
as white, even though I did not consider myself either white or Black." In June
1967, Mártinez wrote a paper to SNCC's Atlanta headquarters titled "Black,
White, and Tan" to chronicle the racism faced by Mexicans in the United States
and "show . . . [the] linkage between Black and brown struggles."[81]

Her position paper was critical of both white and Black responses to the expulsion. Mártinez emphasized that if SNCC wished to engage seriously with
third world liberation movements, they would have to reconceptualize their
racial ideologies and the organization's relationship to the color line. She feared
that SNCC's newfound commitment to the so-called third world, solidified at
a May 1967 staff meeting, would be "yet another rhetoric which will be con-
tradicted by its daily conduct." Mártinez felt that the commitment to Black
separatism in SNCC was incompatible with third world movements, especially
those in Latin America, because Latin American revolutions, she argued, drew
"class, not color lines." She warned, "If SNCC is to establish contact with Latin-
Americans, it must realize that it will be working with white-looking people
sometimes." Mártinez acknowledged the global reach of anti-Black racism by
citing the stark political and economic inequality in Brazil, but she suggested
that in Latin America "color as such lack[ed] the vicious reality you find in the
U.S." With the successful Cuban Revolution and the Puerto Rican *Independistas*
in mind, Mártinez saw Latin America as a region on the brink of revolution.
However, she overstated the extent to which Latin America's revolutions were
racially liberatory and downplayed the severity of anti-Black racism throughout
the region.[82]

In addition to a meditation on race and solidarity, "Black, White, and Tan"
served as a release valve for Mártinez's growing frustration with SNCC's racial
ideologies. Writing after the Kingston Springs decision to expel white activists, Mártinez defended white organizers put in a seemingly impossible position. "How could they defend themselves," she asked, "when attacked for their

whiteness." Like Varela's earlier discussion of white womanhood, Mártinez's use of "they" and "them" in reference to white people suggests she saw herself as racially non-white, even if those in SNCC disagreed. She wrote: "From time to time, the question of whether I was to be classified as white or Mexican (i.e., non-white) has come up in SNCC. People talked about me but never asked *me* what I considered myself." She went on to make clear that she had always identified as Mexican, and therefore non-white. However, in SNCC she found herself reclassified. "One day," she continued, "I found myself unable to vote in SNCC because I was 'white.'"[83]

Varela also grew increasingly exasperated with what she saw as a turn toward ideology and away from community organizing—a move she felt was out of sync with SNCC's roots. The decision to expel white people from SNCC, Varela thought, was a decision made by a "small minority of cultural nationalists, new to the organization."[84] It was also a decision Varela had little intention of heeding. Her work was, as she put it, "determined by local organizers and supported by [her] own fund-raising, it would go on no matter how anyone voted in SNCC."[85] Despite her diligence and refusal to bow to the views of a small minority, Varela noted a tangible shift in the way she was treated in SNCC. The difference in treatment was also a reflection of the deep internal divides within SNCC at the time.[86] Returning to the South after the late 1966 decision to expel white people, Varela was met with varied responses. Some SNCC workers recognized Mexican Americans as not white and therefore did not see the exclusion as affecting Varela, and they, like many of the local people working with Varela, did not change how they treated her. Others stopped speaking to Varela causing "hurt and anger." Certainly, "hurt and anger" was likely an understatement for the well of emotions the expulsion brought on for Varela and other white activists who had given so much to the movement.

Some historians see this decision to expel as a failure to understand the complexity of Latino people's racial identity. Analyzing SNCC's decision to expel white people, and by extension Latino people, historian Lauren Araiza writes, "For all its groundbreaking philosophy and activism, [SNCC] continued to view race through the lens of Black/white and therefore still had difficulty grappling with Latino identity by 1967."[87] Part of that is certainly true. While SNCC talked about its desire for third world unity, its post-1965 practices indicated a commitment to Black nationalism that excluded non-Black Latino people.

This disjuncture between movement rhetoric and local practice, however, should not suggest that SNCC's decision to expel Latino people along with white people reflected an inability to comprehend how to fit Latino people within a Black/white frame. Instead, the largely Black and southeastern staff knew that in the South it was not, in fact, about Black and white. Instead, race was ordered around Blackness, and those Latino people who were non-Black— even though they may not have been fully white—were not subject to the same types of racism as Black southerners.

The expulsion, recast in light of the history of Latino people in the South, highlights the regional nature of SNCC's racial vision. SNCC's racial politics were born in the US South. Just as white southerners were able to accept non-Black Latino people into whiteness because of their distance from Blackness, Black SNCC organizers ultimately eschewed these relationships for similar reasons. In this moment, SNCC's decision exposed that race was different across geography and that the multiracial solidarities formed in Los Angeles and Chicago did not translate easily to the South. SNCC understood that in the South, non-Black Latino people were not experiencing Jim Crow in the same way that Black southerners were and, therefore, could not be the organizing engine behind its dismantling.

The formal expulsion of Latino people from SNCC did not slow the organization's efforts to claim a commitment to domestic and global struggles of third world peoples—often with the assistance of the very Latinos no longer on SNCC staff. In the months after the expulsion, Carmichael and other SNCC leaders would make appearances at several gatherings of third world movements, aligning with the struggles of all oppressed peoples in the United States and around the world. In 1967, Stokely Carmichael would attend both the Organization of Latin American States (OLAS) in Cuba and the Organization of Solidarity with the People of Asia, Africa, and Latin America (OSPAAAL) in Puerto Rico. Because Carmichael did not speak Spanish, Betita Martínez did the lion's share of translation and introduced Carmichael to revolutionary leaders with whom she had built connections.[88]

At OLAS, Stokely Carmichael performed his role as the darling of the revolutionary movement sitting for a nearly two-hour press conference and offering a stirring speech about solidarity and cross-racial unity that was met with a standing ovation. In the speech he lamented the "divide-and-conquer" trick used to keep "Mexican-Americans and Spanish-speaking people" separate from African Americans. "Our destiny," he declared, "cannot be separated from the destiny of the Spanish-speaking people in the United States and of the Americas." A powerful orator, Carmichael held the audience's rapt attention, as he imagined a utopian "America" that spanned from "Tierra del Fuego to Alaska" and was rid of the oppression under which most of the hemisphere was being crushed.[89]

Even as Carmichael gestured to the power of the third world uniting, he emphasized the particular importance of the global Black diaspora. In the same speech in which he foregrounded the intertwined destinies of African Americans and Spanish-speaking people, he added, "Many Latin American nations are populated by descendants of slaves brought from Africa, like ourselves. Our hands are extended to them in particular as brothers in the indivisible, worldwide struggle against racism."[90] While he acknowledged the structural ramifications of the legacy of colonialism on Latin America as a whole, he singled out Black Latin Americans, highlighting the particular burden faced by those both struggling against colonialism and anti-Black racism.

This emphasis on Black Latin Americans mirrored SNCC's ongoing negotiation of their relationship to domestic third world struggles. In the same speech he gave to the OLAS, Carmichael noted that the divide and conquer had been, at least somewhat, successful. "At the present moment," he began, "the power structure has [sown] the seeds of hate and discord between African-Americans and Spanish-speaking people." The two groups, he continued, "view each other with suspicion and sometimes, outright hostility."[91] And although he never stated it explicitly, the expulsion made clear that while SNCC saw itself in alliance with "Spanish-speaking communities," it was the global Black diaspora with which the organization felt most connected.

Certainly, Carmichael's speech reflected the changing nature of global politics in the late 1960s, and it also reflected a deeply local, and particularly southern, story about race. Carmichael, who spent months on the ground in Lowndes County, Alabama, building the LCFO and years before that in the Mississippi Delta registering Black voters, was deeply affected by southern Black politics.[92] Carmichael's complex transnational vision was echoed in the alliances formed among domestic Latino organizations.

In 1967, SNCC was invited to the New Politics Conference in Chicago by Reies López Tijerína, the leader of the Southwestern Hispano Land Grant movement—a movement dedicated to reclaiming land stolen in the years following the Treaty of Guadalupe Hidalgo.[93] SNCC's communications director, and later Georgia State legislator, Julian Bond called on Varela to host Reies to make him "feel more at home among us."[94] The invitation for Varela to participate exposed a seeming contradiction within SNCC. Varela could be excluded for her "whiteness" and then, at the same time, be called on to represent SNCC as a (non-white) Chicana woman.

According to Varela, Reies was eager to work with SNCC because they had two Chicanos as organizers. However, as she expressed in a letter to SNCC staff member Ethel Minor, "It was hard for him to understand when I explained a little of the reality of that—that some Black people still see us, Chicanos and Puerto Ricans—as white—and still do not trust us, and perhaps would not trust him." When Reies asked, "But don't they read about what we are doing to the anglo?" Varela responded that "east of the Mississippi very little news is carried about his struggle."[95] Her response, gesturing to east of the Mississippi, was more precisely a reference to the Southeast. Despite her efforts to translate the parallels of the two struggles to Mississippi, many, as her comment suggests, remained skeptical about the potential to build these cross-racial alliances.

Southern Black organizers likely saw how activists like Varela, Mártinez, and Zapata were able to access privileges of whiteness and felt this jeopardized their capacity to be at the center of a movement to dismantle white supremacy in the South. Even though the non-Black Latino participants attempted to use their racial position in service of the movement, their ability to undergo these dangerous assignments also shined a light on the fundamentally different re- lationship to Jim Crow that non-Black Latinos had compared to their Black counterparts in SNCC. Even as the Chicano movement expanded in the West and narratives of third world unity coalesced around the globe, SNCC's position in the Southeast made them keenly aware of the limits of multiracial unity in a region where a diverse cross section of people could benefit from whiteness as long as they were not Black.

In some ways, the stories of non-Black Latino activists in SNCC ended where it began. Betita Mártinez and Maria Varela, who were radicalized and drawn to SNCC after facing the cruelty of anti-Latino racism, were drawn back to struggles that centered Latino communities. SNCC and the South were formative spaces in the development of their politics and identity, and by the end of the 1960s, they found themselves engaged in Chicano and Mexican American movements.

After meeting Varela, Tijerina described her as "a true fighter" and a "very brave girl." He recruited her to work with his organization, *La Alianza*, where she helped him craft a message that would better appeal to African Americans. Varela continued to support *La Alianza* for about a year but remained involved in social justice struggles in the Southwest for decades. Varela, who had been called "Mary" while in the South, left Mississippi for the Southwest where she was once again "Maria." Mártinez would become a leader in the Chicana feminist movement where she would eschew her prior name, Elizabeth Sutherland, and instead adopt Betita Mártinez.[96] Having experienced the pain of exclusion from SNCC, it seems likely that both Varela and Mártinez would find comfort in movements that concentrated their efforts on building Chicano power.[97] Non-Black Latino people, although they were driven south by what they identified as interconnected forms of anti-Latino and anti-Black racism, ultimately left because of the realization that, in the South, they occupied a racial position that made their working in solidarity with southern Black communities more difficult.

The history of Latino people in the South during the civil rights movement reveals a racial system fraught with contradictions and inconsistencies. Southern white supremacy could at once violently exclude and disenfranchise Black citizens for their racial "otherness" and, at the same time, assimilate non-Black Latino people. Whiteness, then, was a permeable and constantly shifting category that relied on reifying Blackness as an unassimilable "other" that anchored racial hierarchies.

Tracing the history of non-Black Latino people in the Deep South through their initial arrival, their participation in civil rights organizing, and their eventual expulsion from SNCC, offers insight into how race worked in the 1950s and 1960s South. Their stories show that in a time and place where race was so highly mediated, the categories of white and Black were filled with internal diversity. However, Latino people's experience shows that rather than alluding or complicating this color line, Latino people fit into southern racial systems. This was not because non-Black Latino people were seen as "white" but rather because they were not Black. Jim Crow, this history suggests, was both more flexible and rigid than previously imagined.

Alternatively, those who were Black, including Black Latino people and African Americans, found that their Blackness outweighed any other form of difference. Fatima Cortez, unlike the non-Black Latino SNCC workers, endured Jim Crow segregation alongside southern African Americans. The flexibility of Jim Crow that offered non-Black Latino people access to whiteness was matched by a rigidity around Blackness that strictly circumscribed the lives of African Americans, Black Latino people, and other Black people in the South.

This dual capaciousness and rigidity of Jim Crow had important ramifications for the South's social movements. That Varela and Mártinez were ultimately pushed out of SNCC exposed that the organization saw "Blackness" as the central axis of oppression rather than status as a so-called third world or colonized person. That vision was rooted in SNCC's intellectual and activist origins in the South. For generations the centrality of Blackness to the southern racial order meant that Mexican, Chinese, Italian, and Arab immigrants at different times could come to the South and distance themselves from Blackness to gain access to white privileges. White supremacy had for so long mapped the boundaries of Jim Crow life as limited to Black and non-Black that SNCC, too, was entrenched in this racial order and could not imagine a South with space for racial pluralism.[98]

As was the case with Karla Galarza, these lines around Blackness were enforced by Black and white southerners alike. It was, after all, a Black administrator who first attempted to expel Karla, and a vote of entirely Black SNCC workers that removed Varela and Mártinez. One way to read the story of Latino people in SNCC is as a failure to create cross-racial alliance. Alternately, as I would argue, we can instead read this moment as a shrewd assessment by Black activists of how race functioned in the South. Although Latino people could work in concert with SNCC elsewhere in the country, in the South, they were like the many other non-white/non-Black groups who had benefited from Jim Crow and therefore could not be the vanguard of the movement to dismantle Jim Crow.

Over the twentieth century, Black and Latino alliances would continue to both falter and prosper. As Latino people moved to the South in larger numbers in the 1970s and 1980s, the racialization of these communities shifted notably. At the very moment that formal segregation was coming to a close, an increasingly working-class, undocumented, and darker-skinned population of Latinos began to make the Southeast home.[99]

■ ■ ■ ■ ■ ■ ■ ■ ■ ■ ■ ■ ■ ■ ■

CHAPTER FOUR

I Love My Mexicans

Constructing the Hardworking

Immigrant, 1980–2000

I n 1999, at the age of eleven, Jose Montoya decided to travel to the United States from Guanajuato, Mexico. Most of his family had already come to the United States and were split between California and Texas. He decided, however, to join his brothers in a new destination for Latino immigrants: Dalton, Georgia. Upon arrival, he enrolled in the local middle school where he struggled because he did not speak any English. "It was difficult to understand, to learn," he remembered. In the 1980s and early 1990s, the majority of recent arrivals, like Montoya, did not speak English. Montoya was happy to eventually find a group of teachers from Monterrey, Mexico, who were recruited to work in Dalton's public schools as part of the Georgia Project (discussed later in this chapter), designed to help the growing Latino population in the schools. The Monterrey teachers, he remembered, "were good people and they helped me to understand, to learn."[1]

Despite the support of the teachers from the Georgia Project, Jose did not make it to graduation. He dropped out at seventeen to find a job. Like the vast majority of Latino people in Dalton, his work began and has remained rooted in the carpet industry. He began at a company that made carpet for cars where he did quality checks on the carpets. Two years later he worked in Dalton's next biggest industry, textiles, at a company that produced, washed, stained, and packaged fabrics for clothing. Another two years later, he found a job at one of the major carpet companies in the area where he worked for the next thirteen years.[2]

A lot about Jose's story was typical of immigrants to the South. He was part of a large number of new Latino immigrants to the area—many drawn there as a result of political and economic shifts in the United States and Mexico.

The year 1986 represented the beginning of the large-scale migration of Latino people to the region as a result of the passage of the Immigration Reform and Control Act (IRCA), the amnesty program that normalized the immigration status of nearly 3 million undocumented immigrants in the United States. Free to move for the first time, many sought areas like Dalton that were slower in pace and had lower crime rates, where they could live a more tranquil life than they could in major cities like Chicago and Los Angeles. Over the 1980s and 1990s, Latino migrants would remake the social, economic, and cultural landscape of Dalton, Georgia, and the South more broadly.

Other parts of Jose's story are particular to Dalton. His encounter with the Georgia Project, for example, was not widely shared across the South. This program recruited teachers from the Universidad de Monterrey in Mexico to work alongside Dalton's public school teachers to help the newly arrived students. The program, funded in part by federal grants and in part by the area's largest carpet companies, was an innovative approach to supporting Latino students. However, as Jose came to understand, this effort was not nearly enough to combat the cultural, linguistic, and economic barriers to graduating high school.

Describing the changes he witnessed in his time in Dalton, Jose said, "I've seen that the Hispanic community has contributed *muchisisisisímo* [very, very much]. . . . I can't say that without the Latino community there is nothing," he continued, "but I can tell you that Hispanics have contributed a lot because this city is growing every day more and more and more. Contributing with work, with their shops, with their businesses."[3] Jose's celebration of the economic contribution of Latino people would be repeated again and again by both Latino and non-Latino Daltonians. The warm welcome of this community, it seemed, was predicated on their ability to infuse the small Appalachian town's economy with new life.

In the 1970s and 1980s, as food processing and other industries recruited Mexican and Central American workers for low-paying jobs, many southern localities became home to growing Latino populations. By the 1990s, many southern cities and towns were experiencing explosive growth in their Latino populations. In Georgia, for example, between 1995 and 2008, the Latino population grew nearly 1,000 percent.[4] Dalton, Georgia, was one of the many communities that grappled with this rapid demographic change during this period. As the number of Latino people grew, southerners developed racial scripts to understand the new immigrants. Through the 1960s, Latino people had benefited from a provisional whiteness in the South, but the massive changes in population would make that impossible by the 1980s. Although some southern

Dalton, Georgia. Jacob Boomsma/Shutterstock.

communities embraced an overt anti-immigrant politic that shunned Latino people as a drain on precious resources, Dalton proved much more welcoming.

Dalton, located ninety miles outside of Atlanta, is a community well-known for its massive carpet production. Known as "the carpet capital of the world," as late as the early 2000s, Dalton manufactured fully two-thirds of all the carpet in the United States.[5] Beginning in the 1980s, a tight labor market, coupled with the continued growth of the carpet industry, caused Dalton's carpet industrialists to look beyond the white Appalachian labor force that had served them for decades. Mirroring strategies employed by Georgia's poultry industry since the 1970s and 1980s, carpet mills began to recruit workers from Mexico.[6]

This migration looked very different than the smaller migrations previously examined in this book. Many of those in Washington, DC, were dignitaries or government workers who benefited either from citizenship or diplomatic status. Those in the South during the civil rights movement were first- and second-generation Mexican Americans and Puerto Ricans. All were citizens and part of established Latino communities outside of the South. The Latino people who arrived in Dalton were far more mixed in their immigration and class status. Many early immigrants arrived in Dalton as a second destination in the United States, having already spent time in traditional settlement sites like California and Illinois. Those who arrived in Dalton reported back to their friends and family both in the United States and Mexico that "allá se trabaja

adentro" (up there you work indoors).[7] Many heeded the call to join the growing community in Dalton. Over the course of the 1980s and 1990s, Dalton was
remade as the Latino population grew.

As these new migrants arrived in larger numbers, they altered ideas about
race in the region. Because of the early and rapid arrival of Latino people to
Dalton, a great deal has been written about the composition of these communities, how they were formed, and the challenges they faced.[8] Alternatively, this
chapter considers how Dalton's story can be better understood in the long history of Latino communities in the South. It also pays particular attention to the
racial scripts established in this period and how an emergent Latino identity
was formed in relation to Blackness and anti-Blackness.

The last thirty years of the twentieth century were crucial in the history
of Latino racialization in the South. In Dalton, during these years, different
groups of Latino people, industrial elites, and local Daltonians jockeyed over
what this new Latino population would mean for Dalton and the future of
race in the region. Dalton is a case study in race making in the post–civil rights
movement South and the ways that white liberals, carpet industry elites, and
Latino people—three groups with remarkably different goals—all employed the
image of "hardworking" Latino immigrants to define what "Latino" or "Hispanic" meant in a community where ideas about race were in flux.

The story of Latino people in Dalton, Georgia, is neither one of crushing
oppression under the weight of enduring southern white supremacy, nor one
of liberal efforts uplifting those in need. Instead, it is a story of varied groups
using new Latino southerners to struggle over the legacy of Jim Crow and the
civil rights movement, the globalization of labor, and a rapidly shifting racial
order. Together, these groups shaped the transition of Latino people from provisionally white to Hispanic in the late twentieth-century and early twenty-
first-century South.

If in an earlier time Latino migrants were able to move through the South
as provisionally white, the combination of a growing Latino population and
the integration of the South into the rest of the country through Sunbelt expansion resulted in the loss of that status. Indeed, it was in this moment that
Latino people began to lose the privileges they had enjoyed in earlier decades.
However, non-Black Latino people were importantly able to continue to reap
certain benefits as a result of their non-Blackness in this period. Indeed, even
the embryonic forms of Latinidad that were forming in the South were always
juxtaposed against US Blackness.

Over this period other forms of southern Latino racialization gave way to an increasingly solidified "Hispanic" category. Some of the earlier ideas about Latino people, like the exoticism of Pedro at South of the Border, endured in this period as the South became increasingly enmeshed in the national culture.[9] Ideas about Latino people as exotic, dangerous, drunk, and hypersexual formed in the long histories of race in the West and Southwest began to permeate a region whose ideas about race had been rooted in the genocide of Native populations, chattel slavery, and the subsequent racial regimes formed to protect white supremacy.

And yet, even as ideas about Latino people began to mirror much of the rest of the country, Dalton's response to new Latino populations was quite different than the anti-immigrant vitriol circulating in legislation, like the Save Our State Initiative, better known as Proposition 187, in California. This 1994 ballot initiative, which received broad support from non-Latino Californians, sought to establish a punitive surveillance and deportation apparatus that would make life nearly impossible for undocumented immigrants in California.[10] In sharp contrast, in Dalton, Georgia, efforts were made to establish bilingual education programs and to celebrate the "hardworking" nature of Hispanic people.

The trope of the "hardworking" Hispanic immigrant emerged throughout the 1990s and early 2000s. During this time, thousands of Mexicans and Mexican Americans arrived to work in manufacturing and agriculture in the Southeast. Latino people, however, did not migrate to the region by coincidence. Rather, industries drove migration through active recruitment of Latino workers. This included Dalton's carpet industry, which enticed thousands of Mexicans and Mexican Americans to the small Georgia community and helped construct the image of Latino people as uniquely hard workers as a way to legitimize their presence in these new jobs, which, at times, displaced local workers.

Latino people also utilized the discourse of "hardworking" immigrants to make claims on the local economy by insisting that the influx of their labor helped save the carpet industry. As a result, they argued, their community deserved resources. They appropriated and extended white narratives about Latino people as hardworking and family oriented to access both social capital and actual capital in the form of programs like the Georgia Project. However, in the process of embracing these images, Latino people also participated in the anti-Black rhetoric that praised Latino laborers as "hardworking," while using Black people as the shadow against which they were compared. Although earlier generations of Latino southerners had distanced themselves from Blackness as a way to ascend into whiteness, this generation grappled with their new racial difference by managing the boundaries between brown and Black.

This period saw the formation of powerful racial scripts that circumscribed the coalescence of a coherent "Hispanic" category. The language of "hardworking" permeated into philanthropic programs that supported the Latino community. Efforts like the Georgia Project, partially funded by the carpet industry, were legitimated through the veneration of members of the Latino community, who were deemed worthy as a result of their industriousness, family values, and Christian faith. Of course, these ideas about the "values" of the Latino community were projections more than facts, and they became important ways to police inter- and intraracial interactions.

Emergent Latino Migration to Dalton

Before the arrival of Latino people, Dalton, Georgia, was a predominantly white community. As was the case with many white-majority communities, this was a result of generations of racial removal projects. This included the genocidal campaigns and removal of long-standing Cherokee populations in the area. More contemporarily, it meant the exclusion of African Americans from Dalton's workforce—pushing them out of the area.

In the early twentieth century, attempts to introduce Black workers to the mills led to labor clashes led by white workers who refused to work in an integrated industry. Historian Douglas Flamming found that from the 1890s to the 1910s every time mill owners attempted to hire Black workers, white millhands staged walkouts, formed unions, and led political campaigns against those who attempted to integrate the mills.[11] Eventually, southern mill managers bowed to white labor and maintained a white-only workforce. As late as the 1950s and 1960s, when Dalton had transitioned away from textiles to primarily carpet production, mill jobs were still reserved for white workers.[12]

This history left a legacy in Dalton that could still be felt in the 1980s. While Black people represented about 30 percent of Dalton's population in the 1890s, by the 1930s, they accounted for only about 10 percent of the population. The Black Dalton population remained at around 10 percent through the 1990s. However, being systematically excluded from the county's biggest industry had financial consequences. In 1995, 7 percent of white households in Whitfield County, of which Dalton is a part, had annual incomes over $75,000, while only 0.7 percent of Black households did. Victor Zúñiga, a Mexican scholar who came to Dalton as part of the Georgia Project, said, "African American people are invisible in Dalton." He said that while African Americans worked as maids, cooks, nannies, and waiters in wealthy Daltonians' homes, few lived in the city limits.[13] As a result, by the time the first Latino people arrived in Dalton, it was a majority-white city by design rather than by happenstance.

The first Mexican immigrants were recruited to Dalton by a construction company in 1969 by way of Dallas, Texas, as part of a dam construction crew. When twelve of the original crew decided to stay in Dalton, they formed the first Latino community.[14] In 1974, Dalton's poultry plant recruited a second group of thirty male and female laborers from El Paso, Texas. These migrants resided in local hotels and spent their days in the plant. Most left after a few months.[15] Recruitment sped up after the passage of the IRCA, when more workers were willing to relocate to the Southeast as a result of the normalization of their citizenship status.

The large-scale migration of Latino people did not begin until the 1980s when local and national changes in policy and industry came together to create an inviting environment for immigrants in Dalton. In 1986, petroleum prices fell and inflation in Mexico reached triple digits. Wages also sank to their lowest point in 1987.[16] Many Mexicans fled a rapidly spiraling economy seeking jobs in the United States.[17] Additionally, in 1986, President Reagan signed the IRCA, which authorized the legalization of 3 million undocumented immigrants, many of whom would go on to gain legal permanent residency. The law also reconfigured seasonal migration patterns, allowing some migrant farmworkers who had moved around the United States following the different seasonal crops to now invest in a life in one place as citizens.

Georgia had already overtaken the Midwest as the termination point of migration from Florida. Georgia was closer, it was cheaper to get to, and it had just as many jobs—in this case, picking Georgia's growing Vidalia onion crop. Some migrants chose to remain permanently in the Southeast when the picking season was over. As many as six in ten of the Southeast's foreign-born agricultural workers established their legal status through the IRCA process.[18] This legislation gave those immigrants from the West and Southwest, now with newly normalized legal status, the ability to safely leave those regions with large and long-standing Latino communities and search for higher wages in new places. Many of them headed to the Southeast.[19]

In addition to these national transformations, several economic changes in the Southeast promoted an increase in Latino migration to the region. The expansion of major southeastern cities and their surrounding suburbs, the growth of the poultry industry, the relatively loose enforcement of immigration law, and the low cost of living all made the South an appealing place for new Latino migrants to move.[20] One labor contractor recalled that in the 1990s he had refused to take workers north of the North Carolina–Virginia border. Above that line, he suggested, labor laws were more tightly enforced.[21] This was more than a cultural practice. Virginia and North Carolina represented two different regions under the Department of Labor, and, as scholar David Griffith writes, "The two regional offices have approached labor law enforcement with varying degrees of enthusiasm." More specifically, the Atlanta regional office, which governed North Carolina and regions south, was far less strict than Philadelphia's, which was in charge of the area north of the Carolinas.[22]

It was not only this confluence of global and regional events but also active recruitment and enticement that drew Latino people to the Southeast.[23] During this time, in the 1980s and 1990s, southeastern companies began to experiment with recruitment schemes to bring undocumented Latino workers to the region.[24] Leading the recruitment effort were agricultural and poultry processing companies. Even with all the factors pushing Latino laborers into the United States in general and the South specifically, companies wanted to ensure they could bolster their workforces with this new migrant stream. Many began to actively recruit Latino workers from across the United States and Latin America. Starting as early as 1977, Mississippi-based poultry company BC Rogers Poultry began to recruit Mexican migrants from El Paso, Texas.[25] Later, the same BC Rogers company formed the "Hispanic Project" that, from 1994 to 1998, attempted to recruit Latino people from Miami to work in poultry processing plants. In Charlotte, North Carolina, large numbers of Mexican men were recruited and brought in trucks by Texan subcontractors.[26] The same was true in Dalton, where, by 1997, the workforce of the nearby ConAgra plant was 80 percent Latino.[27]

Those Latino workers who were recruited and able to find jobs quickly spread the word. Some reached out to family in Mexico and elsewhere in the United States encouraging friends and family to join them in the Southeast, where there were plenty of jobs, a low cost of living, and warm weather. Even more important, it was a place where people could live a peaceful life, both in terms of the more rural settings and the freedom from some of the hyperpolicing Latino people endured in traditional settlement sites like Los Angeles, Chicago, and New York City. Together, the pull of the South with its access to jobs and some respite from fear of deportation and the push of economic instability in Mexico made the Southeast an attractive Latino settlement destination.

Many Latino people were recruited through incentive programs created by the companies. Workers received a bonus for each new worker they recruited and an additional bonus if the recruited workers stayed on beyond a certain time frame.[28] Employers blamed a tight labor market and labor shortages for the initial recruitment of these workers. However, scholars examining the Mississippi poultry industry suggest that many of these "labor shortages" were, in fact, socially constructed.[29] In the case of BC Rogers Poultry, leaders claimed the labor shortages resulted from rampant "absenteeism and welfare" and that there "just wasn't enough people" available to do the work. As one woman told scholar Laura Helton, "If they were paying ten or twelve [dollars] an hour, people would be coming from all over the country for those jobs."[30] Immigrants, according to many industry leaders, were recruited to the South because of labor shortages. This was not, however, a shortage of workers but of cheap and precarious labor.

In Dalton, Georgia, a nearly identical dynamic emerged. Reginald Burnett, a consultant for the carpet industry, noted of Dalton's longtime residents, "We knew that there was a bunch of people who said 'I want to work, but I want to earn $15 an hour. If I can't have $15 an hour I will walk.'" The unwillingness of Dalton's white and Black populations to work at the carpet industry's established wages, Burnett continued, "created [an] opening for somebody who was willing to come in and work for six, or seven, or eight dollars an hour and put in eight hours of work instead of sitting on his duff by the machine."[31]

Underlying the reference to "absenteeism and welfare" was a pervasive anti-Blackness undergirding Latino recruitment. In the case of Georgia, historian Julie Weise interviewed the Aguilar brothers who recruited Mexican workers for Vidalia onion and peach farmers who remembered one of the growers telling them, "If you bring me more Mexicans, I'll let them go," signaling to nearby Black workers.[32] Non-Black Latino people leveraged similar language about race and industriousness. One Latino person working in poultry at BC Rogers in Mississippi said, "You hear that Blacks don't want to work. I don't know if it's true or not. Poultry work is difficult. I'm not minimizing that, but Hispanics do it."[33] The claim of labor shortages then, anthropologist Angela Stuesse writes, "offered a palatable way to talk about racist perceptions of Black laziness, a discourse promoted heavily by the neoliberal Right in the early 1990s."[34]

Throughout the 1970s and 1990s, the poultry industry, along with construction, would lead the charge in recruiting Latino workers to the South. Poultry, however, was brutal work that took an extreme toll on the bodies of the workers. Anthropologist Steve Striffler reported of his nearly two years working in a chicken plant that nearly all the line workers in the poultry plant had finger, wrist, hand, arm, shoulder, or back injuries. Many were forced to undergo surgery to be able to continue working.[35] Indeed, repetitive movement injuries, extreme temperatures, and accidents as a result of employer negligence made working in poultry, and meat processing more broadly, particularly dangerous.[36]

Often those poultry workers who were able left for Dalton's carpet factories where the work posed fewer threats to their lives.[37] Their choice to leave poultry for carpet, however, should not be seen as a celebration of carpet factories. Work in carpet mills often required handling dangerous and corrosive chemicals. Juan García, a worker in a Dalton carpet mill, complained of the toll the chemicals took on his body. "It was rough," he said. "You wore gloves but some of the chemicals were rough. The cracks of your hands would just bleed. That stuff would burn." The chemicals, García recalled, "were very reactive to water if you had over [a certain] amount . . . it would flame up bad. . . . We had known those to explode and the roof come off." Carpet companies also required long shifts from their workers. Although the carpet companies claimed to employ people to work only three twelve-hour shifts each week, García was working twelve-hour shifts six or seven days a week at ChemTech. Sometimes, he remembered, they "would go months without a day off."[38] Others struggled with the scorching temperatures inside carpet factories. Many actively sought out the few factories with air conditioning to avoid toiling in the humid heat of Georgia summers. Carlos Noriega, who worked in several carpet plants, including Shaw and Mohawk, remembered that it could be ninety degrees outside and inside the plants the temperature could rise to ninety-five or ninety-eight degrees—a particularly grueling temperature in which to conduct physical labor for hours.[39] Despite these conditions, people continued to flee poultry work for carpet jobs when possible.

Not satisfied with absorbing those workers leaving poultry plants, Dalton's carpet industry began to actively recruit Latino workers. World Carpets CEO Shaheen Shaheen recalled that in the early 1970s, his company ran vanpools throughout northwest Georgia into Tennessee looking for workers. In the 1970s, he said there were 4,000 job vacancies in Dalton.[40] When local labor seemed tapped out, carpet manufacturers began to mimic poultry plants' recruitment of Mexican labor. After the passage of IRCA, many of the Latino people who came to Dalton were citizens, but over time, this population grew to increasingly include undocumented workers. Some local leaders have estimated that as much as 30 percent of Dalton's Latino population was undocumented.[41]

The carpet industry was the economic center of Dalton, Georgia, producing stark concentrations of wealth and poverty. Because the cost of shipping carpets was so high, few carpet factories ever left Dalton, even after the passage of the North American Free Trade Agreement (NAFTA) and other neoliberal policies that made relocation potentially cheaper. A chief executive of one of Dalton's largest carpet producers, who was born and raised in Dalton, said that if it was not for the carpet industry, he and everyone else in the community would be "poor red-dirt farmers." He was glad that technological advances allowed his company to remain in Dalton and not have to relocate to either a larger city like Atlanta or another country.[42] As a result, many of the carpet companies were multigenerational family companies, and the executives and upper-level management mostly stayed in Dalton.

By the early 1970s, Dalton was home to "more millionaires per capita than any other city in the nation," and by the mid-1980s, "two-thirds of all U.S. carpet mills were located in Georgia," most of which were in the Dalton district. Although the recession in 1981–82 caused a brief drop in production, the 1980s and 1990s remained profitable for the carpet industry. In the 1980s, Dalton carpet industrialists faced the consequences of growing at such a rapid rate— a labor shortage. In Whitfield County, unemployment dropped to 3.8 percent, and workers were driving from several counties away to work in Dalton's carpet mills and in other carpet-related jobs. Whitfield County's unemployment rates remained lower than both national and state levels throughout the 1970s and 1980s. Having seemingly run out of the labor of local Appalachians, carpet capitalists looked farther south and began turning to Mexican labor to "provide some relief from the regional labor shortage."[43]

The growing Latino population was good for business in Georgia, especially the carpet industry. According to historians Randall Patton and David Parker by 1990, "the Census Bureau reported more than 3,500 Mexican immigrants in Whitfield County," a massive increase from the estimated 200 immigrants in 1980. Only four years later, in 1994, "unofficial reports placed the number of Mexican immigrants closer to 10,000."[44] By the 1990s, Latino people represented a sizable portion of Dalton's population and showed no signs of leaving.

The Mexican immigrants who had fueled the carpet industry for nearly a decade were laying down roots and establishing community in Dalton. Church officials reported that in 1997 "Hispanic baptisms accounted for 250 of the 260 total baptisms performed [at] St. Joseph's Catholic Church in Dalton." The Dalton Housing Authority reported that "approximately 40 percent of their public housing clients were Hispanic." However, the growing presence of Latino people was felt nowhere more deeply than in Dalton's public schools. In 1989, the Latino population was 3.9 percent. In 1993, Latino students overtook African Americans as the largest non-white minority at 14.9 percent. By the 1998–99 school year, Latino students made up 41.6 percent of the student body, only 3 percent shy of the percentage of white students in Dalton public schools.[45] Erwin Mitchell, lawyer and former Georgia congressman, commented on the demographic change saying, "All that we needed to do was to look at who is shopping, eating, working, and playing beside us."[46]

Forging Dalton's Latino Community

As the Latino population continued to grow in places like Dalton, Latino communities began to emerge. Latino people formed civic and community organizations that provided economic, social, and cultural resources to develop a collective voice for engaging in Dalton's political system. Born to Mexican parents in the United States, Joana Sandoval grew up in Michigan and came to Dalton in 1989 after graduating from college, hopeful she would be able to find work. Despite her ability to speak English fluently and her college education, Sandoval struggled to find a job. Being Latino, Sandoval felt, blocked her from jobs for which her education should have made her qualified. When she first moved to Dalton, she joined a small community of about a hundred Latino people, and that community began to grow not long after her arrival. Most of the new immigrants were poor, few spoke English, and many were undocumented. Sandoval recognized a community starved for resources and attempted to fill some of the gaps in service.[47]

She began by assisting immigrants eager to take advantage of IRCA. She partnered with her friend Jim Baird, who was known to many as "El Gran Gringo," and they started helping people with their applications. Eventually, every evening a group of volunteers gathered to help recent immigrants fill out IRCA applications or other immigration paperwork. Sandoval and Baird began to work with Reverend Lloyd Trip, an associate minister at the First Baptist Church, and the project grew. With the help of Latino business leaders Norberto Reyes, Hector Alanis, Gilberto Esparza, and Saúl Adame, Centro Latino was born.[48]

The group expanded its purview and began to offer English classes, which got so big that Sandoval recalled she had to "scream so people could hear [her] when we would have the classes."[49] Sandoval and Centro Latino worked to meet the quickening pace of those in need of their services. By 1990, the organization had grown into a nonprofit agency serving Latino families as a "liaison between the Spanish and English-speaking communities." This multiservice agency offered classes in both English and Spanish, as well as citizenship classes, income tax assistance, legal assistance, help with legal documents and driver's licenses, housing assistance, and citizenship application assistance. They also organized dance festivals, poetry contests, and the Copa Centro Latino soccer tournament.[50] By 2000, Centro Latino was helping nearly 900 people every month and had an annual operating budget of more than $85,000.[51]

These community organizations grew rapidly both because of the continued growth of Latino migration and the social capital many immigrants brought with them to Dalton. Two researchers engaged in the Georgia Project noted that many of the immigrants that came to Dalton were migrating not from Mexico, but instead from California, Texas, or Illinois. In a survey of immigrant families in Dalton's public schools, researchers found that 62 percent of fathers and 50 percent of mothers had lived in another US destination before coming to Dalton. Parents had accumulated between five and nine years of migratory experience in the United States before arriving in Dalton.[52]

Dalton's "newcomers" had experience with longer established Latino communities. For example, several of the individuals leading Dalton's rapidly growing soccer league had previous knowledge from their time in the well-established soccer federations of southern California. The success of these communities in mobilizing social capital meant that by the end of the 1990s in Dalton, "Latinos owned more than 60 small and medium size businesses, had organized soccer leagues which grouped hundreds of players and were running for public office."[53] Organizations like Centro Latino, therefore, grew as quickly as they did both because of the scale of immigration and because its members had a wealth of knowledge from previous Latino communities which helped build the infrastructure of Dalton's Latino community.

The carpet industry, as was the case with the Georgia Project, played a role in the funding and functioning of Centro Latino. The organization's budget was composed mostly of private donations from local businesses; notably, of the top five major donors (more than $1,000), three were carpet industry elites. Beaulieu International, Shaw Industries, and Durkan Carpets each donated several thousand dollars to the organization.[54] Two of the members of the Centro Latino board were the diversity manager of Shaw Industries and the human resources representative of Beaulieu International. Their board also included a representative from the local National Association for the Advancement of Colored People (NAACP) and Erwin Mitchell from the Georgia Project.[55]

The creation and expansion of these organizations became important engines in the construction of the hardworking trope. The industriousness and
hard work of Dalton's Latino community, Latino leaders argued, sustained and
allowed for the expansion of the carpet industry. If carpet managers were excited to extoll the virtue and industriousness of their Latino employees, Latino
workers were only too eager to confirm their own importance in the carpet
economy. In June 1999, in one of Dalton's Spanish-language newspapers, *El
Tiempo*, Rafael Carballo penned an op-ed defending the Georgia Project and
connecting the education program with the critical role Latino workers played
in the local economy. "The whole of the Dalton community has to confront
the reality that Dalton's demographics have changed," Carballo wrote. "It has
been the Hispanic community that kept the manufacturing and agricultural
industries on their feet in Dalton. It's a fact that without the labor of Hispanics,
the economies of Dalton and Whitfield County would have hit rock bottom."[56]

Carballo connected Latino people's dominant presence in the workforce to
their growing population in the schools. "We are Dalton's labor force, and we
make up half of the student population. . . . It's about time that we cooperate,
that we speak up, and that we are respected," he implored. Carballo saw the
growing economic power of Latino people as another cause for increased respect in the school system. He argued that Latino residents were more than just
workers—they were hardworking, tax-paying members of the community, and
that entitled them to better treatment in the schools. "We pay taxes through
our pay checks and in all of our food and goods purchased. In other words,
it is we who should demand that our money is used for the well-being of our
children," Carballo wrote.[57] Unlike other Georgia Project fundraisers, Carballo
did not simply ask for resources, he also sought respect. He appropriated the
praise of carpet capitalists to make demands on the local community. If Latino
people were truly a godsend, as many in the carpet industry proclaimed, they
should be treated as such.

Carballo's emphasis on the industry and work ethic of Latino people was
a shared sentiment among many in the community. When researchers from
the Universidad de Monterrey created an "assessment of the Hispanic Community in Dalton," they found that Latino people had much to say about their
work ethic and their labor, and that the "human capital potential" of the Latino
community had strengthened the region and would continue to help grow industry in the area. Latino families, the report found, were "aware of the fact
that they provide Dalton with the necessary labor force for continued regional
development."[58] Latino workers knew that their labor drove the success of the

region and took a particular pride in their "work ethic." According to the report, Latino workers emphasized that "they carry out the most strenuous work at the company and that in turn the rest of the people in the area need the Hispanic community for just this purpose."[59] Latino people insisted that the influx of their labor had helped save the carpet industry, and, as a result, they needed resources, like the Georgia Project, to support their community. They appropriated and extended white narratives about Latino people as hardworking and family oriented to access both social capital and actual capital.

Centro Latino was not alone among Latino organizations working to advance the public perception of the Latino community. If Centro Latino represented the Latino community's efforts to mobilize social and cultural resources to assist newcomers, the Alianza Comunitaria Latino Americana (ACLA) focused on building the economic power of the Latino community. ACLA was a group of Mexican, Colombian, Puerto Rican, and other Latino businessmen and women. Led by Saúl Adame, a successful floor-covering professional, the group brought together Latino elites. Ted Hamman, an educational anthropologist working in Dalton at the time, described the ACLA as an effort by white elites to create a Hispanic Chamber of Commerce that brought together Latino business owners who sought to raise the profile of Latino people in Dalton by promoting their entrepreneurial class.

The ACLA, unlike Centro Latino, had few links with working-class Latino people and new immigrants and instead focused on growing the Latino middle class.[60] Among those involved in ACLA was Alonso Acosta, a young radio and television journalist who was a member of one of the first Latino families to settle in Dalton. He hosted a radio show called *La Voz de Dalton* and was the editor and publisher of *La Presna*, one of four Spanish-language newspapers in Dalton. Also active in the group was Teresa Sosa, the head of one of the first Latino families to arrive in Dalton in the early 1970s. Sosa, who was active in the Catholic church, organized Mexican Independence Day in Dalton for several years in addition to orchestrating community celebrations and parties that featured Mexican folk dance. Most participants in the ACLA were like Acosta or Sosa—they had either excelled in the business community or were strong advocates of cultural life for Latino people in Dalton.[61] Members included restaurant owners, radio hosts, newspaper editors, and church members who hoped to "envision their own and their families' future in Dalton."[62]

In its vision statement, ACLA emphasized how the "Latin American community has become a vital part of the economic growth of the area with approximately 70 owned businesses and employment opportunities to help offset the tight labor market." More than cogs in the carpet machine, a burgeoning middle class, ACLA suggested, was creating jobs and helping grow the local Dalton economy as entrepreneurs in their own right.[63] Members of the community emphasized the impact Latino people had on the Dalton economy as both laborers and consumers.[64]

Regardless of their different emphases, both Centro Latino and ACLA expressed a clear commitment to the language of "family values." Hard work, family, faith, and community uplift were the central pillars of the image that Dalton's Latino residents sought to project. Leaders in ACLA wrote that Latino people in Dalton felt that "family and religion [were] priorit[ies]" in the lives of Latino community members, and as a result the rest of Dalton "benefitted from the [Latino] community's positive (spiritual and family-centered) values."[65] In ACLA's vision statement, they wrote: "Strong family values are reflected in the heritage of this community with the goal of contributing to the community and improving their quality of life."[66] Eager to shed the negative stereotype of Latino immigrants as unattached men, criminals, and heavy drinkers, ACLA and Centro Latino emphasized their commitment to family and community to appeal to white Daltonians.

Echoes of anti-Blackness also permeated this emphasis on family values. Responding, in part, to stereotypes about dysfunctional Black families, the Latino focus mirrored that of conservative politicians on the Right. Research suggests that, in many cases, Latino people in the South distanced themselves from southern African Americans.[67] This desire to differentiate themselves from African Americans emerged from an overidentification with whiteness and a belief in negative stereotypes about Black people and communities, which scholars suggest are both carried from home countries and reinforced in the United States.[68] For example, one social service provider in North Carolina said, "Hispanics complain that African Americans have too many children out of wedlock, are all on welfare, and resent the Hispanics for taking jobs."[69] Some scholars find more optimistic moments of collaboration between Black and Latino communities.[70] Clearly, however, non-Black Latino people continued to find their racial footing by defining themselves either as aligned with or distinct from Blackness.[71]

The respectability politics focus on hard work and family values required tight policing of the boundaries of the Latino community. Many Latino people in Dalton felt that "there [was] more work in Dalton than there are hands."[72] Francisco Palacios felt strongly that work in Dalton was abundant and those who were not working were simply choosing to be out of work. When his relatives came from California to Dalton, he witnessed, as he put it, how easy it was for them to "find a job when they get here." "When you live in the U.S.," he continued, "if you don't want to work, it's because you are lazy. We can find jobs. None of us are afraid to kill chickens if we have to."[73] Most Latino people who came to Dalton were beneficiaries of a tight labor market and found that the wages were higher than elsewhere in the country and significantly higher than in Mexico.

Palacios's claim that those who did not find work were simply lazy was coated in language of racial uplift. Hardworking Latino people, Palacios felt, could move up in life, and those who did not were reflections of individual failure. Moreover, in Palacios's eyes, Dalton was particularly well positioned to welcome the incoming Latino workers. Quoting Erwin Mitchell, Palacios said, "Dalton is a city not afraid to change, and I agree."[74]

Some Latino people also attempted to safeguard their image in Dalton by distancing themselves from what they saw as some of the more damaging elements of their own community. In the 2000s, as Latino immigration continued, some of Dalton's more established Latino residents felt a shift in the type of immigrants coming to Dalton. They feared that the influx of Latino people from California brought with them drugs and gang violence that the Latino community had previously been free from. When talking about this new population, Joana Sandoval said that if "it scares us, you can imagine how the Anglos feel! You know, [these newcomers] are stepping on our territory, too. We have convinced a lot of the Anglo community that we are hard-working family people and now this comes in."[75]

Sandoval's frustration suggests there was internal discord within what most Anglos probably saw as a unified Latino community. It also made clear how intentional the leaders of Centro Latino, like Sandoval, had been in crafting a certain image of Latino people in Dalton. Sandoval bemoaned these newcomers because she and other leaders in the community had "convinced" the Anglo community that Latino people were "hardworking family people." The newcomers, she felt, were disrupting this carefully crafted image.

Others, like Rafael Carballo, took aim at parents as the cause of unrest. "Hispanic parents are not present in Dalton's schools, and we have to stop this immediately." In his larger polemic, he indicted the schools for failing Dalton's Latino students; however, at the end, he turned his focus to the parents. He argued that students' lack of success was also partly the responsibility of absent parents. If family was going to be a central value for Latino people, Carballo and others ensured that those failing to meet standards were publicly held responsible for their children's subpar education.[76] Even as Centro Latino and ACLA attempted to describe Latino people as Americans who embodied values of hard work and commitment to family, perhaps even to a greater extent than other Daltonians, the realities of a diverse community threatened to muddy this image.

Other Latino people feared that the growth in new migration in the 1990s and 2000s threatened their position as members of the "hardworking" Latino community. A Mexican woman who had moved to Dalton in the 1970s reported to researchers Víctor Zúñiga and Rubén Hernández-León that the newly arrived immigrants "were really bad, because they worked so hard. . . . It would take us two or three hours to creel a machine. When they got here, they would do it in a half-hour. It was really ugly. People worked liked [sic] that because they weren't legal. They were afraid of losing their jobs and worked overtime to pay for those jobs."[77] Her comment pointed to the fragility in the status of the hardworking immigrant. Even within the Latino community, this woman suggested, there were growing fractures around labor and who was willing to work under these new conditions. There were always those in more desperate straits willing to work harder for less, and the carpet industry was only too quick to continue recruiting increasingly vulnerable workers. Moreover, it pointedly demonstrated that the labor capacity of Latino people had nothing to do with race and everything to do with the extent of their precarity.

There was, in fact, a changing demographic nature of Latino immigrants over the decades. Before IRCA the vast majority of migrants were men migrating alone. Zúñiga and Hernández-León point to two subsequent waves after the passage of IRCA. The first wave, from 1987 to 1992, saw more women than the pre-IRCA migration (although overall still fewer women than men), and the second wave, from 1993 to 1998, saw women surpass men as the fastest-growing group of Latino people migrating to Dalton.[78] As women and children grew as a proportion of the immigrant population, new institutions in Dalton felt the impact.

The Georgia Project

Public schools became a key site in the unfolding politics of Latino immigration to the South. One day in 1994, former Georgia congressional representative Erwin Mitchell comforted his youngest daughter who came home after a long day working as a paraprofessional at Roan Elementary School in Dalton. "We have all these little Latino children," she lamented, "and no teachers who can speak Spanish."[79] His daughter was observing something that had been

Erwin Mitchell and students. Courtesy Richard B. Russell Library for Political Research and Studies, University of Georgia Libraries, Athens.

developing for nearly two decades. Between 1976 and 1997, the Latino student population in Georgia had grown from 2,000 to 33,600.[80] Mitchell understood his daughter's concern; he had observed the changes in Dalton, too. "I had noticed more brown-skinned folks in the community," he recalled. "I had no earthly idea what was happening in Dalton, Georgia." He exclaimed, "In Northwest Georgia, at that time 1 out of every 3 children was brown-skinned," and with a slight provocation he noted, "more brown-skinned than Black-skinned." Eager to help his daughter, Mitchell began to investigate what Dalton's public schools were doing to deal with the new population. He quickly discovered that little was being done and the school board was mostly caught up in "hand wringing" about what to do for the new Latino students.[81]

When Mitchell began to tackle the question of educating Spanish-speaking students, he reached out to his lifelong friend and fellow Daltonian Robert "Bob" Shaw, the chief executive officer of Shaw Industries, one of the largest carpet manufacturers in the world. It is not surprising that Mitchell reached out to Shaw, given that he, and other carpet industry leaders in the area, had an established history with philanthropy that served the growing Latino community. This included the funding of Grupo Juevnil, a youth group at the local Catholic church, Saint Joseph's. Carpet philanthropy also funded several teams in the enormously successful Dalton soccer league and organized a Cultural Expo at the local convention center, which included folk dances, traditional food, and a Mass honoring the Virgin of Guadalupe.[82] Many of the carpet companies also offered some adult education programs, mostly English classes, for their Spanish-speaking workers. These courses had limited success, in part because of the intense time and energy demands of carpet jobs.[83]

Shaw was even more receptive to the idea of supporting Mitchell's vision given that Shaw had just completed a successful joint venture with the Mexican corporation Grupo Alfa to sell carpet throughout Latin America. In response to Mitchell's request, Shaw reached out to Roberto Delgado, the owner of Versax Industries in Mexico, to look for Mexican teachers. Delgado put Shaw in touch with the Universidad de Monterrey, and the early visions of the Georgia Project were born.[84] The coalition that formed included Erwin Mitchell, Bob Shaw, Roberto Delgado, and Victor Zúñiga of the Universidad de Monterrey. Eleven of the eighteen members of the Georgia Project committee were carpet executives and represented every major carpeting company, including Aladdin/Mohawk, Shaw Industries, Durkan Patterned Carpet, World Carpets, Beaulieu, and Allied Fibers.[85] Although the carpet industry invested relatively little money in the Georgia Project, they maintained a great deal of control over the program.

Mitchell also secured a federal government grant for Title VII funding, otherwise known as an Emergency Immigration Grant. This funding was designed as a stop-gap measure to provide aid from 1997 to 1999 to help school districts deal with new Spanish-speaking students in their classrooms.[86] At the local level he was able to get the Dalton City Council to "grant the school system $350,000 a year for three years to pay some of the costs."[87]

This was not the first time that the federal government had intervened to support Latino migrants to the region. The Migrant Education Program (MEP) was established in 1966 as part of Lyndon Johnson's War on Poverty. The program, which largely served Black migrant farmworkers, started to see some migration from "Hispanic/Spanish-speaking" communities in the early 1970s. Washington County, North Carolina, first used these funds in 1971 to assist the children of Latino, mostly Mexican, migrant farmworkers. Throughout the 1970s, the proportion of Spanish-speaking students in North Carolina's MEP remained low, but by 1987, they accounted for one-third of the program participants, and by 1989, they accounted for one-half. The Georgia Project, therefore, was not alone in its effort to navigate the changing population of their schools.[88]

It took a few years to get off the ground, but the Georgia Project began in earnest on March 19, 1997, when an accord was signed between the Universidad de Monterrey and the City of Dalton and the County of Whitfield. The accord defined the terms and outlined the four key functions of the Georgia Project.[89] First, the Universidad de Monterrey would offer teaching assistants to aid with bilingual education in the Georgia public schools. Second, teachers from Dalton and Whitfield County schools would participate in an "intensive Spanish and Mexican Culture Program," in which they would "spend four weeks of intensive Spanish instruction as well as immersion in cultural activities at the Universidad de Monterrey." Third, the Universidad de Monterrey would conduct a "comprehensive study of the Dalton/Whitfield community" to "reveal detailed demographic information related to the Hispanic community." The information would then be used to help develop programs to foster "community leadership; adult biliteracy; and parent, school and industry programs." Finally, the Universidad de Monterrey committed to assist the Georgia school systems with the "development of a bilingual education program."[90] The Monterrey Accord, as it came to be known, institutionalized the work that Erwin Mitchell and others had done to create this program.

In the summer of 1997, the Georgia Project sent twenty-four Dalton teachers to the Universidad de Monterrey for a month. There they received four weeks of Spanish instruction with a focus on colloquial Spanish, as well as immersion in cultural activities, instruction in Spanish and Mexican history and culture, and training in English as a Second Language methodologies.[91] From the images of that summer, it is clear that nearly all, if not all, of the teachers who traveled to Mexico from Georgia were white. This was not surprising given that only 1 of the 301 teachers in Dalton public schools was Latino in the 1996–97 school year.[92] Angela Hagris, a sixth-grade teacher in Whitfield County who traveled to Mexico for the program, remarked: "I can't wait to get back in class and share what I learned with my students." She continued, "Now I know so much more about where some of my kids come from and can relate to their different heritages."[93]

The next phase of the Georgia Project involved inviting fifteen teachers, known as the "Monterrey girls," from the Universidad de Monterrey to live and work in Georgia.[94] In the beginning, logistical challenges plagued the program. Difficulties acquiring visas forced the arrival of teachers to be delayed twice, and by April 1997, it was clear that the visas would prevent them from beginning in the summer. The teachers finally arrived on October 9, 1997, after

Georgia Project teachers. Courtesy Richard B. Russell Library for Political Research and Studies, University of Georgia Libraries, Athens.

the school year had already begun.[95] Bob Shaw provided transportation for the teachers, easing some of the cost at the beginning of the Georgia Project.[96]

Billy Bice, the superintendent of Dalton public schools, was excited to incorporate the Georgia Project into the schools. In anticipation of the program, Bice met with eight school principals in Dalton and found widespread enthusiasm. In a letter to the head of the Georgia Project in Monterrey, Bice calculated that Dalton public schools could benefit from a total of sixty-eight teachers from Monterrey. He conceded that it was "perhaps an unrealistic number" and that even half of that number would be wonderful. Bice and the Dalton principals seemed eager to bring the Georgia Project to their schools in as broad a capacity as possible.[97]

In March 1998, six months after the Georgia Project teachers arrived, Dalton High School held a welcome assembly titled "Everyone at Dalton High Smiles in the Same Language." The assembly represented the commitment by the Dalton public schools, and the Dalton community more broadly, to integration through multiculturalism. To advertise the event, the school created a flier featuring a clip art photo that a decade later would look like a caricature of multiculturalism. It included children from different regions of the world wearing only the most visible markers of their ethnic difference and holding hands in an arc at the top of the page. One girl wears a kimono, a young boy is in a sari, and another boy dons a bullfighter's uniform. Perhaps visitors were lucky that serapes and sombreros were not featured in the cultural mosaic.

The assembly's theme coupled with the imagery sends a complex message. On the one hand, everyone is unified as part of one human race; on the other hand, children can be easily sorted into taxonomies of difference based on their country of origin. The assembly at once highlighted the Georgia Project teachers' differences and subsumed that difference into a homogenous Dalton High School. This theme encapsulated the constant struggle of white liberals between a desire for color-blind subjugation of difference and an increased focus on multiculturalism, which highlighted difference in often exaggerated ways and alienated children of color.

Sandra Benítez Crow, one of the Monterrey teachers, recalled that some of the new students "used to cry for two or three weeks. But if they saw me, and I'd just speak to them in Spanish, they changed—their faces would be like, 'Oh, somebody speaks Spanish!'"[98] At other times, children would be inconsolable, and Crow would have to "cancel [her] schedule, just to be with that kid the whole day." Crow and the other Monterrey teachers were much more than translators or teacher's assistants; they were serving as social workers, therapists, and cultural translators for children who felt foreign in their new school. They served as crucial lifelines for children in the classroom and for parents who otherwise would have struggled to be involved in their children's school life because they did not speak English.

The need for the Monterrey teachers grew exponentially each year. Crow remembered that in the first year she had thirty students and then more than fifty in the second year. By her third year she had nearly eighty students. "The number of Spanish-speaking children in the school," she recalled, "was just growing that fast."[99] Data confirms Crow's observation. In the 1989–90 school year, Latino pupils made up less than 4 percent of Dalton's public schools' students. By the 2000–2001 school year, they made up more than 51 percent of the student body—a majority.[100]

As part of the Georgia Project mandate, a group from the Universidad de Monterrey conducted a study to assess the demographic and social situation of the "Hispanic Community" in Dalton. Among the several topics addressed in this report, the researchers focused on discrimination and community integration. Even with the presence of the Monterrey teachers, the researchers found, some children were forbidden from speaking Spanish at school and were punished if they disobeyed.[101] Parents, too, felt frustrated by the school system. Although parents were always invited to academic events, the small number of Georgia Project teachers meant that bilingual interpreters were not always present. As a result, parents would have to rely on their children to interpret.[102] The report suggested that, despite the supports offered by the Monterrey teachers, the Dalton public schools were still far from a welcoming environment for all Latino students.

The Georgia Project teachers made a huge difference in making Latino parents feel welcome in the schools, but structural problems prevented full involvement by many parents—for example, Dalton lacked adequate public transportation; in most households, both parents worked for a carpet company and therefore had conflicting schedules; language barriers persisted for those who did not have a Georgia Project teacher in their child's classroom; and many felt a larger sense of alienation from the Dalton community and judgment from teachers in particular.[103] The Georgia Project, while it helped ameliorate the sense of alienation for some parents, could not resolve these structural issues. The same carpet industry that helped conceive and fund the program that sought to better incorporate parents in their children's education was also creating the work schedules that made that participation nearly impossible.

The local newspaper, the *Daily Citizen-News*, celebrated the Georgia Project as "an unusual relationship with business and industry that should have been formed long ago . . . specifically in regard to communication barriers with the Hispanic community here." After all, the paper noted, "Our Hispanic neighbors are here because local businesses gave them jobs" and therefore those businesses should "accept some responsibility beyond hand[ing] out a regular paycheck." The business community agreed that the Georgia Project represented such a "step toward accountability."[104] Even as states rolled back labor and environmental regulations for factories like those in Dalton, investment in programs like the Georgia Project allowed carpet industrialists to portray themselves as corporate citizens who served the community they occupied. By investing in the education of their workers, like the mill owners of an earlier generation, they successfully courted new immigrant labor while projecting an image of Dalton as a racially progressive haven that helped facilitate the integration of Latino immigrants into its school system.

This nonprofit program, created in conjunction with local business elites, represented a profoundly different reaction to Latino newcomers than that seen in nearby localities like Gainesville, Georgia, where the Ku Klux Klan reemerged in response to rapid immigration.[105] The project was a boon for many who desperately sought resources for bilingual education in a state that was actively retracting funding for education and debating "English-only" amendments.

Dalton, however, was not immune from some of these anti-immigrant sentiments. Erwin Mitchell lamented in an editorial in the *Daily Citizen-News* that "[Hispanics] have been virtually ignored—even hated by some simply because of their presence." He went on that this hate was particularly misplaced because Latino people were hardworking, "filling some of the toughest manual jobs around," and exhibited "intensive familial ties."[106] While Mitchell bemoaned the general neglect of Latino people, those in Dalton were not entirely free from the anti-immigrant sentiment that had taken hold in Gainesville and other parts of the country.

Francisco Palacios remembered struggling with anti-Latino racism when he first arrived in Dalton. Palacios was born in San Francisco, California, and spent his early childhood there. He spent his later childhood in Mexico, and in 1994, he moved to Dalton where he worked as a translator. He was hired by the newspaper to help sell ads and found that people were "shutting doors in [his] face" because he was Latino. When he worked as the editor at a Spanish-language newspaper, *El Informador*, he would have to cross a picket line of white protestors from the group Citizens Against Illegals.[107] The anti-immigrant group that Palacios had to face down on his way to work successfully lobbied local officials to support a partnership between the Dalton Police Department and Immigration and Naturalization Services (INS).

This partnership spawned what would become the Immigration Task Force in 1995 using money from a federal grant. The task force had two goals. The first goal was "to become a positive force for changing the image of the police in the Hispanic community." To this end, members of the task force had to be bilingual by the end of their first two years in the program. The second goal was to "act as a liaison with the Immigration and Naturalization Services . . . , participating in illegal alien sweeps and deportation activities."[108] These goals were obviously at odds with one another. Dalton police officials estimated that 40 percent of the Latino workers hired in the carpet plants were undocumented and that some 90 to 100 percent of the labor force at these plants was undocumented.[109] These police officers were attempting to serve as a "positive force" in the same communities that they were terrorizing with immigration raids that tore those communities apart.

Dalton was not the only community with increasing numbers of undocumented workers, and the federal government was also taking notice. The 1990s saw several operations at the US-Mexico border with the goal of making cross-ing so dangerous that it would deter future immigrants. Among them were Operation Hold the Line in 1993 and Operation Gatekeeper in 1994. These ef-forts did not stop at the US-Mexico border, and in 1995, Operation SouthPAW (Protecting American Workers) brought deportation raids to six southeastern states.[110] Four thousand people were detained and deported in these states, and 1,351 of those deportations came from Georgia.[111]

In 1995, as part of Operation SouthPAW, the INS and the US Border Patrol raided several major carpet mills in Dalton.[112] In 1997, when the INS was ac-tively checking for undocumented immigrants in the Dalton area, they appre-hended more than 300 people in three days at interstate points surrounding Dalton. Raids continued throughout the mid-1990s, but by the late 1990s, they had mostly ceased. One historian attributed this to Latino workers becoming a more stable part of the workforce in Dalton over the 1990s.[113] However, even though partnerships like these made life inhospitable for many, Latino people continued to settle in Dalton citing the relative safety and security they felt there compared with other parts of the country.

The Carpet Industry and the Construction of the "Hardworking" Latino

Because the carpet industry drove Dalton's Latino population growth, carpet elites also played an important role in shaping ideas about race in Dalton. They actively supported the creation and implementation of the Georgia Project, and, because so many of them lived in Dalton, they felt a personal stake in supporting the growing Latino community on which their companies relied. Unlike poultry or other multinational corporations that also recruited Latino workers to the South, most of the leaders in the carpet industry remained in Dalton and saw firsthand the consequences of their companies' recruitment. As a result, the Georgia Project represented a complicated fusion of paternalistic and charitable longings of local white Daltonians and emergent racial scripts created by the industrial sector.

Some of the warm welcome that immigrants received in Dalton was likely a result of what historian Mary Dudziak has called Cold War civil rights. In the midst of the Cold War and in the wake of the civil rights movement, Dudziak argues, many people in the United States became increasingly concerned with the appearance of racial injustice and made conscious efforts to perform racial harmony.[114] These efforts to enact racial equity became particularly potent with the arrival of Latino people to the US South. Indeed, Angela Stuesse writes of white Mississippians, "While seemingly incongruous championing Latinos may effectively enable white individuals to discount their own anti-Black sentiments. After all, goes the logic, how could they be 'racist' given their advocacy on behalf of the area's newest minority?"[115] Julie Weise found something similar in Charlotte, North Carolina, where white Christian southerners sought to reconcile the history of segregation by building community with Mexicans.[116] The embrace by white Daltonians of the "hardworking immigrants" in their midst was likely infused by this desire to reimagine the region as a place beyond the legacy of Jim Crow.

The Georgia Project represented one manifestation of this desire, but it was not alone. Religious communities elsewhere in the Southeast opened their doors to the new Latino migrants eager to engage in the kinds of missionary work they were used to, but this time in their own backyards. Church volunteers in Georgia framed the farmworkers they aided, as Weise writes, "as charity cases," and in the process "elid[ed] the fact that the workers worked and carefully avoiding any implications that farmers might bear some responsibility for their poverty."[117] This combination of charitable desires and agricultural need created a new political formation that Weise calls "pro-immigrant conservatism."[118] This political ideology both made room for the complex paternalism and admiration white southerners held for "hardworking" Latino migrants. At the same time, it supported conservative policies that ultimately made life much harder for those same migrants as well as their poor and working-class Black counterparts in the region.

Erwin Mitchell used similar rhetoric to garner support for the Georgia Project. Extolling the value of the program, Mitchell claimed, "Nothing is more important than to teach these children the ways of America." Teaching these "unpolished jewels" was a civic duty that Georgians should rally behind.[119] Reflecting years later on the immigration of Latino people to Dalton and the Georgia Project, Mitchell said that "these folks were coming to fill the jobs that were really critical at that time." The carpet industry, he went on, "was just running out of people and they needed these people." He emphasized, "they were good workers . . . and with rare exception were all model contributing members of the community."[120] Here Mitchell fused together the discourses of Latinos as hardworking and valuable community members that carpet elites would refine. Latino people, in Mitchell's estimation, were deserving of any assistance they received through programs like the Georgia Project because they filled necessary jobs and were model community members.

The framing of Latino people as "model contributing members of the community" serves as both praise and policing. Praising Latino people as vital members of the Dalton community helped soothe the post–civil rights movement anxieties that many white liberals felt. They could both rhetorically and financially support this non-white group without having to confront or be reminded of the legacies of Jim Crow and the civil rights struggle. However, this praise also had the accompanying implication that resources should be available only to those Latino people who were "model" and "contributing." Latino people, then, were only deserving of support as long as they were productive and fit within the scripts of southern family values.

This paternalistic charity also represented an investment opportunity. "The bottom line," Erwin Mitchell said, "is that by emphasizing the education of these students, we're going to have an educated labor force for your community."[121] Educating students was both an emotional and a financial commitment for Mitchell and the carpet elites. They could simultaneously serve children who genuinely needed help in getting bilingual education and look to the future for a better-educated workforce. Those promoting the Georgia Project, Mitchell demonstrates, internalized and repurposed the discourse of productivity from the carpet industry as part of their appeal for funds.

In Mitchell's petition to carpet philanthropists, he melded the language of multiculturalism and "the American dream" with productivity and investment. Mitchell certainly was devoted to the Georgia Project for reasons beyond its ability to create a more productive Dalton, but his decision to use the language of productivity and investment suggests that his fundraising efforts needed to incorporate industrial concerns. The language of investment, however, was certainly a slippery and dangerous slope. If Latino people were worth educating because of their productivity, economic downturn or misfortune would seemingly be the death knell of any interracial support. The emphasis on Latino people being deserving because of their labor potential helped solidify a discourse that both allowed carpet elites to participate in new forms of paternalism and, at the same time, suggested that if Latino people were unwilling to endure the increasingly grueling labor in the factories, their families would no longer be deserving of resources.

For carpet manufacturers, programs like the Georgia Project helped strike a balance between an investment in the community and an investment in their workforce. In a letter to Tommy Maybank, president of Maybank Textiles, Shirley J. Lorberbaum, vice president of Mohawk Industries, exclaimed the successes of the Georgia Project. "In the long run," she wrote, "it is our community that truly benefits from the Georgia Project." Lorberbaum continued, "We gain better employees, better citizens, better people." Lorberbaum's word order is important. The Georgia Project produced, first and foremost, better employees. Lorberbaum looked forward to a still undocumented, English-speaking work-force that could more efficiently produce carpet.[122]

In another fundraising letter Lorberbaum expounded on the benefits of the Georgia Project for local business. In reference to the growing immigrant pop-ulation, she wrote, "The students of today will play a major role in the suc-cess of our community tomorrow. Industry, of course, will employ many of them, but EVERY business in Dalton/Whitfield will benefit from a well-educated population. These students will earn better jobs with the opportunity for ad-vancement."[123] Her letter makes clear that the carpet industry saw many of these young students as likely future employees. Some Georgia Project students would certainly have improved job prospects that may have facilitated their exit from Dalton, but for many in the carpet industry, the Georgia Project also functioned as early worker training. Elsewhere, Lorberbaum emphasized that "these are the people" who will become "customers and . . . employees in the years to come." She asked, "Isn't investing in their future now a great way of improving your business in the future?" As she did in her first letter, in which she implied that people's status as future employees outweighed their status as citizens or persons, Lorberbaum layered the language of investment and profit onto an issue of education and citizenship. The bottom line, it seemed, was never far from her mind.[124]

Lorberbaum's reference to Latino people as customers, as well as workers, fit squarely within the growing efforts to market to Latino consumers during this period.[125] As Latino people came to constitute a larger portion of Dalton, and the national population, their value as workers was matched by their value as consumers. Lorberbaum sought to appeal both to the Latino labor that her carpet company desperately needed and to the growing Latino population in Dalton, many of whom were building homes that also required carpet.

For carpet elites, the narrative of the hardworking immigrant allowed them to participate in what they saw as racially progressive ideology. Their invest-ment in the Georgia Project demonstrated they both supported their Latino workers and were willing to invest in the community that their companies' hiring practices had transformed. Latino immigrants, carpet manufacturers argued, were hardworking, family people, and the Georgia Project demon-strated their financial commitment to this population. Scholar James Engstrom has noted that these laudatory expressions were distinct, not because of the celebration of the immigrant "work ethic," but rather because of "how quickly the discourse about hard work and loyalty switched from one ethnic group to another." Carpet industry executives had consistently praised the white, native-born Appalachian workers in the past, but it was now Mexicans who were seen as "godsend[s]" and the "lifeblood" of the carpet industry.[126] The narrative of the hardworking immigrant also allowed them to normalize both the displacement of white Appalachian labor in the mills and the expectations of increased output from Latino workers. If Latino people were all hard workers, as carpet elites claimed, slow-downs, refusals to work, and strikes would have violated the racial scripts that had been constructed. It therefore helped solidify the idea that Latino people were naturally hyperproductive as a function of their race.

Carpet elites unabashedly celebrated the arrival of Mexican workers and the revitalizing effect they had on the carpet industry. "Certainly, we couldn't support our rug and carpet manufacturing industry without our Latino population," argued George Woodward, president and chief executive officer of the Dalton/Whitfield County Chamber of Commerce. Woodward saw the relationship as symbiotic between industry and Latino workers: "We provide an opportunity for people to come to a nice area of the country and find some good paying jobs."[127] A report by Kennesaw State University researchers confirmed that Woodward's opinion was widely held among Chamber of Commerce members. The Chamber of Commerce, researchers found, "indicate[d] that Hispanic labor migration saved the mills and plants in the Dalton area." Researchers also found that Hispanic laborers were "lauded by the employers for their strong work ethic."[128]

The "need" for Latino workers also fed another common refrain from the carpet capitalists: that the influx of labor prevented the relocation of carpet factories to Mexico. According to Jeff Lorberbaum, chief executive officer of Mohawk Industries, the new immigrant labor truly was a godsend. In fact, he said the company "considered moving some of its facilities in the 1990s" because of a "concern we wouldn't be able to have a labor force to fund the plants and factories."[129] Vance Bell, the executive vice president of Shaw Industries, noted that if immigrant labor "had not moved from Mexico to this area," the carpet industry "may very well have had to move facilities down there."[130] Statements like Bell's and Lorberbaum's stoked fears in the region that carpet might leave for greener, or in this case cheaper, pastures. By preserving the threat of leaving the area, they maintained tighter control on the few white and Black workers they hired. It also meant that many feared challenging the carpet industry's welcoming embrace of the Latino community.[131]

Carpet executives were able to perform the paternalistic appreciation for Latino people while also simultaneously naturalizing the body-breaking pace of labor by praising "the work ethic of the new immigrants" and the "industriousness and tirelessness of Mexican immigrants."[132] "I love my Mexicans," said Durkan Spinning Mill manager Sonny Buchanan. "They go out there and run their jobs. They're loyal. The white people are just the opposite—they bounce around. These Hispanics are helping us out."[133] The paternalism inherent in many of the corporate carpet practices was made personal in Buchanan's declaration that he loved *his* Mexicans. Buchanan's comment, which was both possessive and infantilizing, highlighted the chasm between labor and management in the carpet industry. It also demonstrates the extent to which management internalized the paternalistic ethos of the company's public relations presentation. Although Buchanan's bald condemnation of white workers' lack of loyalty was exceptional, much of the rhetoric used by carpet capitalists included an element of comparison. "Hispanic" workers were loyal, whereas Black and white workers refused to accept their labor conditions.

Latino people, those in the carpet industry argued, had the capacity to work harder, longer, and faster than their white or Black native-born peers, and, for that reason, they could be expected to maintain a grueling production pace that others struggled to meet. Chad Harris, the manager of Four Square Chemical and Finishing, offered a similar account of how hard the Latino immigrants he hired to dye cotton at his Georgia plant labored. In 1997, Harris paid Mexican employees eight dollars an hour, nearly 50 percent more than he had paid the native-born workforce a few years prior. Even with the increased pay, Harris reported that he still "comes out ahead." The explanation he offered was that "Hispanic employees work harder and produce more . . . [they] are just fantastic workers." He continued, "They don't call in sick, and when they come, they really work." Hispanic workers, he noted, "work twice as hard as Americans for the same wages."[134] Comments like those of Harris presented immigrants as naturally harder working and more eager to produce at higher and higher rates. Harris successfully cast immigrants as having a natural propensity for hard work, and, as a result, their increased production was a reflection of their "willingness" to work hard rather than of increasingly arduous labor expectations and conditions.

Latino people in Dalton, however, understood the underlying roots of their widely lauded "work ethic." Jose, who worked in the carpet industry most of his adult life said, "I am not saying that the [white] people here do not like to work . . . what I see is that many [Latino] people come with an economical need. That is what makes us work more, put more effort into work, work harder, because maybe we need the money more . . . and we don't want a problem of them firing us."[135] As Jose's comment suggests, the pace of work had little to do with race and much more to do with the tenuous economic position of Latino workers.

The open praise of the "loyalty" and "industriousness" of immigrant workers served two purposes. First, it undercut Black and white workers' ability to organize for better working conditions because management could employ, and more easily control, undocumented workers whose status made them more vulnerable. Second, it characterized Latino people as being somehow innately more hardworking than their native-born peers, effectively eliding the harsh working conditions under which these superhuman feats of labor were performed. It therefore worked to naturalize the hyperproductive labor these workers did and made invisible the embodied consequences of this type of work.[136] What this rhetoric obscured was that a large proportion of the workforce was undocumented. The mixed-status nature of much of the workforce and their families was an open secret that undergirded the celebrated Latino work ethic.

The carpet industry was certainly not alone in their emphatic and paternalistic praise of the Latino "work ethic."[137] Throughout the South, industries that were increasingly reliant on Latino labor used racial scripts about hardworking Latino people to legitimize their largely undocumented and highly exploited workforce. In Kentucky, Latino workers were celebrated for their diligent care of the state's thoroughbred horse population.[138] North Carolina's fishing and seafood processing industries similarly touted the unique work capabilities of Latino laborers.[139] Perhaps most important, the poultry industry throughout the Southeast in the 1990s and early 2000s promoted the idea that Latino people were hardworking and values-driven people who helped uplift their industry and the surrounding communities.[140] One manager in the poultry industry told anthropologist Angela Stuesse, "I will tell you strictly my opinion. I'm crazy about 'em. . . . They're providing the work that otherwise would go undone in our country. . . . I don't know what our poultry industry would do without our Hispanic guests."[141] His reference to his Latino workers as "guests" certainly foreshadowed the ways those in the South would eventually seek to expel the very populations that saved their industries and communities. In Dalton, Chamber of Commerce president George Woodward said, "Thank goodness that when we needed to fill these jobs, we had people to come in to keep the carpet investment here." He continued, "In general, these are people with strong family values—red, white, and blue values."[142]

One of the consequences of the discourse of "hardworking immigrants" was that it helped explain the hyperproductivity of Latino workers. If carpet factory owners were to be believed, Latino people were capable, at the level of their genetic material, of producing at a much higher rate than their Black or white peers. In a 1998 interview, Charles Parham, the vice president of manufacturing at Queen Carpet, said, "Hispanics have been a salvation of our carpet industry." Latino workers, he went on, were "wonderful workers." Executives found that "by and large the experience of the company with Hispanic workers has been positive," in part because "Hispanic workers are compliant and not demanding."[143]

In addition to drawing broad generalizations about "Hispanic workers," the native-born white and Black workers are clearly the unnamed referent against which Latino workers were being compared. Parham's comments, while taken at face value seemed to affirm the industriousness of Latino labor, matched a widely held view that Latino people were a more manageable constituency than Black Americans. However, this view, anthropologist Arlene Dávila argues, "not only generalizes the structural vulnerability of the undocumented Latino worker onto the entire Latino population, but also, and more problematically, turns such vulnerability into a 'positive' character trait."[144]

In other cases, the comparison was made explicit. Comparing Mexican and African American workers, a plant manager in a north Georgia poultry plant told scholar David Griffith that you could tell the work ethic of the two groups by looking at workers returning from the bathroom. Mexican workers "nearly ran back to their positions on the line," he noted, "while African Americans took their time, stopping along the way to talk to other workers."[145] A similar dynamic emerged in the Atlanta construction industry where employers expressed a preference for Latino workers over both white and Black US-born workers because they worked harder for longer hours and with less complaint.[146]

This comparison between Black and Latino southerners had effects outside of the workplace. In Dalton, for example, the arrival of Latino people in Dalton's East Side neighborhood stretched to its limit the city's already strained low-income housing. A large section of northeast Dalton became so densely occupied by Latino residents that it was referred to as "Little Mexico" by the white population.[147] As Latino people "gain[ed] a reputation among local landlords for being more prompt with rent payments and better at keeping up properties than other types of tenants," white and Black residents of Dalton's low-income housing found themselves displaced.[148] Similarly, the private and public interest in programs like the Georgia Project, which served a largely non-Black Latino population, rested on the logic that these students represented similar potential as their parents. Black Daltonians—who had been pushed out of the labor market and then public housing—did not receive the same kinds of infusions of funds into their children's educational promise.

Black Daltonians both participated in and were critical of this hardworking narrative. Sociologists Rubén Hernández-León and Víctor Zúñiga found that Black Daltonians "expressed an admiration for the entrepreneurial capacity and social capital of the newcomers." However, they also noticed that white people were "catering to Latinos and providing things for Latinos to adjust"—resources like business and housing loans and educational opportunities from which Black Dalton had been barred.[149]

Just as in earlier periods, for non-Black Latino people, it was against Blackness that they would be defined by neighbors and employers—and it was also how they came to define themselves. Adrian Gánadra, a sixth grader in Dalton, struggled in school because, as he said, "kids made fun of me because of my skin." At times they would call him Black as a way to tease him. Gánadra struggled to adjust to life in Dalton as a result of the racism he endured in his school. "Sometimes I don't really wish I was white, but sometimes just to get away from racism. . . . I don't wish I was white, I just wish I was in Mexico with other people like me."[150] The decision to use the taunt of "Blackness" against Gánadra suggests that his classmates saw Latinidad and Blackness as distinct racial categories and that Blackness was the ultimate insult you could wage against a peer.

In the late 1980s and 1990s, Latino racialization shifted from provisionally white to Hispanic or, in some cases, Latino.[151] This new racialization initially cohered around the idea of Latino people as hardworking immigrants who brought superhuman labor and family values to the rapidly growing South. The hardworking Latino immigrant was an ostensibly positive racial script. This group was heralded for bringing much-needed labor to industries ready to expand and family values to a religiously conservative part of the United States ready to eschew the legacies of racism and Jim Crow. This new form of racial difference did not contain the vitriol or fear that categorized Latino racial scripts in other places in the country. However, this seemingly positive portrayal of Latino people was insidious for multiple groups: Latino laborers driven to more grueling labor expectations, local Black and white workers pushed out of the labor market, and Black southerners who often served as the unnamed referent against which "hardworking" and "family values" were weaponized.

The category of "hardworking" also did not protect hard-won resources for

Latino people when budgets became tighter. By the spring of 1999, the Georgia Project was defending itself against claims that it was too expensive to remain viable. Superintendent Billy Bice announced that the Georgia Project would end in Dalton's public schools that spring when the three-year federal grant ran out.[152] In its place, the assistant superintendent of curriculum instruction, Sheila Evans, proposed a "Language Development Action Plan," replacing the Georgia Project with "language academies." These academies would offer students a "crash course in English for a semester or two before entering regular classes full-time" and would serve Spanish-speaking students in separate classrooms as opposed to the Georgia Project model, which kept Spanish-speaking students in integrated classrooms with the assistance of a translator.

Suspicious of such a program, Erwin Mitchell reached out to experts to see if it could be legally challenged.[153] Although it does not appear that Mitchell pursued this line of legal reasoning by taking Dalton public schools to court, his inquiry pointed to one of the most problematic elements of the new plan: it supported a new form of segregation. The Georgia Project directed resources to ensure that students could remain in classes with their peers, whereas this new model proposed removing all Spanish-speaking students (effectively removing much of the Latino population) and segregating them until they were proficient in English. Aside from the questionable pedagogical merits of such an approach, it also reinforced the increasingly segregated nature of Dalton public schools.[154]

The following two years remained tense, and funding continued to be a source of conflict between the Georgia Project and Dalton public schools. However, in May 2001, Dalton public schools ended their relationship with the Georgia Project. In an email to one of the coordinators of the Georgia Project In Monterrey, the Dalton public schools Board of Education announced that it had come to the decision to "hire 11 Monterrey teaching assistants as paraprofessionals," thereby reducing their numbers and demoting them professionally. In 1996, Bice had conservatively estimated the need for nearly sixty-eight teachers from Monterrey to handle the influx of Spanish-speaking students. Five years later, when the population had grown exponentially, even just eleven teachers proved too expensive for Bice and Dalton public schools. Ultimately, four years after the project was inaugurated in the "carpet capital of the world," it was gone from Dalton.[155]

As Latino students populated Dalton schools in higher numbers, echoes of segregation academies and white flight began to ring louder. Dalton's Catholic churches found that when the churches began to fill with the new Latino population, white parishioners began attending churches in Fort Oglethorpe, Georgia, and Chattanooga, Tennessee.[156] Additionally, a Georgia Project study funded by the Department of Education found that "as a result of the increase in the Hispanic population of the public schools a significant number of Anglo families have withdrawn their children and sent them to private schools." Between 1989 and 1997, white student enrollment in Dalton public schools dropped from 81 percent to about 49 percent.[157] Some white families chose to leave the county, and others chose to remove their children from the state's public schools entirely. Many crossed the nearby border to send children to private schools in Chattanooga.[158]

As many white families fled Dalton, more Latino families continued to arrive. Between 1990 and 2000, Whitfield County grew from 3.2 percent to 22.1 percent Latino.[159] Over the same decade that Dalton's Latino population grew by 600 percent growth, the city was also becoming home to a more established Latino community. Those who had migrated a decade earlier had become a part of the Dalton community. Since Jose Montoya's arrival in 1999, Latino people had become an integral part of Dalton. Discussing his connection with Dalton, he said, "I have my Mexican roots, my parents are Mexican, I'm Mexican. However . . . this country, this city has given me a lot, it has given me a lot of opportunities and I am grateful . . . because I've been put in Dalton because God has helped me."[160] Dalton, a place that had at one point felt foreign to Montoya, had become a home. By his own estimation, nearly 90 percent of his family was in Dalton, and his cousins had formed a successful construction company. Indeed, rather than a "new destination," as so many social scientists would describe cities like Dalton in this period, it was becoming a hub of both Latino migration and deep community formation. In the process, spaces like Dalton were redefining how race worked in the US South.

Between the 1970s and the start of the twenty-first century, what had begun as a racial description saturated with praise—"the hardworking Latino"—eventually deepened the growing chasm of racial difference among white southerners and non-Black Latino people. By the end of the 1990s and the beginning of the new millennium, the label of "Latino" was evolving in the Southeast once again. The economic boom in the region began to contract, and in 2001, the September 11 terrorist attacks would reconfigure American ideas about race, immigration, and belonging. Southern Latino people would find that the era of "hardworking" immigrants had come to a close.

■ ■ ■ ■ ■ ■ ■ ■ ■ ■ ■ ■ ■ ■ ■

CHAPTER FIVE

The Aliens Are Here

From Hardworking to Illegal, 1990–2011

On June 29, 2010, two young women concluded their fourteen-day hunger strike at the center of downtown Raleigh, North Carolina, across from the North Carolina Legislature Building. Rosario Lopez and Viridiana Martinez, along with Loida Silva, had spent the previous two weeks surviving on Gatorade and Pedialyte while sitting outside the legislature in the heat and humidity of the North Carolina summer. Before the end of the strike, Silva was taken to the hospital to be treated for a combination of dehydration and heat stroke. All three women had lived in central North Carolina since they were children and were members of the NC DREAM Team. All three were pursuing higher education and had discovered how limited their educational and professional futures had become in North Carolina as a result of a growing number of pieces of legislation aimed at undocumented immigrants in the state. Jose Rico, also a member of the NC DREAM Team, remembered being proud of "those three strong women." He recalled, "They decided to take direct action. . . . They were tired of living in the shadows . . . and not being able to have the same opportunities that everyone had."[1]

The young women hoped their hunger strike would push Senator Kay Hagan, a Democrat from North Carolina, to cosponsor the Development, Relief, and Education for Alien Minors Act, more widely known as the DREAM Act. Although Kagan never cosponsored the bill or even voted in support of it, the hunger strike raised the profile of the growing number of young people in North Carolina who were undocumented and unafraid. The hunger strike ended with Lopez and Martinez leading community members in singing "We Shall Overcome," an anthem of the southern civil rights movement. The group called on the legacy of the civil rights movement as both a source of strength to continue their protest and a way to make their struggles legible to the southern context.[2]

NC DREAM Team during hunger strike, June 17, 2010, Raleigh, North Carolina. Justin Valas/ Flickr, CC BY-NC-ND 2.0.

Nine months later, Martinez and Rico traveled to Georgia to join undocumented students from around the country to protest Georgia's legislation that banned undocumented students from attending the top five public schools in the state. They recognized that the fight the NC DREAM Team had started in Raleigh was the same fight being waged by undocumented youth throughout the South. Rico described his reason for participating: "Because there are . . . all of these bills popping up in North Carolina, there is a ban in South Carolina, there [is] just around the country the same thing."[3] Following a march through Atlanta, Rico and Martinez, along with five other students, donned graduation caps and blocked a street that stretched from the Georgia State University campus to the state capitol. As the students were arrested, the crowds chanted "No papers, no fear, immigrants are marching here!" and, perhaps referencing their southern location, "Education not segregation!"[4]

"We have learned from the past," Rico said. "In the 1960s when the Civil Rights Movement was going on, it took a lot of people to do a lot of civil disobedience, people getting arrested forty times in order to change things."[5] In seeming affirmation of the parallel drawn by Rico between the modern-day fight of undocumented youth and the civil rights activists of the 1950s and 1960s,

Georgia representative and former leader of the civil rights organization, the Student Nonviolent Coordinating Committee (SNCC), John Lewis came out in support of the students saying, "I got arrested . . . 40 times. I was beaten, left bloody, but I didn't give up. And you must not give up."[6] In just over sixty years, Latino people had evolved from being not-Black to having their struggle aligned with the southern legacy of the civil rights movement.

Inspired by the civil rights movement, the groundswell of national protests against anti-immigrant legislation was growing. On December 16, 2005, the Sensenbrenner Bill, also known as the Border Protection, Anti-Terrorism and Illegal Immigration Control Act of 2005 (HR4437), was passed in the US House of Representatives. Although the bill did not become law, it sparked protest across the country, led by immigrant and Latino communities fighting back against the tough anti-immigrant legislation. Through March and early April 2006, demonstrations fanned out across the country: 20,000–40,000 in Washington, DC; 100,000–300,000 in Chicago; 300,000 in New York City; and an estimated 1 million in La Gran Marcha in Los Angeles.[7]

However, it was the number of marches in the South opposing the bill that perhaps signaled to many that the geography of Latino settlement had changed.[8] Marches took place not only in cities like Atlanta and Charlotte but also (to a lesser degree) in rural areas. For example, in April 2006, an estimated 2,000 people protested in Tifton, Georgia, against both the Sensenbrenner Bill and Georgia's statewide anti-immigrant bill, SB529.[9] For some parts of the United States, these marches were yet another moment in the long history of Latino activism; in the South, however, it was one of the first times that Latino people had participated in a mass political mobilization. Southern Latino participation in these marches demonstrated how much had changed in the fifty years since Karla was kicked out of Margaret Murray Washington Vocational School or the thirty years since Maria Varela, Elizabeth Martinez, Luis Zapata, and Fatima Cortez stood alone as Latino activists in the civil rights movement. As the protests of these young women and the widespread participation in national mobilizations against anti-immigrant legislation show, there was a growing sense of a shared political identity amongst Latinos in the South.

As a result of the mounting legislation and xenophobia, as well as the growing Latino social movements across the South, many Latino southerners found themselves becoming more aligned with African American communities. Referred to by some as the "twenty-first-century civil rights movement,"[10] these immigrants' rights protests marked yet another shift in Latino people's racial position in the South. If in the 1990s many southern Latino people identified

Latino population growth in new-destination states in the South

State	Percentage change, 1990–2000	Percentage change, 2000–2010
Alabama	207.9	144.8
Arkansas	337.0	114.2
Georgia	299.6	96.1
Kentucky	172.6	121.6
Mississippi	148.4	105.9
North Carolina	514.2	111.1
South Carolina	211.2	147.9
Tennessee	278.2	134.2
Virginia	105.6	91.7

Source: US Census data from Social Explorer, www.socialexplorer.com/explore-maps.

as "hardworking" to racially distance themselves from southern African Americans, the racialization of Latino southerners as "illegal" drew into sharp relief the ways southern Latino and Black communities faced connected struggles. No longer "provisionally white," many Latino southerners now identified as racialized minorities.

Despite the increasingly unsafe conditions for Latino southerners in the late twentieth and early twenty-first centuries, migrants continued to come to the South to rejoin family and community members and seek work in the growing agricultural, manufacturing, construction, and food processing sectors.[11] Between 1990 and 2000, the Latino population grew 308 percent in six southern states.[12] Between 2000 and 2003, the South saw 22 percent overall growth in its Latino population, whereas traditional settlement states (Illinois, California, New Jersey, and New York) saw only 11 percent growth.[13] Places like Dalton, Georgia, maintained consistent growth even after their first wave of migration in the 1990s. The continued increase in Latino migration was, in part, a result of industry leaders continuing to recruit Latino labor to the Southeast.

Another important dynamic of this continued migration was that women and children increasingly accounted for the migrant population in the early 2000s. Men who migrated to the South in the 1980s and 1990s established footholds and then brought partners and children who had stayed behind to reunite with them in their new hometowns. As a result of this migration, southern towns saw spikes in the number of Latino people in their schools and public places. Many schools, like Dalton Public Schools, saw double-digit growth in the percentage of Latino students. Latino families increasingly populated stores, local parks, and hospitals. Although the change had been happening for years, it was in this period that many southerners began to feel it in their social lives.[14]

Some southerners found Latino people's growing presence in these spaces problematic. Previously, many people had viewed Latino migrants as "birds of passage" moving through the Southeast for work, but the growing presence of women and children made it clear that they were settling in and putting down roots in the community.[15] As a result, Latino people increasingly found their movements and lives policed, not only by local and federal law enforcement but also by their neighbors and fellow community members. A new wave of anti-immigrant legislation enshrined these changing ideas about race.

This book began with Latino people finding space in whiteness in the Jim Crow South, and it ends sixty years later with Latino people linking their contemporary struggle to the lineage of the southern civil rights movement. If the 1990s represented the beginning of a coherent "Hispanic" racial identity, the early 2000s solidified the association between that identity and "illegality." The early 2000s also saw the emergence of a growing activist movement of Latino southerners combatting the mounting anti-immigrant legislation in the region.[16] Over this period, the South began to look increasingly like the rest of the country in ideas and legislation governing Latino populations.[17] The rhetoric that surrounded Proposition 187 and other anti-immigrant legislation elsewhere in the country had arrived in the South, if a decade later.

To trace the consequences of the evolution of racial scripts about Latinos in the South during this period, this chapter looks at changes in policy both as they were discussed by lawmakers and felt on the ground. To do this, I use the unfolding debates about immigration legislation and oral histories. These oral histories are both from existing databases, including the Southern Oral History Program at the University of North Carolina at Chapel Hill, and original oral histories I collected with Latino college students in the Birmingham, Alabama, area. North Carolina and Alabama were two of the hubs of both the anti-immigrant legislation that characterized this period and the emergent protest energy that followed the introduction of this legislation. The oral histories are drawn from a mix of documented and undocumented, younger and older, Latino people living in Alabama and North Carolina. What is still missing from these oral history collections and many of those documenting the "Nuevo South" are the voices of Black Latino people. The anti-Black racism that often renders "Black" and "Latino" as separate, rather than overlapping as they often are in people's lives, bleeds into the archive of the Latino South.[18]

The question of when and why this anti-immigrant sentiment began to appear in the South continues to unfold. Historian Julie Weise has argued compellingly that the anti-immigrant tide in the South originated in the 1990s and early 2000s during times of economic prosperity when Latino people's growing economic success gave them the ability to move to previously all-white exurbs. Weise argues that it was a Latino presence in previously white spaces that threatened white people's position and resulted in the anti-immigrant tide. Scholar Perla Guerrero, alternatively, argues that it was the rapid demographic change that sparked a local grassroots effort by white Arkansans to police and limit the growing presence of Latino populations in the state.

My own research emphasizes national and international shifts that helped spark this anti-immigrant moment. Starting with the September 11 terrorist attacks, both politicians and local southerners began to talk differently about Latino people. Instead of hardworking, good, family people, the threat of the terrorist "other" loomed over Latino communities.[19] In addition to changing attitudes, September 11 opened the door for an unprecedented expansion of the security state. This included the adoption of 287(g) programs that facilitated collaboration between local, state, and federal police in targeting undocumented immigrants. The September 11 attacks both increased anti-immigrant sentiment and gave states the necessary funding and latitude to marshal the power of the state in support of those views.[20] Seven years later, the Great Recession accelerated many of the anti-immigrant sentiments and policies that were beginning to cohere in the South. By 2010, the South was home to some of the most draconian anti-immigrant legislation in the nation, and Latino people were in the sights of many politicians.

Race had changed dramatically for many Latino people in the South over the course of the second half of the twentieth century. For decades, they were not raced in any consistent way in the South. By the first decade of the twenty-first century, Latino (or Hispanic at the time) had become a hardened racial group, thereby losing the instability that had defined the category in an earlier period.

September 11 and the Hyperpolicing of Illegality

The September 11 terrorist attacks forever changed life for those in the United States. The nation watched in horror as nearly 3,000 people died in targeted attacks in New York and Washington, DC. Surging American patriotism in the aftermath of the attacks became jingoism and anti-immigrant sentiment in the days and weeks that followed.[21] Muslim and Arab-descended peoples felt this most intensely as hate crimes rose and the creation of the "Muslim registry" treated many in those communities as potential "terrorists."[22]

Perhaps unexpectedly, September 11 also reshaped southern Latino racialization and identity in the region. The violent growth of xenophobia in the wake of September 11 was not reserved solely for Muslim and Arab Americans; Latino people, too, found themselves subjected to increased scrutiny and suspicion. Additionally, the xenophobia growing in the wake of the attacks was militarized with a rapidly expanding security state that, in addition to profiling and targeting Muslim and Arab Americans, created the conditions for the growth of the detention and deportation of undocumented Latino people in the US South.[23] Latino communities, who previously received a tempered welcome as "hardworking immigrants" in the post–civil rights movement South, found themselves increasingly attacked as foreign and illegal.

Despite a lack of evidence linking any of those involved in the September 11 attacks with Latin America, one part of the national narrative became focused on protecting US borders from national threats both in the Middle East and south of the border. One Fox News anchor worried that "Bin Laden–funded operatives [would] ride the rails undetected from Mexico along with hundreds of thousands of undocumented workers."[74] Fusing two recurring conservative talking points—terrorism and "illegal" immigration—this news anchor drew on the nation's fear in the aftermath of September 11 to reignite anger and anxiety about undocumented migration. Another woman called to complain to her local newspaper in Greenville, South Carolina, about her concern that terrorists could take advantage of the "looseness of our border with Mexico."[25] This fear that the problem with Mexican immigration would help fuel future terrorist attacks was echoed in conservative circles.

With this kind of anti-Latino rhetoric emerging after the attacks, Latino southerners were subject to the post–September 11 rise in xenophobia. As immigration scholar David Hernández writes, "Merging traditional arguments for and against immigration, with fears of international terrorism, politicians from both sides of the aisle have reframed the immigration debate, suggesting that immigrants are the cause of the nation's security vulnerabilities."[26] It was in the context of 9/11 that immigrant men became "dangerous criminal aliens."[27] September 11 activated a rising tide of hate against immigrants and became fuel for anti-"illegal" immigration advocates.[28]

The reverberations of September 11 were felt in places like Dalton, Georgia; and the same place that Latino people had been heralded as hardworking, they now found themselves targets of suspicion and fear. Carlos Noriega remembered how life changed in Dalton, Georgia, after the attacks. "After 9/11, it got hard. It was more difficult for us as Latinos because . . . they look at us as though we cause[d] the [9/11] attacks. . . . Since we [Latinos] are from outside [the United States]," he continued, "they think that we [foreigners] are all the same, [that we are] terrorists or something like that."[29] Jose remembered that in North Carolina things "exploded" after the attacks and a "lot of people . . . became racist."[30] Both men felt the shift after 9/11 in how non-Latino southerners saw the Latino community.

The swell of both xenophobia and policing in the post-9/11 years made life increasingly challenging for Latino southerners throughout the region.[31] Sociologist Jennifer Jones interviewed Latino people in Winston-Salem, North Carolina, who commented on how difficult life became after September 11. One of her respondents, Diego, who came to Winston-Salem from Guerrero in 1999, reported that before 9/11 finding work was easy. "But now," he said, "after the attack on the Twin Towers, it's been a bit more difficult. . . . With the war, they already had the rules to check on the people more and more. Then the raids. Now the economy. So, yes it's a lot more difficult now."[32] Another woman Jones interviewed, Mayra, said, "You know things started getting worse in 9-1-1 [9/11], and after that, the focus shifted to immigrants. Hispanics are not the only immigrants, and they had nothing to do with 9-1-1! They are not here to hurt anyone."[33] A Guatemalan poultry worker in Mississippi told anthropologist Angela Stuesse, "We only come to work, and we want to do it well. We don't want them to see us as criminals, as terrorists. We are the terrorists of the tomatoes, the oranges, the chickens. Nothing more."[34] This poultry worker's defense of himself suggests he was aware of how undocumented Latino migrants were increasingly racialized as dangerous alongside Muslim and Arab American migrants. September 11 injected new life and power into legislation targeting undocumented Latino people. It created both the ideological and legislative groundwork for what would emerge in the Southeast—waves of anti-immigrant legislation focused on undocumented Latino people.

Many Latino people could feel the way the post–September 11 period further limited their mobility. Yazmin Garcia Rico's mother arrived in North Carolina before September 11, so it was, as Rico reflected, "really easy for her to come without documents." "But when I came," she continued, "with my oldest brother, it was after 9/11, right after 9/11, so it was very challenging."[35] In addition to making the trip to the United States more perilous, the racial discourse about Latino populations also changed. Rafael Prieto Zartha recalled the 1990s as a good time to be in Charlotte, North Carolina: "The people were very friendly, and we felt like an exotic (laughter) . . . element in the city." However, he recalled, "When I came back . . . after the attacks, things had changed. . . . It had started on the anti-immigrant way."[36] Federico Van Gelderen remembered it similarly. He blamed irresponsible rhetoric on the part of politicians in the wake of the September 11 attacks. "Unfortunately, [Latino people] went through more rejection than I was expecting. September 11 . . . changed everything in our minds. . . . Unfortunately, we got caught in the middle of that."[37]

As national attitudes grew increasingly hostile toward Latino and Arab Americans, September 11 also generated a massive expansion of the security state that targeted these groups, among others. This targeting of Latinos however, was not unprecedented, and it built on a legislative infrastructure created to police and criminalize Mexican migration. Initially part of the 1996 Illegal Immigration Reform and Immigrant Responsibility Act (IIRAIRA), 287(g) programs grew in popularity after September 11. These 287(g) programs were collaborations among federal, state, and local authorities, and they allowed the Department of Homeland Security to deputize state and local law enforcement officers to enforce federal immigration law.[38] In doing so, these programs expanded the reach of the federal government into the lives of everyday people.

The attacks on September 11 had shown a spotlight on the failure of interagency cooperation and an inability of state and federal agencies to communicate. To many state officials, 287(g) programs seemed to be a powerful antidote to these security gaps by expanding the reach of federal agencies into local police stations. As sociologist Helen Marrow notes, there was little interest in the 287(g) program between 1996 and 2001, but after 2001, states clamored to join. The first 287(g) agreement was signed by Florida in 2002; a year later, Alabama joined, and seven years later, by 2009, sixty-seven state and local agencies in twenty-three states were participating in the program.[39] Sheriff Jim Pendergraph of Mecklenburg County, North Carolina, an early supporter of the 287(g) program, invoked September 11 when he testified to Congress that his primary support for the program grew out of the need to protect against "those cross-ing our porous borders looking to cause harm and commit acts of terrorism against the United States." He warned, "This is a serious Homeland Security issue."[40] These 287(g) programs gained strength in the Southeast and resulted in local officials playing unprecedented roles in detaining and deporting un-documented immigrants.

Latino people felt the world changing around them as their status as hard-working newcomers gave way to the cruel moniker of "illegal alien." As Antonio, who came to North Carolina from Mexico in 2006, told sociologist Jennifer Jones: "People that have been here even longer [than I] used to say that back in the 1990s when someone saw a Hispanic, the first reaction was curiosity. . . . The treatment was different. . . . Hispanic . . . has a negative connotation now. Hispanic is illegal, unauthorized, poor, nothing to offer to the society, criminal, gangster."[41] Data on hate crimes confirm Antonio's observation. Between 2003 and 2006, the number of hate crimes against Latino people grew in the South as did the number of anti-immigrant hate groups.[42]

Other scholars suggest that one cause of the increased alienation of Latino people from southern life was the growing collision between the middle-class dreams of Mexican/Mexican American and white suburban/exurban parents and community members.[43] Latino people wanted to buy homes in middle-class neighborhoods and send their children to public schools—both of which made white suburbanites feel under attack, ultimately leading to the end of, as Weise puts it, the "South's history of tenuous accommodation to Mexican immigrants and Mexican Americans."[44] Additionally, the southern economy was slowing after the boom times of the 1990s, and tighter labor markets led to growing suspicion by some southerners of their new immigrant neighbors.[45]

Between 2000 and 2004, only a few immigration laws and ordinances were under consideration; then, in 2005 alone, forty-five immigration laws were passed in the Southeast.[46] Legislation ranged in severity, but most included some kind of mandate that businesses use the federal E-Verify program to screen employees for legal status; a restriction of access to social services, in-cluding health care; and a mandate that local law enforcement check the legal status of those arrested and report them to federal immigration authorities, regardless of the severity of the crime.[47] Anti-immigration law during this time period was not a uniquely southeastern phenomenon, but its largely unprece-dented nature in the region made it acutely felt.

Although not solely responsible for the fixing of "illegal" to "Latino," 9/11 accelerated the anti-immigrant and anti-Latino sentiment that was only just

emerging in the South. There, 287(g) programs became increasingly popular and were justified, in part, by the memory of September 11. Years after
the terrorist attacks, in an interview about her support of controversial anti-
immigrant legislation, Sue Myrick, a congressional representative for North
Carolina, invoked the historical moment, saying, "Everybody keeps forgetting
9/11. The bottom line: We have no idea who is in our country, and we have no
idea who comes across the borders, both north and south."[48] Myrick, who was
described affectionately by her North Carolina colleague Congressman Mark
Souder as being "concerned about immigration laws before being concerned
about immigration laws was cool," was also a fierce advocate for the 287(g)
program. Representative Souder and Representative Myrick fused fears of terrorism and fears of so-called illegal aliens in their 2006 testimony on Capitol
Hill in support of the 287(g) program.[49] Representative Myrick testified that she
was troubled by the "very real possibility Islamic fundamentalists have slipped
into our country to commit acts of terror." She implored, "When are we going
to wake up in America?"[50] Myrick mobilized fears of September 11 to justify
more stringent enforcement of the US-Mexico border—explicitly linking the
movement of undocumented Mexican immigrants across the border with those
responsible for the attacks on September 11. Although other parts of the country had seen a "Latino threat" narrative cohere in earlier decades, it was after
September 11 that Latino people began to be seen as a "threat" in the South.[51]

The 287(g) programs were designed to target serious and violent criminals,
but they rarely worked that way. Paul M. Kilcoyne, a deputy assistant director
of Immigration and Customs Enforcement's Office of Investigations, said that
the programs would focus on "criminal organizations, those individuals who
pose a threat to border security," rather than "the landscape architect that had
a broken headlight."[52] Even though a 2007 Immigration and Customs Enforcement (ICE) fact sheet noted that "the 287(g) program is not designed to allow
state and local agencies to perform random street operations [nor is it] designed
to impact issues such as excessive occupancy and day laborer activities," many
southeastern localities took the opportunity to screen everyone who came into
contact with law enforcement.[53]

It was in the South that what immigration policy scholars have called the
"universal model of enforcement" emerged.[54] Designed to target as many
undocumented people as possible, regardless of their criminal history, this
universal model made minor infractions legitimate grounds for deportation.
In places like North Carolina and Georgia, local officials used their authority to enforce federal immigration law expansively and screened anyone they

suspected of being "illegal"—regardless of the reason they came into contact with law enforcement.[55] A broken taillight, in this new policing regime, could end in deportation.[56]

Although local authorities always maintained that these laws were not racial profiling, Latino communities disproportionately felt the impact. In Dalton, Georgia, the leader of the local organization, Coalition of Latino Leaders, America Gruner, recalled the painful early days of 287(g) in Dalton. In Latino communities, she remembered, "Houses were abandoned and businesses were closing because a lot of people were detained and deported."[57] Dalton was not alone in Georgia as Cobb, Gwinnett, and Hall counties also signed 287(g) agreements.[58] These counties' law enforcement officials also targeted Latino communities. In Gwinnett County, between 1999 and 2011, the sheriff's department reported that 93 percent of inmates held on 287(g) detainers were Latino.[59] In Dalton, where Latino people had once been heralded as the "lifeblood" saving a community industry, they were now targeted as threats to national security.

The confluence of the changes in migration streams, legislation, and the economy meant that Latino people faced increased attacks as "illegal" and "alien." A campaign ad for a North Carolina congressional candidate began with the *Twilight Zone* theme music followed by a narrator saying, "The aliens are here, but they didn't come in a spaceship; they came across our unguarded Mexican border by the millions. They've filled our criminal courtrooms and invaded our schools. They sponge off the American taxpayer by clogging our welfare lines and our hospital emergency rooms."[60] The ad—not so subtly—suggested that Latino migrants were fundamentally different from native-born southerners. Anthropologist Leo Chavez notes that Latino people were often referred to as an "invading force" as part of the construction of what he calls "The Latino Threat." The production of these ideas, according to Chavez, was part of a process of objectification and dehumanization of Latino people.[61]

The attacks grew so omnipresent that "Latino" became synonymous with "illegal" during this time. Perla Guerrero argues that it was in this era that "the construction of Latina/o immigrants as 'illegal' became a defining characteristic; it ceased being one part of a whole and became the whole that defines the parts."[62] "Illegal" had become the primary racialization of Latino southerners. As new anti-immigrant legislation emerged, what it meant to be "Latino" and "illegal" became increasingly perilous.

Latino people were beginning to be seen by many southerners as "illegal" and potentially dangerous at the exact moment that local police were given more power to detain and deport than ever before. Although September 11 is largely remembered for the negative impact it had on Muslim and Arab American communities, a secondary consequence was the growth of the state's capacity to remove undocumented people from the United States.[63] September 11 was a watershed moment for the evolution of southern Latino racialization because it opened the door for increased local power to deport and fueled an already growing tide of nativism.

Anti-Immigrant Legislation, the Great Recession, and the Deepening of Racial Boundaries

Demographic change and a sluggish economy fueled the harsh legislation and xenophobia from the first wave of anti-immigrant sentiment in the early 2000s; it only got worse after the nation faced the worst economic downturn since the Great Depression. In December 2007, the United States entered what would become known as the Great Recession, which resulted from the confluence of the housing bubble bursting in 2005–6, the decline in value of mortgage-backed securities, and the collapsing of several banks. Collectively, this economic collapse was known as the subprime mortgage crisis. Household net worth, the value of the stock market, and housing prices all collapsed in this period and, by many accounts, did not rebound until the early 2010s.

At the national level, it became clear that the Great Recession would follow in the legacy of the Great Depression with its sharp rise in anti-immigrant sentiment.[64] States began to enroll in higher numbers in 287(g) agreements and pass their own state-level anti-immigrant legislation. By 2009, sixty-seven law enforcement agencies (ranging from municipalities to entire states) were enrolled in 287(g) agreements.[65] All of these efforts were cloaked in language that echoed the repatriation efforts during the Great Depression: the removal of unwanted immigrants would ensure "real" Americans (white Americans) had the jobs and resources necessary to survive the recession.[66]

Emblematic, in many ways, of this legislative wave was Arizona's SB1070, also known as the Support Our Law Enforcement and Safe Neighborhoods Act, which Governor Jan Brewer signed into law in April 2010. SB1070 required law enforcement officials to determine the immigration status of anyone they stopped, detained, or arrested (including lawful stops where no crime was being committed or discovered). The law also made national headlines for its controversial clause that allowed law enforcement officials to stop anyone who "appeared illegal" to see their papers, even if they were not committing or suspected of committing a crime. This law became known by many as the "show me your papers" law, and it enshrined racial profiling of Latino people into Arizona state law. One of the law's key goals was to create attrition through enforcement or, put differently, create such difficult conditions that undocumented immigrants would "self-deport."[67]

Many states in the South took SB1070 as a model—and made it tougher. In April 2011, a year after SB1070 was signed into law, Georgia passed HB87 (officially titled the Illegal Immigration Reform and Enforcement Act of 2011).[68] HB87 was the first of the SB1070 copycat bills to pass and was described by many as one of the toughest anti-immigrant laws in the country.[69] The bill required the use of E-Verify in all businesses with more than ten employees, it allowed police to determine the immigration status of citizens stopped in the course of police business, and it increased the prison time and fines associated with using fake documents and assisting undocumented immigrants.[70] In addition to this legislation, in October 2010, the Georgia Board of Regents passed a law that banned undocumented students from enrolling in the state's most popular colleges. For those schools that undocumented Georgians could attend, they would be ineligible for in-state tuition. This law effectively made college in Georgia prohibitively expensive for many.[71] This included those Latino students who grew up with the Georgia Project in Dalton, Georgia, and who were now unable to attend their local Dalton State College.[72] Latino southerners were no longer a racial oddity or potential site of paternalistic charity as they had been in the 1990s; now, they were a racial threat to be managed through punitive legislation and policing.

This growing anti-Latino sentiment was more easily weaponized as a result of the policing infrastructure created in the wake of September 11. Successive generations of anti-immigrant legislation created a complex web of laws that empowered police and made life for undocumented people ever more difficult. If the terrorist attacks on September 11 opened the door to new forms of immigration control and nativist ideology for the nation, it was the wave of southern anti-immigrant legislation in the wake of the Great Recession that solidified those ideas about Latino people in the region.

South Carolina Governor Nikki Haley followed Georgia and Arizona's lead and signed a similar bill into law in June 2011.[73] Like previous laws, this bill required police to check the immigration status of those suspected of being undocumented—regardless of the reason they were stopped. Like Arizona's law, the South Carolina bill made not carrying official identification while traveling in South Carolina a misdemeanor for adults in the state.[74] In a press conference about the law, South Carolina state senator Larry Grooms said of undocumented immigrants, "They cling together in illegal communities and bring with them drugs, prostitution, violent crimes, [and] gang activity."[75] The bill, therefore, was not simply an expansion of the immigration enforcement apparatus in the region; it was a harbinger of a new way of thinking and talking about undocumented immigrants (and by extension most Latino people) in the South.

Mississippi also tried to follow suit by introducing its own anti-immigrant legislation. In 2011, thirty-three different bills were introduced by Mississippi lawmakers designed to, like SB1070, create a culture of self-deportation. Different bills called for the denial of public benefits to undocumented people, restrictions on immigrants' ability to rent apartments, and even an "English-only" mandate.[76] Although it did not become law, the bill that came the closest was SB2179, which passed in the Mississippi State Senate. SB2179 made not carrying immigration papers a crime and authorized state, county, and local police to perform immigration checks at any time, including at traffic stops.[77] The failure of any of these Mississippi laws to go into effect, scholars argue, is the result of strong Black/brown coalitions, often led by powerful Black legislative caucuses that fought these anti-immigrant measures.[78]

Even as the racial scripts about Latino people transformed during this time, hierarchies endured that shaped which parts of the Latino community were most impacted by the growing tide of criminalization. Color, for example, evinced continued importance as darker-skinned Latino people bore the brunt of this new racial order. Jose recalled of his childhood and adolescence in Alabama that his parents, both Latino, had very different experiences of race. Jose's mother had "very pale skin," while his father had "very dark skin [and] jet Black hair."[79] He remembered that his mother had to go into restaurants before his father to ask for a table; when his father asked for a table, he was rebuffed. Darker-skinned Latino people, like Jose's father, continued to experience more instances of racism, but this racism now had a growing police and security apparatus to enforce it. Without a state to protect them or a space in provisional whiteness, darker-skinned Latino populations became particularly vulnerable to the southeastern deportation regime.

Color, both in Latin America and the United States, continued to structure how Latino people were racialized in the US South.[80] Irving arrived in North Carolina in 2000 and remembered how his own understanding of race changed in the move. While in Mexico he recalled his parents' desire for their children to marry white "para mejorar la raza" or to improve the race through whitening. Describing the long reach of *mestizaje*—a deeply rooted racial ideology for many in Mexico—he remembered being described as "guero," or light skinned, in Mexico.[81] "I was always labeled white in Mexico and I was fine with it," Irving remembered. However, he continued, "When I came here . . . I was no longer guero, I was Mexican."[82] Although race changed for Irving, the underlying white supremacist values of mestizaje endured.

The fact that color is a powerful force within Latino communities is hardly a surprise given the extensive scholarship on the topic. What is different in this case is that in previous decades in the South color mattered differently. In earlier periods, the provisional whiteness of darker-skinned Latino people was certainly less secure than that of their lighter-skinned peers. However, they always maintained access to the institutional mechanisms of whiteness (schools, housing, employment). Darker-skinned Latino people in Washington, DC, may have faced individual moments of Jim Crow segregation, but those isolated incidents did not result in housing or school segregation. Braceros who came to Arkansas and were Jim Crowed could appeal to the Mexican government and regain their status in provisional whiteness.[83] This is all to say that many dark-skinned Latino people did face discrimination in the South before the 1980s. However, those moments of exclusion did not result in structural or institutional forms of marginalization.

From Economic Lifeblood to Economic Burden

Each piece of legislation, no matter the state, shared a common concern about the "taxpayer" and keeping jobs for "Americans." South Carolina Governor Nikki Haley, in her announcement of the new legislation, said, "What we're saying is this state can no longer afford to support people that don't come here the right way and we are now going to do something about it."[84] Nathan Deal, governor of Georgia, said of his own state's anti-immigrant legislation, HB87, "States must act to defend their taxpayers."[85] Supporters parroted this focus on taxpayers and budgetary concerns. "They're using all these services and not giving back into the system," Stone Mountain, Georgia, resident Catherine Davis argued. In Mississippi, the chair of the Mississippi Federation for Immigration Reform and Enforcement, Rodney Hunt, said, "Illegal immigration eliminates a lot of jobs for people who want to provide for their families. Passing this bill will open up more jobs and lower unemployment for the state."[86] Twenty years earlier, Latino people were celebrated as the hardworking lifeblood fueling the economies of these southern communities; now those same people were deemed "illegals" draining state and city coffers.

Through the construction of "the illegal," Latino people were no longer legitimate recipients of white paternal protection and instead became dangerous and unwanted members of many southern communities. For decades, industries in the South used elaborate recruitment schemes to bring (mostly undocumented) Latino workers to the region. Now, state and local authorities were attempting to expel the very people who had rejuvenated their local economies. Carpet manufacturers in Dalton, poultry processing in Georgia and the Carolinas, and the construction industry throughout the Sunbelt all had employed different strategies to bring Latino people—more specifically, undocumented Latino people—to work.[87] This was, perhaps, most striking in Alabama—a state where in 2002 Gold Kist poultry had installed billboards that read "Mucho Trabajo en Russellville, Alabama" [There's plenty of work in Russellville, Alabama], and bought radio ads in Mexico to entice new workers to the heart of Dixie.[88] Despite this history of recruitment, Alabama's own version of post–Great Recession anti-immigrant legislation was one of the harshest in the region.

Alabama Governor Robert J. Bentley signed the Beason-Hammon Alabama Taxpayer and Citizen Protection Act, or HB56, into law on June 9, 2011.[89] Like SB1070, HB56 required police to detain any person they had "reasonable suspicion" was in the country unlawfully. The law prohibited undocumented migrants from receiving any public benefits at either the state or local level. It made it illegal for undocumented immigrants to attend public colleges or universities and required K–12 schools to check the immigration status of their students. The law also banned landlords from renting to undocumented people and made it unlawful to hire undocumented workers.[90] It was not the first time that Alabama's state government had passed harsh anti-immigrant laws; however, this law was among the widest-reaching and most powerful pieces of legislation.

In this new wave of anti-immigrant legislation, lawmakers emphasized the risk and burden that Latino immigrants posed to the community. Alabama representative Micky Hammon fiercely defended the anti-immigrant legislation he introduced in the state senate. Referencing the provision that required schools to check students' citizenship status, he said, "God bless [these children] but, they're a burden."[91] However, even as the racial scripts changed, echoes of the hardworking immigrant reverberated. In defending HB56, Representative Kerry Rich said, "I like the Hispanic people. Most of them are hard workers . . . have good family values . . . are good Christian, church-going people. The ones that I have a problem with are the ones that come here and create all kinds of social and economic problems."[92] Representative Rich did not clarify how he was able to discern between the "good" and "bad" Hispanic immigrants.

Birmingham-based Latino activists and students remembered how these laws successfully created a culture of "self-deportation" as they saw their friends and families vanish before their eyes.[93] Delores recalled that when HB56 passed, once "thriving Hispanic enclaves" in the Birmingham area were "deflated." Karen remembered that HB56 "scared a lot of people away," and that her parents seriously considered returning to Washington State once the bill passed. "A lot of people left," Enrique remembered. "We started with a small group [at school], and then it kept getting smaller and smaller." Maria also remembered a school announcement made the day after HB56 passed to her majority-Hispanic school: "We had an assembly for Hispanic students and [the administrators] were like, 'If you need to go, it's okay. No big deal. . . . Just give us a phone call and we'll send your records wherever.'" Twelve years old at the time, Maria remembered feeling overwhelmed by the fear of having to move and the responsibility put on her to make these seemingly impossible choices.[94]

Those who stayed in Alabama found that life had become much more difficult. For example, jobs that were once reliable became riskier as employers took advantage of the new law to commit wage theft.[95] After HB56, Roshell remembered that her father, who painted homes for a living, came across people who refused to pay him once the work was done. In one incident a woman refused to pay him and threatened to call ICE if he took his complaint any further. Similarly, her mother, who was also undocumented, worked cleaning homes and found that her employers regularly deducted wages from their agreed-on price. Roshell's mother had no recourse for the wage theft. Before HB56, Roshell remembered that undocumented people could be employed anywhere and "it wasn't a big deal" to be paid under the table. After HB56, "Things [became] very strict," Roshell continued, "so people . . . get into riskier situations . . . and then the risk is like, am I going to get paid this week or next week?"[96] Across the nation, life for undocumented Latino people became more challenging in the years after the Great Recession, and the South was no exception.[97]

In December 2011, ICE officials began raiding Latino neighborhoods in Alabama. A report by the Southern Poverty Law Center (SPLC) included accounts of agents interrogating young children about their parents and the consistent terror these raids wrought on Latino communities.[98] The raids also had a secondary impact—normalizing the deportability of these immigrants. Anthropologist Nicholas De Genova writes about the "spectacle" of the border and illegality and the work it does to "produce the law and the terms and conditions for the 'illegality.'"[99] In this vein, the public ICE raids in places like Alabama, Mississippi, Georgia, and North Carolina helped erase the long and complex history of Latino populations in the region. These raids cast Latino immigrants as "illegal aliens" rather than as a generation of immigrants who responded to the call of southern industry, which was, at the time, desperate for their labor. As economic conditions shifted, so too did the racialization of Latino immigrants.

Many of those migrating to the South were fleeing economies decimated by free trade agreements and violent civil wars funded by the United States. Another crucial shift happening at this time was in the origin countries of Latino migrants. In the 1980s and 1990s, it was overwhelmingly Mexican and Mexican Americans who were migrating to the US South. By the early 2000s, the migrant population was increasingly composed of Indigenous people from Latin America, including Purépecha immigrants from Mexico and Maya immigrants from Guatemala.[100] Adding to the already steady stream of migration, these new populations were often darker skinned and unable to access many of the resources already built by Latino communities because of the language barrier.[101] Additionally, Indigenous immigrants faced racism both in the United States and in Latin America.[102] By recasting undocumented immigrants as "illegals," conservative legislators and activists worked to erase the economic and geopolitical conditions under which Latino people arrived in the South. The category of "Illegal," De Genova argues, works to conceal the reality of these migrants as "asylum seekers."[103]

It is hard to disentangle the national and international forces from the economic and demographic influences occurring in the South during this time. As the early 2000s continued, Latino people played a growing role in powering the southern economy. More industries relied on their labor, more businesses relied on them as consumers, and more consumers relied on their businesses. However, the central economic role of Latino people, rather than offering protections, made them increasingly vulnerable to racist othering.

If, as many argue, a key function of the category of race is to fuel capitalism,[104] the solidification of Latino people as racialized others was also a by-product of their growing integration into the southern economy. The production of these racial categories helped objectify and dehumanize workers to legitimize brutal working conditions, deportation sweeps, and racist violence. In the era of the Galarzas or SNCC, Latino people were not as integral to the southern economy and, therefore, their racial position did not need to be managed as tightly. With Black workers providing a great deal of the industrial and agricultural labor in the South before the 1990s, white supremacy relied on and helped produce the unequal conditions that kept Black workers locked into debt peonage, convict lease systems, and eventually neoliberal hyperexploitation. As Latino workers came to share this position with Black workers, their racialization began to look more similar.

Some, like *New York Times* writer Diane McWhorter in 2018, drew stark parallels between the struggles of undocumented Latino people in the South with earlier forms of anti-Black racism. Alabama's HB56 mandate that the state maintain a database of "illegals," McWhorter wrote, recalled the "antebellum ads spotlighting runaway slaves." "The law," she continued, "still exempts domestics, observing the plantation hierarchy of 'house Negroes' and 'field hands.'"[105] McWhorter saw the contemporary discrimination against Latino people in Alabama as part of a direct lineage that could be drawn to slavery and Jim Crow. Scott Douglas III, the executive director of Greater Birmingham Ministries, agreed with McWhorter, comparing the law's provision punishing anyone harboring an undocumented immigrant to the fugitive slave acts of the nineteenth century. "The difference," he said "between the fugitive slave act and this current law is then they punished you for helping somebody trying to escape, now they punish you for helping somebody trying to come here. So it's still the same thing."[106]

However, the long history of Latino people in the South cautions against making such facile comparisons.[107] Scholar Tiffany Willoughby-Herard offers a different connection between the contemporary exploitation of Latino workers and the history of slavery. She argues that rather than thinking about the working conditions of contemporary undocumented people as "like slaves," we should think about the history of slavery as producing the conditions in which this kind of hyperexploitation can occur. It is the historical and contemporary exploitation of Black communities in the South, she argues, that laid the groundwork for the kinds of inequality and racialization that contemporary Latino communities are facing.[108]

Writing about undocumented immigrants in Georgia, scholar Lorgia Garcia Peña makes a similar argument. She writes that "anti-immigrant racism emerges out of the same colonial capitalist structures that engendered slavery and continues to sustain the existence of Black and Brown immigrant subjects in the afterlife of slavery."[109] The legacy of anti-Black racism in the South, in this formulation, created the conditions for the exploitation of non-Black Latino people. These histories of slavery and anti-Black racism in both the United States and Latin America also produced powerful incentives for non-Black

Latino people to weaponize anti-Black racism as a form of protection and so-cial mobility.

Over the first decade of the new millennium, a great deal changed for Latino southerners. In the 1990s, Latino people began to form a coherent racial group, but in the first decade of the 2000s, that racialization took on a decidedly neg-ative meaning. Largely cast as "illegal," Latino people struggled to find new footing in the region that so many had moved to in order to find work and a peaceful life. That life of rural calm was being dismantled by legislation that made living and working in the Southeast more dangerous for many Latino communities. Sociologist Jennifer Jones calls this shift "reverse incorpora-tion." "Latinos in North Carolina and elsewhere," she writes, "saw their status decline rapidly from valued worker, volunteer, parent, and neighbor to highly vulnerable positions as unwanted and deportable subjects."[110] This shift from "wanted" to "unwanted" remade the nature of southern Latino activism and racial identification.

Unsurprisingly, as a consequence of this change, some Latino southerners began to see themselves increasingly aligned with southern African American communities.[111] In this new era of policing, Latino communities were experi-encing the kinds of surveillance that had long been weaponized against Black communities. Enrique recalled of his life in Alabama, "You have a perimeter that you know you cannot cross. And if you do then you're going to be pun-ished."[112] He then recounted one of the times that lesson was confirmed: When driving through a small town in Alabama to get gas, he was pulled over. The police officer said Enrique clearly was not from around there and gave him two tickets. Enrique felt that he was a target of racial profiling and that not "being from around here" was more about his race than his hometown. These kinds of encounters with police officers likely mirrored many of the stories of Black Alabamians.

The challenges faced by Latino and Black southerners had other striking parallels. After 9/11, the "controlling image"[113] of Latino men began to look much like that of Black men.[114] Represented as criminal, illegal, and poten-tially dangerous, both Black and Latino men were incarcerated at increasingly high numbers. While mass incarceration started in the 1970s, the Great Re-cession accelerated the expansion of private prisons and their new extension, immigrant detention centers. After the Great Recession, state enforcement of 287(g) agreements and increasingly punitive legislation made Latino people more vulnerable both to arrest and detention. Jim Pendergraph, the sheriff of Mecklenburg County, North Carolina—a locality that participated in a 287(g) agreement—testified to Congress that the arrests resulting from this new enforcement had pushed his jails to capacity. "So many illegal immigrant criminals have been identified through my 287(g) program," he began, "it is causing me a jail space problem."[115] Black and Latino people were facing the connected network of racial profiling, hyperpolicing, and mass incarceration.

It is also likely that Black Latino people experienced this hyperpolicing even more acutely than non-Black Latino people.[116] In fact, "The State of Black Immigrants Report," by the Black Alliance for Just Immigration and the New York University Immigrant Rights Clinic, shows that in the US Black immigrants, many of whom are Latino, are disproportionately targeted for deportation on criminal grounds as a result of the mass criminalization of Black people in the United States.[117] Sociologist Tanya Golash-Boza found similarly high rates of deportation of undocumented Jamaican and Dominican immigrants. She notes, for example, that around a quarter of all criminal deportees are deported based on drug charges; however, these percentages are much higher for Jamaicans (80 percent) and Dominicans (40 percent).[118] Despite this, the national and regional narratives around deportation have largely focused on non-Black immigrants from Latin America. These anti-immigrant laws, which expand the grounds for criminalization and deportation, as much as they have an impact on non-Black Latino people, disproportionately affect Black Latino and Black immigrants more broadly. Garcia Peña similarly finds that Black Latino diasporic subjects face this double form of policing. She writes, "They can be shot by the police and arrested by the immigration authorities."[119]

At the interpersonal level, too, how some Latino southerners understood themselves vis-à-vis southern African Americans shifted. "I think that Blacks and Hispanics are minorities, and I feel like they go through a lot of the [same] struggles," Birmingham resident Enrique said. "Hispanics deal with being put in a category of . . . illegal immigrants . . . and Blacks go through the struggle of profiling [as criminal]." He continued, "So I think they both go through the same struggles in their own different ways, but they can relate to each other in a way."[120] Another Alabamian, Jose, made the argument that Black and Latino communities shared certain values: "Hispanic and Black people have a very similar . . . heritage." He elaborated, "A very strong value in the family, people taking care of other people."[121] Drawing connections around shared "values" marked a significant departure from an earlier period when Latino people's value as "hardworking" stood in almost explicit contrast to the myth of the "lazy" Black worker.

For as many people like Jose or Enrique who saw the linkages between Black American and Latino communities, many others continued to draw the distinction, emphasizing their difference from Black communities.[122] Eduardo, an immigrant from Quetzaltenango, Guatemala, living in North Carolina, talked in an interview with sociologist Helen Marrow about how white employers would ask Black and Hispanic employees to work and Hispanic workers would instantly respond, "Yes," while Black workers complained about the difficulty. He explained that Hispanic people "like to work" and that is why "white Americans always talk to Hispanics."[123] Lidia, an immigrant from Oaxaca and also in North Carolina, like Eduardo, emphasized work ethic. She said that Latino people, unlike Black Americans, "are not public charges. They are hardworking people who come here to fight for a better well-being for their families."[124]

Others, like Edgar, emphasized criminality. When discussing the relationship between Black and Latino communities, he said the tension was a result of Black people robbing several Latino people in North Carolina. "They don't want to work," he said, "they want easy money . . . and the rumor is that they steal money . . . so there isn't a good relationship between Black people and us."[125] What is interesting about Edgar, and many others interviewed, is that they also discuss the racism they faced. He recalled how racism shaped the experiences of immigrants and how, by 2008 when he was interviewed, he felt that many people in the United States no longer needed immigrants the way they had in an earlier period.[126] In Edgar's case, he both saw the way racism circumscribed his life and fiercely defended the difference between his community and the local Black community. Anti-Black racism, as in earlier periods, continued to configure the boundaries of Latinidad.[127]

It is, perhaps, not surprising that the distinction between Black/not-Black endured into the twenty-first century. Indeed, even as Latino people were pushed to the margins of southern society, many non-Black Latino people retained their deeply held anti-Black ideologies. The same way that ideas about mestizaje and color were introduced in Latin America and reinforced in the United States, the pervasive anti-Blackness in Latin America found a welcome home in the US South.[128]

Between 2000 and 2011, the peace and quiet many Latinos had hoped to find in the South was becoming increasingly elusive. Over this period Latino migration, as in the rest of the country, began to slow. A steady stream of migration continued, but it was not at the pace of the previous decades.[129] In the first decade of the new millennium, Latino populations shifted from being seen as "hardworking" to being seen as "illegal" and were subject to a proliferating number of state and federal laws that made life throughout the United States more perilous. As race changed for Latino southerners, some things stayed the same. Citizenship, race, class, color, and other identities continued to structure how Latino people were racialized in the South. However, the most important factor in shaping Latino racialization was still their relationship to Blackness.

I n 1967, the same year that Latino people were expelled from the Student Nonviolent Coordinating Committee (SNCC), Richard Enriquez, the grandson of Daniel and Alice Soto, was born in the Mississippi Delta. Although Enriquez was the first in his family to be born in Mississippi, by that point, his parents and grandparents had both spent years in the Delta. After the move from San Antonio to the Mississippi Delta, the family had already begun to put down roots, and Richard's birth only deepened their growing sense of home in the Delta. Describing his family's decision to stay, Richard said, "[In] the Delta we felt at home."[1]

Isabel Rubio had a similar story. She was born in McComb, Mississippi, in the mid-1960s to parents of Mexican descent who were both from the US South. Her mother had been born in New Orleans, Louisiana, and her father in Mississippi. Part of the early generations of Latino people born in the region, Enriquez and Rubio would watch the South change dramatically over their lifetimes.

In 1971, Rubio was six years old and in first grade when her all-white elementary school followed federal mandates and was forcibly desegregated. Describing her memory of the desegregation she said, "I didn't really think anything about it." She noted that a segregation academy had opened nearby but her father chose not to send her there. Enriquez had a similar memory of the civil rights era. Describing his parents' experience of the era he said, "I don't think it was something they were really aware of."[2] In both their retellings, the civil rights movement did not interfere with their daily lives.

Rubio moved to Birmingham, Alabama, in the 1990s and began to reconnect with her self-described "Latino roots in Mexico." Her travels Mexico, she remembered, "began to point me in [the] direction in terms of my interest in working in community." Around 1995, Rubio remembered that alongside her personal evolution, Birmingham was also experiencing a demographic revolution. "Birmingham was beginning to change," Rubio recalled, "and we saw a lot more Latinos come to Birmingham."[3] In 1999, Rubio worked with a coalition of community leaders to officially form the Hispanic Interest Coalition of Alabama (HICA), which served as a clearinghouse for the scant resources available for Latino migrants to the state.[4]

Rubio's evolution from a young woman in an all-white school to a leader in an emergent southern Hispanic organization illustrates the important shift that occurred in the post–civil rights movement South. HICA, where she later became executive director, served Birmingham's rapidly growing Latino population, which looked very different from Rubio and her family. Rubio's father was an architect, her mother stayed at home, and Rubio received her bachelor's degree from the University of Southern Mississippi and her master's degree from the University of Alabama at Birmingham.[5] In contrast, most of those who HICA served were new migrants to the region. Many came from Mexico or the US West and Southwest, and they worked in the growing manufacturing and agricultural sectors of the Southeast. Yet Rubio's shift in identity from a young woman embedded in the white social life of McComb, Mississippi, to a self-identified Hispanic advocate in Birmingham, Alabama, suggests something about how race was changing in the post–civil rights movement era. Those like Isabel Rubio and Richard Enriquez, both of whom had been born in a South, where they were "provisionally white," were now part of a growing "Hispanic" community.

At the core of this book has been an exploration of how Latino people experienced race in the South before and after the large-scale migration of Latino people in the 1970s and 1980s and how this group, over these years, became Latino. It is about how in Isabel's lifetime she could be a part of a white supremacist institution like segregated schools and then become a leader in an emerging Hispanic community. Over the second half of the twentieth century and the opening decades of the twenty-first, non-Black Latino people in the US South transitioned from being categorized as "provisionally white" to being deemed "illegals." This evolution in the racial status of a group runs counter to many of our American histories about ethnic groups "becoming white" during their assimilation into American white supremacy.[6] Looking from the vantage point of Karla Galarza's exclusion from a "colored" vocational school for being "not a Negro" and her family's acceptance in Washington, DC's white suburbs, one might think that non-Black Latino people would follow the trajectory of other "provisionally white" populations like the Italians or the Irish. Instead, non-Black Latinos lost the privileges of whiteness over this period and by 2011, had become targets of vicious anti-immigrant legislation and rising nativist sentiment in the South.

This racial evolution was driven by regional, as well as national and global, changes in culture, politics, and the economy. However, most of all, it was fueled by the persistent racial formation that identified Latino people in relation to Blackness. As demonstrated in the first three chapters of this book, Latino people's racial categorization helped to reinforce Jim Crow. Non-Black Latino people, while they remained racially distinct, were able to establish important footholds as white by virtue of their non-Blackness. Jim Crow, which claimed a sorting of just Black and white, included a great deal of racial diversity. However, at the center of Jim Crow's logic was the subjugation of Blackness and Black people. Jim Crow could absorb Latino people by sorting Black and non-Black Latino people into Blackness and whiteness, respectively.

At the same time non-Black Latino people were benefiting from the privileges of whiteness, a proliferation of some of the most damaging images of Latino people at South of the Border suggested they were not "passing" as white. Additionally, with Pedro's leading role and South of the Border's Confederateland, white southerners fused those anti-Latino stereotypes with emergent neo-Confederate identities—formed, in large part, as a response to Black activism against Jim Crow. It was in the civil rights movement that non-Black Latino activists experienced the paradox of being racially non-white and at the same time being excluded for their whiteness or, more appropriately, non-Blackness. The story of SNCC's expulsion of non-Black Latino people reflected a deep understanding of the Black/not-Black division at the heart of Jim Crow. Those who had not lived as Black, regardless of their race, could not be among those leading the charge to dismantle this racial system.

Black Latino people, like non-Black Latino people, experienced this division of Black/not Black in the region. On the topic of Black Latino people, this book opens up more questions than it answers. The stories of Black Latino people demonstrate the deep fractures within any imagined category of Latinidad and the power of Blackness in shaping all racial categories in the region. However, this book has not probed deeply into the diversity of southern Black history and how Black Latino people fit into these communities. Future research on this will certainly reveal new depths to our understanding of the interplay of Blackness, whiteness, and Latinidad in the South.[7]

Even as large-scale migration reshaped the position of non-Black Latino people, Blackness loomed large in their racialization. Before this period, non-Black Latino people had been able to access whiteness through their non-Blackness. However, as examined in the final two chapters of this book, racially distinct categories like "Hispanic" and "Latino" began to cohere in the 1980s and 1990s. The welcome of Latino communities in the 1990s was marked by an emphasis on the "hardworking Hispanic." In this trope, white southerners were able to normalize brutal working conditions and, in part, preserve the foil of the imagined lazy Black worker against whom hardworking Hispanics were defined. In the wake of September 11 and the Great Recession, some Latino communities were finding common cause with southern Black communities because of their experience of segregation, hyperpolicing, and marginalization. In perhaps the most obvious evocation of the parallels, many activists began to call the anti-immigrant laws and practices "Juan Crow."[8] If an earlier period marked non-Black Latino people as provisionally white, this period was increasingly characterized by the growing precarity of Latino people and communities in the South.

The evolution in race for Latino people also draws into sharp relief the political and economic uses of race. In the South, Latino people's racial position was used to preserve Jim Crow, to fuel an expanding manufacturing industry, and eventually to energize white backlash politics. The fact that Latino people moved from provisionally white to "Hispanic" at the moment they made up a larger proportion of the labor force is not a coincidence. As the Latino population grew in size, their characterization as "illegal" only made the hyperexploitation of Latino communities more possible.

What is shared across the broad time period is a racialization defined, in large part, by Blackness. It is anti-Blackness and white supremacy that have defined the contours of Latinidad in the South. Certainly, growing Latino communities are laying claim to their own forms of Latinidad that are far more liberatory and rooted in collective efforts at social change. However, as this book suggests, at the heart of the category of Latino is an effort to define this group as being not-Black. "Latino," while it is a complicated and conflictual category, is one that is always being defined in relation to Blackness. This story, then, is about both continuity and change. It is about the dramatic evolution in the racial status of southern Latino people over the second half of the twentieth century and the enduring role that Blackness has played in shaping the boundaries of that category.

As Latino people continue to make up a larger portion of the American populace, increased attention is being given to the ways these communities are transforming American ideas about race. This story, however, offers a new way to understand this growing population and its effect on the racial topography of the United States. Deep fractures within the category of Latino are based on, among other things, geography and race. Additionally, as the category of Latino has shifted and evolved in the past, so it can once again. Understanding that anti-Blackness is at the core of defining these boundaries encourages non-Black Latino people to be cognizant of the ways they are, at times, invited into white supremacy.

The story of Latino people, as told from the South, suggests that part of the continued fracture around Blackness and whiteness within Latinidad is the long history of non-Black Latino people's relationship to white supremacy. Life for Lila Quintero, a non-Black Latino woman who grew up in Alabama during the civil rights era living in white neighborhoods and attending white schools, was quite different from that of Innocencio, a young non-Black Latino man whose mixed-status family moved to Alabama in the early 2000s and struggled to find safety under an increasingly punitive legal regime targeting undocumented people and their families. Their experiences of race, power, and identity look vastly different. And yet, their stories cannot be entirely disentangled. Both people had their varied *Latinidades* defined, in part, by anti-Blackness.

The history of Latino people and communities cannot be told in isolation and must reckon with both the segregated nature of our histories and the long entanglements with white supremacy. In the South, Latino people were always understood through the lens of Blackness, so Latino racial formations cannot be understood without fully reckoning with this connection to Blackness. If becoming Latino in the South meant distancing from Blackness, those invested in Latino futures must confront anti-Black logics within this category and within this community.

NOTES

Introduction

1. Foley, *White Scourge*; Martinez, *Injustice Never Leaves You*; Johnson, *Revolution in Texas*; Krochmal, *Blue Texas*; Behnken, *Fighting Their Own Battles*; Villanueva, *Lynching of Mexicans*; Zamora, *Claiming Rights*; De León, *They Called Them Greasers*; Gutiérrez, *Walls and Mirrors*; Montejano, *Anglos and Mexicans*.
2. Richard Enriquez interview by author; Mary Enriquez interview by author; Soto interview by Richard Enriquez; Julie M. Weise, "Mexicans and Mexican Americans in the Mississippi Delta," Mississippi Encyclopedia, July 11, 2017, updated June 20, 2018, https://mississippiencyclopedia.org/entries/mexicans-and-mexican-americans-mississippi-delta/. A special thank you to Julie Weise for introducing me to members of the Enriquez family, who have become an invaluable part of my research.
3. Soto interview by Richard Enriquez.
4. Richard Enriquez interview by author; Mary Enriquez interview by author; Soto interview by Richard Enriquez.
5. Aguirre interview by Angela Macias.
6. The term "passing" historically refers to African Americans who chose to live as white. It is a reference, in part, to Nella Larsen's 1925 Harlem Renaissance novel *Passing*. For more, see Hobbs, *Chosen Exile*; Larsen and Bernard, *Passing*.
7. Diaz interview by Sonia Song-Ha Lee.
8. Wilderson, among others, has argued that Black/not-Black is the central antagonism in modernity. This formulation draws, in part, on that understanding. Wilderson, *Red, White and Black*. Jung and Vargas define antiblackness as "an antisocial logic that not only dehumanizes Black people but also renders abject all that is associated with Blackness." Jung and Vargas, *Antiblackness*, 8.
9. Jung and Vargas, *Antiblackness*.
10. The literature on these populations has been dominated by social science scholarship focusing on the emergence of the Latino community in the South in the 1990s and early 2000s. See Odem and Lacy, *Latino Immigrants*; Stuesse, *Scratching Out a Living*; Ribas, *On the Line*; Marrow, *New Destination Dreaming*; Massey, *New Faces in New Places*; Striffler, *Chicken*; Smith and Furuseth, *Latinos in the New South*; Winders, *Nashville in the New Millennium*; Winders, "Changing Politics of Race and Region"; and Winders, "Representing the Immigrant Social Movements."
11. Rakesh Kochhar, Roberto Suro, and Sonya Tafoya, "The New Latino South: The Context and Consequences of Rapid Population Growth," Pew Research Center, Hispanic Trends Project (blog), July 26, 2005, www.pewresearch.org/hispanic/2005/07/26/the-new-latino-south/.

12. Marrow, *New Destination Dreaming*; Massey, *New Faces in New Places*; Winders, "Changing Politics of Race and Region"; Odem and Lacy, *Latino Immigrants*.

13. Florida and Texas do not fit into this study, not as a statement of their legitimate claims to "southernness" but because of the entrenched Latino populations that lived in those states before the 1940s. This is not to participate in "Florida exceptionalism" as critiqued by Paul Ortiz or Texas exceptionalism for that matter. Instead it acknowledges that for the purposes of tracing Latino racial development, these two states were in very different stages than other parts of the South. Ortiz, *Emancipation Betrayed*. Because of the long-standing histories of Mexican, Mexican American, Cuban, and Cuban American populations in Texas and Florida, those geographies were in very different stages of racial formation than in other parts of the Southeast that were just starting to experience Latino migration for the first time in the mid to late twentieth century. Of course, parts of north Florida and east Texas are indiscernible from the other parts of the South discussed in this book. As with other states I discuss, Florida and Texas both include long histories of violent enforcement of white supremacy that fueled economic exploitation of a racialized workforce. Martinez, *Injustice Never Leaves You*; Johnson, *Revolution in Texas*; Hewitt, *Southern Discomfort*; McNamara, "Borderland Unionism"; Ortiz, *Emancipation Betrayed*.

14. This book also opens important questions about region and racial formation. Recent scholarship productively seeks to dismantle myths of "southern exceptionalism" that paint the South as more racist or politically "backward" than any other region in the United States. This literature has demonstrated the long reach of Jim Crow segregation that existed elsewhere in the United States and the various forms of separation and exclusion practices in other regions. This book, while not advancing a southern exceptionalism argument, does pay attention to the confluence of economic, political, and cultural factors that made race work differently for Latino immigrants in the South before the 1970s. Lassiter and Crespino, *Myth of Southern Exceptionalism*.

15. Omi and Winant, *Racial Formation*.

16. Holt, *Problem of Race*, 21.

17. For more on the process of race-making in the United States, see Holt, *Problem of Race*; Holt, "Marking"; Mills, *Racial Contract*; Fields, "Whiteness, Racism, and Identity"; Fields and Fields, *Racecraft*; Omi and Winant, *Racial Formation*; Crenshaw, Gotanda, Peller, and Thomas, *Critical Race Theory*; Molina, *How Race Is Made*; López, *White by Law*; Molina, HoSang, and Gutiérrez, *Relational Formations of Race*; Bonilla-Silva, *Racism without Racists*; Davis, *Women, Race and Class*; and Collins, *Black Feminist Thought*.

18. Mallon, *Decolonizing Native Histories*; Castellanos, Nájera, and Aldama, *Comparative Indigeneities of the Américas*; Coulthard, *Red Skin, White Masks*; Simpson, *Mohawk Interruptus*; Dunbar-Ortiz, *Indigenous Peoples' History*.

19. Historians who have argued against the idea of the South as "exceptional" include Lassiter and Crespino, *Myth of Southern Exceptionalism*; and Weise, "Introduction."

20. For more on the idea of regional racial formations, see Cheng, *Changs Next Door*. For more on regional racial hierarchies, see Pulido, *Black, Brown, Yellow, and Left*. For more on regional racial lexicon, see Molina, *Fit to Be Citizens?*

21. Alcoff, "Latinos beyond the Binary"; Perea, "Black/White Binary Paradigm of Race"; Mendieta, "Making of New Peoples"; Alcoff, "Is Latina/o Identity a Racial Identity?" For a thorough critique of the idea that Latino people are disruptive to US racial ideologies, see Hooker, "Hybrid Subjectivities," 190. Hooker writes, for example, "Ultimately, the trope of *Latinidad*'s racial exceptionalism is derived less from the vagaries of U.S. systems of racial classification and more from arguments Latino political theorists have borrowed from certain strands of Latin American thinking about race, particularly notions of *mestizaje*."

22. Fernández, *Young Lords*; Fernández, *Brown in the Windy City*; Mora, *Making Hispanics*; Fernández, "Becoming Latino"; Oboler, *Ethnic Labels, Latino Lives*; Dávila, "Latin Side of Madison Avenue"; De Genova and Ramos-Zayas, *Latino Crossings*; Aparicio and Chávez-Silverman, *Tropicalizations*; Beltrán, *Trouble with Unity*.

23. There are many valuable critiques of the category of "Latino," especially the work of Cristina Beltrán in *Trouble with Unity*. Perhaps the most salient critique of the category in the context of this book is the way it erases the different experiences of race that many Latinos have. Black Latinos, Asian Latinos, Mestizo Latinos, and others all experience race quite differently and, as such, the term will always fail to capture that complexity. When appropriate, I have modified the term to note these racial differences, using "Black Latino" and "non-Black Latino." My use of "Latino" is not part of a broader dismissal of the very helpful term "Latinx," which emerged in the early 2000s out of queer Latino communities who wanted to find a space beyond the gendered Latino/Latina categories. The "X" in Latinx was an effort to open up space for queer, trans, and gender-nonconforming Latino people for whom binary gender categories were insufficient. Since then, in response to critiques that "Latinx" does not translate easily into Spanish, some have started to use "Latine" as the gender-neutral descriptor of this community. Although both "Latinx" and "Latine" are useful terms, I have opted to use "Latino" in this book because it is the term most frequently used in the communities I am writing about. For more on "Latino" as a category, see Guidotti-Hernández, "Affective Communities"; de Onís, "What's in an 'x'?"; Milian, *LatinX*; Rodriguez, *Queer Latinidad*; and Chavez, *Queer Migration Politics*.

24. Telles, *Pigmentocracies*; Duany, "Reconstructing Racial Identity"; Golash-Boza and Bonilla-Silva, "Rethinking Race, Racism, Identity and Ideology"; Andrews, *Afro-Latin America*; García-Peña, *Borders of Dominicanidad*.

25. García-Peña, "Translating Blackness"; García-Peña, *Borders of Dominicanidad*; Ramírez, *Colonial Phantoms*; López Oro, "Love Letter to Indigenous Blackness"; López Oro, "Garifunizando Ambas Américas"; Flores and Román, "Triple-Consciousness?"; Román and Flores, *Afro-Latin@ Reader*.

26. Kevin Escudero, "Dear Latines: Your Antiblackness Will Not Save You," *Latinx Talk* (blog), November 11, 2020, https://latinxtalk.org/2020/11/11/dear-latines -your-antiBlackness-will-not-save-you/.

27. Figueroa, "Distributed Intensities"; de la Cadena, "Reconstructing Race"; Hooker, "Hybrid Subjectivities"; Hooker, *Theorizing Race*; Wade, *Race and Ethnicity*; Smith, "Symbolics of Blood."

28. Throughout this book, I refer to people and groups as they have identified themselves or, when their racial identity is not clear, as I understand them to be racially—for example, "white Latino" (Latino individuals who are phenotypically white, a framing that also recognizes the enduring presence of whiteness in Latin America and in US Latino populations), "mestizo Latino" (Latino people some may call "brown," including those who are not phenotypically white and do not have an expressed Indigenous identity), "Black Latino" (people of African descent who are Latino and are phenotypically Black), and "Indigenous Latino" (people with an expressed Indigenous identity).

29. For more on the process of Latino as a bottom-up category, see Mora, *Making Hispanics*; Beltrán, *Trouble with Unity*; De Genova and Ramos-Zayas, *Latino Crossings*; Dávila, *Latinos, Inc.*; Oboler, *Ethnic Labels, Latino Lives*; Fernández, "Becoming Latino." For more on Latino as a category of Black and Indigenous erasure, see Rivera-Rideau, Jones, and Paschel, *Afro-Latin@s in Movement*; Román and Flores, *Afro-Latin@ Reader*; and Hernández, "Afro-Mexicans and the Chicano Movement."

30. Román and Flores, *Afro-Latin@ Reader*.

31. Raquel Garza, "Woman Awaited News of Husband at Omaha Beach," Narratives, 2001, Voces Oral History Collection, University of Texas at Austin; Ramírez interview by Raquel Garza.

32. Blanton, *George I. Sánchez*; Blanton, "George I. Sanchez," 569; Dowling, *Mexican Americans*. For an alternative account of how Black and Mexican American communities forged common ground, see Krochmal, *Blue Texas*.

33. Baldwin, *Price of the Ticket*; Foley, *White Scourge*; Rochmes and Griffin, "Cactus That Must Not Be Mistaken for a Pillow"; Bow, *Partly Colored*; Yancey, *Who Is White?*; Waters, *Ethnic Options*; Toni Morrison, "On the Backs of Blacks," *Time*, December 2, 1993.

34. Fernández, *Brown in the Windy City*; López, *Racism on Trial*.

35. López, *White by Law*; Gomez, *Manifest Destinies*.

36. Molina, HoSang, and Gutiérrez, *Relational Formations of Race*, 7.

37. Molina, "Power of Racial Scripts"; Molina, HoSang, and Gutiérrez, *Relational Formations of Race*; Guerrero, *Nuevo South*.

38. Letters between W. A. Brownell and J. C. Robert, October 6 and November 1943, Graduate School Records, Box 1, "Admissions Correspondence" folder, Duke University Archives, Durham, NC.

39. de Leon interview by Sonia Song-Ha Lee.

40. de Leon interview by Sonia Song-Ha Lee.

41. de Leon interview by Sonia Song-Ha Lee.

42. Guridy, *Forging Diaspora*.

43. For more on whiteness as a set of wages or property, see Roediger, *Wages of Whiteness*; Cheryl I. Harris, "Whiteness as Property," *Harvard Law Review*, June 10, 1993, https://harvardlawreview.org/1993/06/whiteness-as-property/. For more

on the legal history of the category, see López, *White by Law*; Gross, *What Blood Won't Tell*; and Pascoe, *What Comes Naturally*. For more on the cultural valences of whiteness, see Hale, *Nation of Outsiders*; and Abel, *Signs of the Times*.

44. Who was white changed dramatically over the late nineteenth and early twentieth centuries as white ethnic groups achieved a new status as "white." Ignatiev, *How the Irish Became White*; Jacobson, *Whiteness of a Different Color*; Guglielmo, *White on Arrival*; Roediger, *Wages of Whiteness*.

45. Hartman, *Scenes of Subjection*; Willoughby-Herard, "More Expendable Than Slaves?"; Sexton, "People-of-Color-Blindness"; Sexton, *Amalgamation Schemes*; Sharpe, *In the Wake*; King, *Black Shoals*; Spillers, "Mama's Baby, Papa's Maybe"; Jung and Vargas, *Antiblackness*.

46. Smallwood, *Saltwater Slavery*; Morgan, *American Slavery, American Freedom*; Morgan, *Laboring Women*; King, *Black Shoals*; Oshinsky, *Worse Than Slavery*.

47. Taylor, *From #BlackLivesMatter to Black Liberation*.

48. Morgan, *American Slavery, American Freedom*.

49. Lassiter and Crespino, *Myth of Southern Exceptionalism*.

50. For racial separation, see Woodward, *Strange Career of Jim Crow*; Woodward, *Origins of the New South*; Ayers, *Promise of the New South*; Connolly, *World More Concrete*; Dailey, Gilmore, and Simon, *Jumpin' Jim Crow*; Du Bois and Lewis, *Black Reconstruction in America*; and Rothstein, *Color of Law*. For lynching and murder, see Feimster, *Southern Horrors*; Hall, *Revolt against Chivalry*; Hale, *Nation of Outsiders*; and Payne, *I've Got the Light of Freedom*. For racial hierarchy, see Hale, *Making Whiteness*. For white purity, see Pascoe, *What Comes Naturally*; and Somerville, *Queering the Color Line*. For the southern landscape, see Abel, *Signs of the Times*; and Raiford, *Imprisoned*. For routine, see Berrey, *Jim Crow Routine*.

51. Hooker, *Theorizing Race in the Americas*.

52. Castro interview by author.

53. Lowery, *Lumbee Indians in the Jim Crow South*; Lowery, *Lumbee Indians*; Bow, *Partly Colored*; Hinnershitz, *Different Shade of Justice*; Loewen, *Mississippi Chinese*; Jung, *Chopsticks in the Land of Cotton*; Quan and Roebuck, *Lotus among the Magnolias*; Weise, *Corazón de Dixie*; Guerrero, *Nuevo South*.

54. Roshell [pseud.] interview by author.

55. Fink, *Maya of Morganton*; Guerrero, *Nuevo South*; Stuesse, *Scratching Out a Living*; Angela Stuesse and Laura E. Helton, "Low-Wage Legacies, Race, and the Golden Chicken in Mississippi: Where Contemporary Immigration Meets African American Labor History," *Southern Spaces*, December 31, 2013, https://southern spaces.org/2013/low-wage-legacies-race-and-golden-chicken-mississippi-where -contemporary-immigration-meets-african-american-labor-history/; Mohl, "Latinization in the Heart of Dixie," 243.

56. Mohl, "Globalization, Latinization, and the Nuevo New South."

57. For more on the formation of a "Sunbelt" region, see Cadava, *Standing on Common Ground*; Dochuk, *From Bible Belt to Sunbelt*; Nickerson and Dochuk, *Sunbelt Rising*; Lassiter, *Silent Majority*; Schulman, *From Cotton Belt to Sunbelt*; and Shermer, *Sunbelt Capitalism*.

58. Robinson and Kelley, *Black Marxism*; Jenkins and Leroy, *Histories of Racial*

Capitalism; Gilmore, *Golden Gulag*; James, *Black Jacobins*; Du Bois and Lewis, *Black Reconstruction in America*; Williams, Palmer, and Darity, *Capitalism and Slavery*; Connolly, *World More Concrete*; Johnson and Kelley, *Race Capitalism Justice*; Woods and Gilmore, *Development Arrested*.

59. Jones, *Browning of the New South*.
60. Márquez, "Juan Crow."
61. Dávila, *Latino Spin*; Molina, *How Race Is Made*; Molina, "Power of Racial Scripts"; Molina, HoSang, and Gutiérrez, *Relational Formations of Race*.
62. McClain et al., "Racial Distancing in a Southern City"; Cruz-Janzen, "Madre Patria (Mother Country)"; Hernández, "Latino AntiBlack Bias"; Golash-Boza and Darity, "Latino Racial Choices."
63. Quoted in Matos, "Legacy of Exclusion," 88.
64. Beltrán, *Cruelty as Citizenship*.

Chapter One

1. Joe Shephard, "Girl Jolts D.C. School System: Defies Edict to Quit Negro Classroom,Student Bases Claim on Equal Facilities; Father Backs Stand," *Chicago Defender*, April 12, 1947.
2. Pepe interview by author.
3. Brilliant, *Color of America Has Changed*; Montejano, *Anglos and Mexicans*; Sanchez, *Becoming Mexican American*; Strum, *Mendez v. Westminster*.
4. Green, *Secret City*, 266.
5. Nunley, *At the Threshold of Liberty*; Masur, *Example for All the Land*; Asch and Musgrove, *Chocolate City*.
6. Barahona, "History of Latinx Students at Duke University"; Weise, *Corazón de Dixie*; unpublished research by the author at the archives of University of Alabama at Birmingham and Duke University, Durham, NC. Parallel stories of Black Latin Americans and Latinos attending southern universities can be found in Guridy, *Forging Diaspora*; and Grillo, *Black Cuban, Black American*.
7. Márquez, "Strange Career of Juan Crow."
8. Candelario, *Black behind the Ears*, 140.
9. Campos interview by Hector Corporan.
10. Weise, *Corazón de Dixie*, 25–27.
11. Although Washington, DC, is considered by many to be a "borderland" between the North and South, it fits into my study because of the convergence of Jim Crow laws and the lack of a long-standing Latino population in the region. It therefore offers an opportunity to assemble the complex set of racial ideas Latino people had to navigate in the Jim Crow era.
12. Mintz, *Caribbean Transformations*; Wade, *Race and Ethnicity*; Whitten and Torres, *Blackness in Latin America*; Duany, "Reconstructing Racial Identity"; Rivero, "Erasing Blackness."
13. Ideas about race were being formed throughout the Americas as early as the seventeenth century and continued to evolve into this period. As such, Latin

American migrants were not encountering Jim Crow without their own ideas about race, which were often rooted in anti-Black and anti-Indigenous ideology. Hooker, *Theorizing Race*; Guridy, *Forging Diaspora*; Gracia, *Forging People*; von Vacano, *Color of Citizenship*; Gudmundson and Wolfe, *Blacks and Blackness*; Dzidzienyo and Oboler, *Neither Enemies nor Friends*; Rivera-Rideau, Jones, and Paschel, *Afro-Latin@s in Movement*; Román and Flores, *Afro-Latin@ Reader*; Andrews, *Afro-Latin America*; Rodríguez-Silva, *Silencing Race*.

14. Hooker, *Theorizing Race*; von Vacano, *Color of Citizenship*; Gudmundson and Wolfe, *Blacks and Blackness*; Vinson, *Before Mestizaje*.

15. Candelario, *Black behind the Ears*, 157.

16. For discussions of Mexican Americans and segregation in general, see García, *Mexican Americans*; Orozco, *No Mexicans, Women, or Dogs*; Márquez, *Lulac*; Blanton, *George I. Sánchez*; García, *White but Not Equal*; and Zamora, *Claiming Rights and Righting Wrongs*. For discussion focusing specifically on school segregation, see Gonzalez, *Chicano Education*; San Miguel, *"Let All of Them Take Heed"*; and Strum, *Mendez v. Westminster*.

17. Ruiz, "South by Southwest."

18. Strum, *Mendez v. Westminster*.

19. Barber, *Latino City*; Amezcua, "Beautiful Urbanism"; Fernández, *Brown in the Windy City*.

20. For more on how Latino people were segregated in urban centers during the 1940s and 1950s, see Barber, *Latino City*; Perales, *Smeltertown*; Fernández, *Brown in the Windy City*; Amezcua, "Beautiful Urbanism"; Lee, *Building a Latino Civil Rights Movement*; Sanchez, *Becoming Mexican American*; Arredondo, *Mexican Chicago*; Otero, *La Calle*; Fairbanks, *War on Slums*; Hoffnung-Garskof, *Tale of Two Cities*; and Perez, *Near Northwest Side Story*. For racial violence, see Fernández, *Brown in the Windy City*; Sanchez, *Becoming Mexican American*; Ramirez, *Woman in the Zoot Suit*; and Alvarez, *Power of the Zoot*.

21. For example, these historians find Latino people increasingly racialized in cities as "non-whites": Arredondo, *Mexican Chicago*; Perales, *Smeltertown*; Barber, *Latino City*; Lee, *Building a Latino Civil Rights Movement*; and Amezcua, "Beautiful Urbanism." Others looking at midwestern cities find a more uneven experience of race—sometimes a "less-than-white" category, sometimes more aligned with white ethnics, and other times the unambiguous racialization as "brown" or Latino. See Fernández, *Brown in the Windy City*; and Innis-Jiménez, *Steel Barrio*.

22. Lee, *Building a Latino Civil Rights Movement*; Bernstein, *Bridges of Reform*; Brilliant, *Color of America*; Fernández, *Brown in the Windy City*; Pulido, *Black, Brown, Yellow, and Left*; Alvarez, *Power of the Zoot*; Arredondo, *Mexican Chicago*.

23. De Oca Ricks, "Ernesto Galarza."

24. Galarza, *Barrio Boy*; Ernesto Galarza, "Pan-American Union Speaks," February 1945, Ernesto Galarza Papers, Stanford University Special Collections, Stanford, CA.

25. Ernesto (misspelled as "Ernest") Galarza Census Record, Year: 1930, Census Place: Manhattan, New York, Page: 8B, Enumeration District: 0517, FHL microfilm:

2341295, accessed September 22, 2022, www.ancestrylibrary.com/discoveryui
-content/view/42577133:6224?indiv=1&tid=&pid=&queryId=50f51c37e0a509781bf
8f01d28dace72&usePUB=true&_phsrc=fdp196&_phstart=successSource.

26. Denning, *Cultural Front*, 277.

27. Asch and Musgrove, *Chocolate City*.

28. Austin, *Coming of Age in Jim Crow DC*; Caplan, "Eat Anywhere!"; Murphy, *Jim Crow Capital*; Catsam, "Early Economic Civil Rights."

29. Green, *Secret City*, 250–62.

30. Green, *Secret City*, 270.

31. "Washington, a Citadel of Racial Prejudice," *Norfolk Journal and Guide*, December 18, 1948, 8.

32. Cobb, *Most Southern Place on Earth*.

33. Asch and Musgrove, *Chocolate City*; Green, *Secret City*.

34. "Pertinent Points about D.C. Bias," *Baltimore Afro-American*, December 18, 1948, 3.

35. Green, *Secret City*, 278–79.

36. Gonda, *Unjust Deeds*; Rothstein, *Color of Law*; Glotzer, *How the Suburbs Were Segregated*.

37. Asch and Musgrove, *Chocolate City*.

38. Asch and Musgrove, *Chocolate City*, 288.

39. Asch and Musgrove, *Chocolate City*; Murphy, *Jim Crow Capital*; Catsam, "Early Economic Civil Rights"; Brown, "NAACP Sponsored Sit-Ins"; Pacifico, "'Don't Buy Where You Can't Work'"; Bates, *Pullman Porters*; Barber, *Marching on Washington*; Austin, *Coming of Age in Jim Crow DC*.

40. Anderson, *Eyes Off the Prize*; Von Eschen, *Race against Empire*; Plummer, *Rising Wind*; Ransby, *Ella Baker*; Singh, *Black Is a Country*; Tyson, *Radio Free Dixie*; Borstelmann, *Cold War and the Color Line*.

41. Phillips, *War! What Is It Good For?*; Theoharis and Woodard, *Freedom North*; Marable, *Race, Reform, and Rebellion*. For more on how returning GIs infused energy into civil rights struggles throughout the country, see Payne, *I've Got the Light of Freedom*; Parker, *Fighting for Democracy*; Woolfolk, "Afterword"; Biondi, *To Stand and Fight*; Chamberlain, *Victory at Home*; Dittmer, *Local People*; Bates, *Pullman Porters*; Tyson, *Radio Free Dixie*; Gilmore, *Defying Dixie*; and Plummer, *Rising Wind*.

42. Candelario, *Black behind the Ears*, 157.

43. Andrew Harrison, "Fairmount Heights, Maryland," *Washington Tribune*, September 18, 1943, 30.

44. Andrew Harrison, "Fairmont Heights and Vicinity," *Washington Tribune*, August 21, 1943, 6.

45. Providencia Marquez's name appears as "Rowdencia Margues" on HeritageQuest online; however, an inspection of the handwritten census revealed this was an error. HeritageQuest Census Data 1940, Year: 1940, Census Place: Washington, District of Columbia, District of Columbia, Roll: T627_567, Page: 2B, Enumeration District: 1-433A.

46. HeritageQuest Census Data 1940, Year: 1940, Census Place: Washington, District

of Columbia, District of Columbia, Roll: T627_562, Page: 7B, Enumeration District: 1-288.

47. HeritageQuest Census Data 1940, Year: 1940, Census Place: Washington, District of Columbia, District of Columbia, Roll: T627_556, Page: 16A, Enumeration District: 1-101.

48. For more on the idea of "forging" community across the Black diaspora, see Guridy, *Forging Diaspora*.

49. Grillo, *Black Cuban, Black American*.

50. Candelario, *Black behind the Ears*, 164.

51. Candelario, *Black behind the Ears*.

52. Willard Townsend, "State Department Bias Results in Red Faces," *Chicago Defender*, February 26, 1949.

53. For further discussion of her experience with segregation in Washington, DC, see Martínez, "Neither Black nor White," 531–33; and Martínez interviews by Loretta Ross, 5–10.

54. Martínez, "Neither Black nor White"; Martínez interviews by Loretta Ross.

55. Pepe interview by author.

56. Loza, *Defiant Braceros*.

57. García, *Mexican Americans*.

58. Menchaca, "Anti-Miscegenation History."

59. McGuire, *At the Dark End of the Street*, 25, 113.

60. Unpublished research by author of censuses for 1930 and 1940 in the Washington, DC; Maryland; and Virginia areas from Ancestry Library, ProQuest.

61. This appears as "Consulo" in the HeritageQuest Database, but it is in fact "Consuelo." HeritageQuest Census Data 1940, Year: 1940, Census Place: Baltimore, Baltimore City, Maryland, Roll: T627_1510, Page: 2B, Enumeration District: 4-72.

62. Weise, *Corazón de Dixie*, 31.

63. The HeritageQuest Database indicates that her name is Victorian Gutierrez. However, an inspection of the handwritten census leads me to believe it was actually "Victoria."

64. HeritageQuest Census Data 1940, Year: 1940, Census Place: Wythe, Elizabeth City, Virginia, Roll: T627_4259, Page: 40A, Enumeration District: 28-18.

65. Todd interview by junior and senior high school students of the D.C. Everest Area School District; Cortez (Todd) interview by author.

66. Candelario, *Black behind the Ears*, 159–60.

67. "Pattern of Segregation as Practiced in Washington," *Norfolk Journal and Guide*, December 18, 1948.

68. "Pattern of Segregation as Practiced in Washington." Her experience, however, stood in stark contrast to that of ethnic Mexicans elsewhere in the United States who daily navigated their own regional racial segregation. In Texas and California, spaces like the movie theater that this Spanish woman successfully entered were segregated for ethnic Mexicans. Camarillo, "Navigating Segregated Life," 662.

69. Erdman, "'Diplomacy, American Style.'"

70. Erdman, "'Diplomacy, American Style,'" 130–31, 136.

71. Erdman, "'Diplomacy, American Style,'" 110.

72. Karla Galarza, Washington Lee High School, 1941 Yearbook, Ancestry Library, ProQuest, accessed September 20, 2022, www.ancestrylibrary.com/imageviewer /collections/2442/images/M-T0627-04246-; Minutes of the Washington, DC, School Board Meeting, "Board Adopts Resolution in RE Case of Miss Karla Rosel Galarza, a Student at the Margaret Murray Washington Vocational High School, Divisions 10–13," April 2, 1947, Charles Sumner School Museum and Archives, Washington, DC (hereafter cited as Minutes of the School Board Meeting).

73. Minutes of the School Board Meeting; "Letter from Interdenominational Council on Spanish Speaking Work in San Antonio Texas," Box 1, Series 1, Folder 3, Ernesto Galarza Papers, Stanford University Special Collections, Stanford, CA.

74. Bartley, *Rise of Massive Resistance*; Lewis, *White South and the Red Menace*; McRae, *Mothers of Massive Resistance*.

75. De Oca Ricks, "Ernesto Galarza."

76. Ritterhouse, *Growing Up Jim Crow*.

77. Bow, *Partly Colored*, 47.

78. Weise, *Corazón de Dixie*.

79. Donato and Hanson, "'Porque Tenían Sangre.'"

80. Unpublished research by author of 1940s yearbooks in the Washington, DC; Maryland; and Virginia area from Ancestry Library, ProQuest.

81. For more on accents, see Burgos, *Playing America's Game*; Lippi-Green, *English with an Accent*; Lozano, *An American Language*; and Rosa, *Looking Like a Language*.

82. Francisco Gonzalez, Roanoke College, Virginia, 1945 Yearbook, Ancestry Library, ProQuest, accessed August 8, 2021, www.ancestrylibrary.com/imageviewer /collections/1265/images/1265_b890599-5?usePUB=true&_phsrc=bHi1&_phstart =successSource&usePUBJs=true&pld=1437795472.

83. Luis Felipe Gonzalez, School of Medicine, University of Maryland, Baltimore, 1952 Yearbook, Ancestry Library, ProQuest, accessed August 8, 2021, www.ancestry library.com/imageviewer/collections/1265/images/1265_b906381-00035?usePUB =true&_phsrc=Cog3&_phstart=successSource&usePUBJs=true&pld=1374268381.

84. Carlos Nathaniel Vicens, School of Medicine, University of Maryland, Baltimore, 1952 Yearbook, Ancestry Library, ProQuest, accessed August 8, 2021, www.ancestry library.com/imageviewer/collections/1265/images/1265_b906381-00060?usePUB =true&_phsrc=Cog3&_phstart=successSource&usePUBJs=true&pld=1374268381.

85. Manuel Rafael Fossas Jr., Baltimore College of Dental Surgery, University of Maryland, Baltimore, 1950 Yearbook, accessed August 8, 2021, www.ancestry library.com/imageviewer/collections/1265/images/42092_920600178_021100026 ?usePUB=true&_phsrc=Cog3&_phstart=successSource&usePUBJs=true&pld =298080395.

86. Robert Hess, Baltimore College of Dental Surgery, University of Maryland, Baltimore, 1950 Yearbook, accessed August 8, 2021, www.ancestrylibrary.com /imageviewer/collections/1265/images/42092_920600178_021100029?usePUB =true&_phsrc=Cog3&_phstart=successSource&usePUBJs=true&pld=298080395.

87. For more on the highlighting of accents as a way to insult the intelligence of Latino people, see Burgos, *Playing America's Game*.

88. Beatriz Bolivar, Marymount High School, Arlington, Virginia, 1950 Yearbook, Ancestry Library, ProQuest, www.ancestrylibrary.com/imageviewer/collections /1265/images/sid_15893061_1950_0035?usePUB=true&_phsrc=DOX8&_phstart =successSource&usePUBJs=true&pId=750448897.

89. Unpublished research by author of 1940s yearbooks in the Washington, DC; Maryland; and Virginia area from Ancestry Library, ProQuest.

90. Campos interview by Hector Corporan.

91. Grillo, *Black Cuban, Black American*, 66.

92. Grillo, *Black Cuban, Black American*, 60.

93. Grillo, *Black Cuban, Black American*, 66.

94. Asch and Musgrove, *Chocolate City*.

95. Denning, *Cultural Front*, 277.

96. "Court Case to Test Right of School Board to Bar Girl," *Baltimore Afro-American*, May 31, 1947.

97. "Court Case to Test Right of School Board to Bar Girl."

98. Shephard, "Girl Jolts D.C. School System."

99. Pepe interview by author; Dr. Ernesto Galarza to Miss Watkins, April 3, 1947, Charles Sumner School Museum and Archives, Washington, DC (hereafter cited as CSSMA).

100. Pepe interview by author; "Court Case to Test Right of School Board to Bar Girl."

101. Minutes of the School Board Meeting.

102. Hamilton, "Cost of Integration."

103. Minutes of the School Board Meeting.

104. Minutes of the School Board Meeting; Galarza to Watkins, April 3, 1947.

105. Du Bois, *Dusk of Dawn*.

106. Minutes of the School Board Meeting.

107. Minutes of the School Board Meeting.

108. "D.C. School Law Faces Challenge: White Girl to Fight Ruling Plans Suit OF MEXICAN DESCENT Father Formerly with Pan-American Union," *Baltimore Afro-American*, April 12, 1947; "White Girl Ordered from Colored School," *Norfolk Journal and Guide*, April 12, 1947; Minutes of the School Board Meeting.

109. "D.C. School Law Faces Challenge"; "White Girl Ordered from Colored School"; Minutes of the School Board Meeting.

110. Wall v. Oyster, No. 36 App. D.C. 50, 1910 U.S. App. Lexis 5949 (Court of Appeals of District of Columbia, December 5, 1910).

111. *Wall*, No. 36 App. D.C. 50, 1910 U.S. App. Lexis 5949.

112. Green, *Secret City*, 299.

113. "Recent Cases."

114. Asch and Musgrove, *Chocolate City*; McQuirter, "'Our Cause Is Marching On'"; McNeil, "Community Initiative."

115. Murphy, *Jim Crow Capital*.

116. Murphy, *Jim Crow Capital*; Asch and Musgrove, *Chocolate City*; Catsam, "Early

Economic Civil Rights"; Brown, "NAACP Sponsored Sit-Ins"; Pacifico, "'Don't Buy Where You Can't Work.'"

117. Asch and Musgrove, *Chocolate City*; Devlin, *Girl Stands at the Door*; "Aim New Blow at D.C. School Bias: Parents Petition Board to Abandon Segregated Policy," *Pittsburgh Courier*, April 1, 1947.

118. Horace Cayton, "Ought to Quit: When Negroes Get in Positions Where They Have to Sacrifice Democracy They Should Resign," *Pittsburgh Courier*, April 19, 1947.

119. Harry Keelan, "Voice in the Wilderness," "Court Case to Test Right of School Board to Bar Girl."

120. Don Goodloe, "Letter to Board of Education Public Schools of the District of Columbia June 26, 1947 from Paul Cooke President of American Federation of Teachers (American Federation of Labor Local 27)," July 1, 1947, CSSMA; "Minutes of the Eighteenth Meeting of the Board of Education, Letter from Unitarian Fellowship," June 4, 1947, CSSMA; Christopher Arthur, "Letter to ACLU from Arthur Christopher Junior, DC Chapter of National Lawyers Guild," November 21, 1947, The Making of Modern Law: American Civil Liberties Union Papers, Gale Digital Database.

121. Galarza to Watkins, April 3, 1947.

122. Pepe interview by author; Galarza to Watkins, April 3, 1947.

123. Galarza to Watkins, April 3, 1947.

124. Galarza to Watkins, April 3, 1947.

125. Galarza to Watkins, April 3, 1947.

126. Galarza to Watkins, April 3, 1947.

127. Despite Ernesto Galarza's national fame and the extensive archival collections on his life, this case is not found in his papers or most of the biographical accounts of his life. This chapter, therefore, adds a largely forgotten story to the biographical record of Ernesto Galarza. Given that Galarza was a giant in the field of Chicano history, it is shocking that no information about the case of his daughter's exclusion from a "colored" vocational school and the subsequent fight for her inclusion is in the biographical, autobiographical, and archival records of his life. In view of how much of his life was spent in the fight for civil rights, it seems a notable and significant oversight.

128. Pepe interview by author.

129. "White Girl to Sue," *Times-Picayune*, April 5, 1947; "White Girl Fights Racial Ban," *Sunday Oregonian*, April 6, 1947; "White Pupil Barred from Negro School," *Toledo Blade*, April 4, 1947.

130. "Una joven de raza blanca insiste en estudiar junto con los negros," *La Prensa* (San Antonio), April 11, 1947.

131. "D.C. School Law Faces Challenge."

132. "Adventures in Race Relations," *Chicago Defender*, April 19, 1947.

133. For more on repatriation, see Fernández, *Brown in the Windy City*; Innis-Jiménez, *Steel Barrio*; Sanchez, *Becoming Mexican American*; and García, *Mexican Americans*.

134. "Galarza Case Based on '40 Census Bureau Action," *Baltimore Afro-American*, April 19, 1947, 11.

135. Keelan, "Voice in the Wilderness."
136. Shephard, "Girl Jolts D.C. School System."
137. "Letter to Mr. Galarza from First Assistant Superintendent of Schools Garnet C. Wilkinson," May 29, 1947, American Civil Liberties Union Papers, Gale Digital Database.
138. Robert L. Carter to Charles Houston, April 9, 1947; Charles Houston to Robert L. Carter, April 10, 1947, Part 03: The Campaign for Educational Equality, Series B: Legal Department and Central Office Records, 1940–1950, Series: Legal File, Group ll, Schools, National Association for the Advancement of Colored People Papers, ProQuest History Vault.
139. Robert L. Carter to H. A. Robinson, May 2, 1947, National Association for the Advancement of Colored People Papers, ProQuest History Vault.
140. Clifford Forster (acting director of ACLU) to Charles H. Houston, May 5, 1947, National Association for the Advancement of Colored People Papers, ProQuest History Vault.
141. Don Goodloe, "Letter to Board of Education Public Schools of the District of Columbia June 26, 1947, from Paul Cooke President of American Federation of Teachers (American Federation of Labor Local 27)," July 1, 1947, CSSMA.
142. For more on the legal strategy of the NAACP, see Goluboff, *Lost Promise of Civil Rights*; and Memorandum by Marian Wynn Perry to the Files, January 20, 1948, In Re: Galarza against the Board of Education of the District of Columbia, Conference with Mr. Clifford Forster and Mr. Jonathan Bingham of the American Civil Liberties Union and Mr. Theodore Leske of the American Jewish Congress, National Association for the Advancement of Colored People Papers, ProQuest History Vault.
143. "Letter to Clifford Forster from Marian Wynn Perry," December 18, 1947, American Civil Liberties Union Papers, Gale Digital Database.
144. "Letter to Clifford Forster from Ernesto Galarza," January 22, 1948, American Civil Liberties Union Papers, Gale Digital Database.
145. Pepe interview by author.
146. Guridy, *Forging Diaspora*; Greenbaum, *More Than Black*.

Chapter Two

1. For more on critical assessments of the "Lost Cause," see Gallagher, *Causes Won, Lost, and Forgotten*; Blight, *American Oracle*; Blight, *Race and Reunion*; Wilson, *Baptized in Blood*; Hale, *Making Whiteness*; Foster, *Ghosts of the Confederacy*; and Owsley, "Review of *The Myth of the Lost Cause*."
2. For the early example of Mexican migrant farmworkers in Mount Olive, North Carolina, see Jane Van Ness, "A 20th Century Version—Christ in the Fields," *North Carolina Catholic*, September 5, 1965, cited in research by Sarah Waugh on migrant education programs in "Latinx NC," *Story Map*, April 11, 2022, https://storymaps.arcgis.com/stories/a9442aef9ca54434b80fb8fb507b2797#ref-n-7TS5fK.
3. The history of South of the Border also foregrounds the role of region in shaping

racial discourse. Traditional literature on Mexican and Latino stereotypes is insufficient to understand South of the Border because it is rooted in the particular histories of conquest and colonization of the West and Southwest. Although South of the Border and its mascot, Pedro, are clearly shaped by these discourses, Pedro's Confederate uniform and presence at Confederateland demands an understanding of the particular history of the South to make sense of these distinct Latino racial formations. For more on the discourses of Mexicans and Mexican Americans nationally, see Aparicio and Chávez-Silverman, *Tropicalizations*; Rodriguez, *Latin Looks*; Alonzo, *Badmen, Bandits, and Folk Heroes*; Bebout, *Whiteness on the Border*; Milian, *Latining America*; Berg, *Latino Images in Film*; Santa Ana, *Brown Tide Rising*; and Chavez, *Latino Threat*.

4. Existing literature on South of the Border situates the rest stop in the southern tourism industry. For example, Nicole King's work, *Sombreros and Motorcycles*, examines how South of the Border shaped race, aesthetics, and southern roadside culture. South of the Border, King argues, created a space of transgression through kitsch and camp that chafed against the norms of the religiously conservative South. My work, however, looks at the experience of visitors at South of the Border.

5. Molina, "Power of Racial Scripts."

6. For more on experiences of white loss during the civil rights movement, see Sokol, *There Goes My Everything*; Roy, *Bitters in the Honey*; Kruse, *White Flight*; and Hale, *Making Whiteness*. For more on how travel and tourism shape regional and national identity, see Cox, *Dreaming of Dixie*; Sears, *Sacred Places*; and Aron, *Working at Play*.

7. Deloria, *Playing Indian*.

8. Anna Griffin, "At 50, Still Love or Hate at First Sight," *Charlotte Observer*, March 19, 2000; "The Schafer Company Traces Its Roots to 1870," *Dillon (SC) Herald*, February 4, 2010; "Our History," South of the Border, accessed September 20, 2022, www.thesouthoftheborder.com/history/; "Borderlines," *Dillon (SC) Herald*, February 26, 1965. For more on Strom Thurmond and the cultural and political conservatism of South Carolina, see Crespino, *Strom Thurmond's America*.

9. Rugh, *Are We There Yet?*; Aron, *Working at Play*.

10. Cox, *Dreaming of Dixie*; Starnes, "Creating a 'Variety Vacationland,'" 145–46.

11. For more on critical Indigenous/Native studies, see Coulthard, *Red Skin, White Masks*; Simpson, *Mohawk Interruptus*; Horne, *Apocalypse of Settler Colonialism*; and Estes, *Our History Is the Future*.

12. Blu, *Lumbee Problem*; King, *Sombreros and Motorcycles*; Lowery, *Lumbee Indians in the Jim Crow South*.

13. Lowery, *Lumbee Indians in the Jim Crow South*; Lowery, *Lumbee Indians*; Blu, *Lumbee Problem*; Bow, *Partly Colored*.

14. Blu, *Lumbee Problem*; King, *Sombreros and Motorcycles*; Lowery, *Lumbee Indians in the Jim Crow South*.

15. Goldstein, *Price of Whiteness*; "Dillon/Latta, South Carolina," *Encyclopedia of*

Southern Jewish Communities, Institute of Southern Jewish Life, accessed June 23, 2016, www.isjl.org/south-carolina-dillon-encyclopedia.html.

16. Ignatiev, *How the Irish Became White*; Lott, *Love and Theft*; Roediger, *Wages of Whiteness*.

17. Starnes, "Creating a 'Variety Vacationland,'" 139–44.

18. "Schafer Company Traces Its Roots to 1870"; "Borderlines," *Dillon (SC) Herald*, February 26, 1965.

19. King, "Behind the Sombrero"; South of the Border website, accessed September 20, 2022, www.thesouthoftheborder.com; Rudy Maxa, "South of the Border Down Carolina Way," *Washington Post Magazine*, January 7, 1979.

20. There is no discernible pattern for when and why his skin color was changed. It is seemingly random.

21. Maxa, "South of the Border Down Carolina Way."

22. Gene Autry, "South of the Border (Down Mexico Way)," lyrics from Genius.com, accessed October 14, 2020, https://genius.com/Gene-autry-south-of-the-border -down-mexico-way-lyrics.

23. Berger and Wood, *Holiday in Mexico*; Wood, *Business of Leisure*; Berger, *Development of Mexico's Tourism Industry*.

24. Gaytán, "'Una Copita Amigo'"; Merrill, *Negotiating Paradise*; Cox, *Dreaming of Dixie*.

25. Ruiz, *Americans in the Treasure House*.

26. Cox, *Dreaming of Dixie*; McPherson, *Reconstructing Dixie*; Duck, *Nation's Region*.

27. Cocks, *Tropical Whites*.

28. For more on the links between "tropical" and Latino, see Aparicio and Chávez-Silverman, *Tropicalizations*. For more on the long history of tropicality as tied to the Caribbean, see Dash, *Other America*. For more on the uses of "tropical" in the production of tourism in the Caribbean, see Strachan, *Paradise and Plantation*; and Thompson, *Eye for the Tropics*.

29. "South of the Border," Manuscripts, Carolina Studios Photographic Collection, South Caroliniana Library, University of South Carolina, Columbia (hereafter cited as CSPC); Postcard Collections from Ace-Hi Advertising, Dexter Press, Hannau-Robinson Color Production, Manuscripts, South Caroliniana Library, University of South Carolina, Columbia.

30. "Pedro Presents South of the Border Award Weening Billboards," South of the Border brochure, 2002, printed by LithoGraphics (Orlando, FL), CSPC; Postcard Collections from Ace-Hi Advertising, Dexter Press, Hannau-Robinson Color Production, Manuscripts, South Caroliniana Library, University of South Carolina, Columbia; "Borderlines," *Dillon (SC) Herald*, March 25, 1965, 5.

31. Koser, "Planned by Pedro"; "Pedro Presents South of the Border Award Weening Billboards."

32. "Pedro's Dischoteque," *Dillon (SC) Herald*, September 18, 1964.

33. Koser, "Planned by Pedro"; "Pedro Presents South of the Border Award Weening Billboards."

34. Cocks, *Tropical Whites*, 4.

35. King, *Sombreros and Motorcycles*, 90.

36. King, *Sombreros and Motorcycles*, 90.

37. Griffin, "At 50, Still Love or Hate at First Sight"; "The Lowry War," *Native American Netroots* (blog), March 12, 2010, http://nativeamericannetroots.net/diary/410.

38. "Pedro Needs Help at South of the Border," *Florence (SC) Morning News*, August 20, 1966.

39. King, *Sombreros and Motorcycles*, 90, 93.

40. Pérez, "Brownface Minstrelsy."

41. Johnson, *Burnt Cork*; Hale, *Making Whiteness*; Roediger, *Wages of Whiteness*; Saxton, *Rise and Fall of the White Republic*; Roberts, *Blackface Nation*; Rogin, *Blackface, White Noise*.

42. Lott, *Love and Theft*.

43. For more on the role of accents and language discrimination in the experience of Latinos, see Burgos, *Playing America's Game*; Lippi-Green, *English with an Accent*; Lozano, *American Language*; and Rosa, *Looking Like a Language*.

44. South of the Border, advertisement, *Florence (SC) Morning News*, July 27, 1969.

45. Erksine Johnson, "In Hollywood," *Enterprise Journal* (McComb, MS), September 20, 1949.

46. Burgos, *Playing America's Game*, 215–22.

47. Rodriguez, *Latin Looks*.

48. Berg, *Latino Images in Film*, 72.

49. Ngai, *Impossible Subjects*, 8, 155–59.

50. Almaguer, *Racial Fault Lines*; Bebout, *Whiteness on the Border*.

51. "'Romance of Old Mexico' in Memphis," *Jackson (MS) Sun*, February 27, 1941.

52. "Mexican Fiesta to Perform," *Daily Tar Heel*, November 15, 1966.

53. Rosaldo, "Imperialist Nostalgia."

54. For more on the role of Blackface and its power in solidifying whiteness, see Ignatiev, *How the Irish Became White*; Lott, *Love and Theft*; Roediger, *Wages of Whiteness*; and Dubin, "Symbolic Slavery," 123.

55. "Pedro Presents South of the Border Award Weening Billboards."

56. "Borderlines," *Dillon (SC) Herald*, August 16, 1961.

57. "Borderlines," *Dillon (SC) Herald*, May 8, 1964.

58. Maxa, "South of the Border Down Carolina Way"; "Borderlines," *Dillon (SC) Herald*, February 26, 1965.

59. King, *Sombreros and Motorcycles*; Koser, "Planned by Pedro."

60. Raiford, *Imprisoned*; Allen, *Without Sanctuary*; Goldsby, *Spectacular Secret*; Abel, *Signs of the Times*; Hale, *Making Whiteness*; Willis, *Reflections in Black*; Willis-Thomas and Willis, *Picturing Us*.

61. CSPC.

62. CSPC.

63. Deloria, *Playing Indian*; Sokol, *There Goes My Everything*; Roy, *Bitters in the Honey*; Kruse, *White Flight*.

64. Kruse, *White Flight*; McMillen, *Citizens' Council*; Bartley, *Rise of Massive Resistance*; McRae, *Mothers of Massive Resistance*; Lewis, *White South and the Red Menace*; Walker, *Ghost of Jim Crow*; Payne, *I've Got the Light of Freedom*.

65. Lau, *Democracy Rising*, 95–98.

66. For more on the civil rights movement in South Carolina, see Brinson, *Stories of Struggle*; Arsenault, *Freedom Riders*; Carson, *In Struggle*; and Moore and Burton, *Toward the Meeting of the Waters*.

67. For more on tourism and cultural representation of Native/Indigenous communities, see Vickers, *Native American Identities*; Dilworth, *Imagining Indians in the Southwest*; Weston, *Native Americans in the News*; Coward, *Indians Illustrated*; and Phillips, *Staging Indigeneity*.

68. Starnes, "Creating a 'Variety Vacationland,'" 146–47.

69. CSPC.

70. CSPC; Deloria, *Playing Indian*.

71. Maxa, "South of the Border Down Carolina Way."

72. In reviewing the digitized editions of the *Green Book* from the New York Public Library from 1949 to 1967 (noting that the digitization of the 1949 edition was missing some information), I saw no mention of South of the Border or its surrounding areas. The closest mention was Mullins, South Carolina, twenty-four miles away from Dillon and South of the Border. *Green Book*, NYPL Digital Collections, accessed March 16, 2022, https://digitalcollections.nypl.org/collections/the-green-book?keywords=&sort=keyDate_st+desc#/?tab=about&scroll=8; The Green Book of South Carolina, accessed March 16, 2022, https://greenbookofsc.com/.

73. Hale, "'For Colored' and 'For White,'" 174; King, *Sombreros and Motorcycles*; King, "Behind the Sombrero," 57–58; Maxa, "South of the Border Down Carolina Way."

74. Blu, *Lumbee Problem*, 12.

75. Bebout, *Whiteness on the Border*; King, *Sombreros and Motorcycles*, 40; Hollis, *Dixie before Disney*.

76. Dr. Peter Capelotti, image from correspondence with the author, October 14, 2020.

77. Blu, *Lumbee Problem*, 12; "Lowry War"; King, "Behind the Sombrero," 40.

78. "Borderlines," *Dillon (SC) Herald*, August 21, 1964.

79. "Pedroland, U.S.A.," undated, Harold and Geraldine Haskins Postcard Collection, South Caroliniana Library, University of South Carolina, Columbia.

80. "Borderlines," *Dillon (SC) Herald*, February 5, 1965; June 27, 1962; August 24, 1964.

81. "Borderlines," *Dillon (SC) Herald*, May 8, 1964; Postcard Collections from Ace-Hi Advertising, Dexter Press, Hannau-Robinson Color Production, Manuscripts, South Caroliniana Library, University of South Carolina, Columbia; "Borderlines," *Dillon (SC) Herald*, June 6, 1962.

82. "South of the Border, Largest Motel-Restaurant-Vacation Spa between New York and Miami," undated, Harold and Geraldine Haskins Postcard Collection, South Caroliniana Library, University of South Carolina, Columbia.

83. "Borderlines," *Dillon (SC) Herald*, May 8, 1964; "Borderlines," *Dillon (SC) Herald*, August 14, 1964; South of the Border, advertisement, *Dillon (SC) Herald*, October 9, 1952.

84. In the 1950s and 1960s, there were few Mexican restaurants throughout the South. It was in the 1950s that the Mexican food chain El Chico began to penetrate the southeastern market such that by 1960 it had a handful of restaurants in Louisiana, Arkansas, and Tennessee. However, most Mexican restaurants remained densely concentrated in the Louisiana-Arkansas area, and it wasn't until the 1970s that large numbers of Mexican restaurants began to appear throughout the entire Southeast. El Chico Annual Report 1972, El Chico Restaurant Records (Collection #1246), Box 1, Folder 5, Smithsonian Institution Collection, Washington, DC.

85. Casa Montez Restaurant, advertisement, *Northwest Arkansas Times*, April 9, 1966; "Offers Real Mexican Food at El Patio," *Northwest Arkansas Times*, December 2, 1946; Plaza Cafe, advertisement, *Northwest Arkansas Times*, July 13, 1940.

86. King, *Sombreros and Motorcycles*, 63.

87. "Borderlines (Yanquis Interested in Proposed Race Track)," *Dillon (SC) Herald*, July 25, 1962.

88. "Borderlines (Confederateland Golf News)," *Dillon (SC) Herald*, July 25, 1962.

89. Koser, "Planned by Pedro," 78; "Confederate Land Dedication Monday," *Dillon (SC) Herald*, August 25, 1961; "Borderlines," *Dillon (SC) Herald*, September 8, 1961; "Confederateland, Unique Spot, Opens with Big Fanfare," *Dillon (SC) Herald*, August 28, 1961.

90. King, "Behind the Sombrero," 64.

91. Koser, "Planned by Pedro," 78; "Confederate Land Dedication Monday"; "Borderlines," *Dillon (SC) Herald*, September 8, 1961; "Confederateland, Unique Spot"; "Editorial: Confederateland and South of the Border Are Tremendous Assets to Dillon County," *Dillon (SC) Herald*, n.d.; Laurie M. Grossman, "South of the Border: Things Are Popping This Fourth of July," *Wall Street Journal*, July 3, 1987.

92. CSPC.

93. Koser, "Planned by Pedro," 78; "Confederate Land Dedication Monday"; "Borderlines," *Dillon (SC) Herald*, September 8, 1961; "Confederateland, Unique Spot"; "Editorial: Confederateland and South of the Border Are Tremendous Assets"; Grossman, "South of the Border."

94. CSPC.

95. Cox, *Dreaming of Dixie*; Cox, *Destination Dixie*; Starnes, *Southern Journeys*; King, *Sombreros and Motorcycles*.

96. "Whose Heritage?," Southern Poverty Law Center, accessed April 3, 2019, www .splcenter.org/data-projects/whose-heritage#findings.

97. Cobb, *Away Down South*, 101.

98. "Confederate Land Dedication Monday"; "Borderlines," *Dillon (SC) Herald*, September 8, 1961; "Confederateland, Unique Spot."

99. Simon, "Race Reactions," 244; Tyson, "Dynamite and 'The Silent South,'" 278; Lowery, *Lumbee Indians in the Jim Crow South*, 251–57.

100. Fahs and Waugh, *Memory of the Civil War*, 237.
101. Guerrero, *Nuevo South*.
102. Du Bois, *Dusk of Dawn*.
103. Hale, *Making Whiteness*; Cox, *Dreaming of Dixie*; Cox, *Destination Dixie*.
104. Editorial, *Atlanta Daily World* (date unknown).
105. CSPC; Cook, *Troubled Commemoration*, 107.
106. "Editorial: Confederateland and South of the Border Are Tremendous Assets."
107. Lois Dove, "Borderlines," *Dillon (SC) Herald*, September 1, 1961.
108. CSPC.
109. Webb, "Tangled Web," 196–99.
110. Thom Anderson, "Confederateland Dedication," *Dillon (SC) Herald*, August 25, 1961.
111. Thom Anderson, "Confederate Battleship Pee Dee Relics Rest at South of the Border," *Dillon (SC) Herald*, August 23, 1961.
112. Grossman, "South of the Border."
113. Bebout, *Whiteness on the Border*.
114. "Pedro Presents South of the Border Award Weening Billboards."

Chapter Three

1. Zapata interview by author, May 19, 2010.
2. There is a wealth of historical research on Latinos' involvement in civil rights organizing in places like Texas (see Krochmal, *Blue Texas*; and Behnken, *Fighting Their Own Battles*) but not in the Southeast. Additionally, Julie Weise has written about the presence of Latinos in the South during this period in her chapter on braceros in Arkansas (*Corazón de Dixie*), but she does not deal squarely with the question of civil rights organizing or Latino involvement.
3. Notably, Lauren Araiza's *To March for Others* is the most thorough account of the linkages between SNCC and the United Farmworkers (UFW), and she gives attention to some of the activists discussed in this chapter, including Maria Varela and Elizabeth "Betita" Martinez.
4. One school of thought on Black/brown coalitions largely grows out of the application of whiteness studies to the experience of Mexicans and Mexican Americans. Exemplary of this school is Neil Foley's work about the "Faustian pact" with whiteness that "offered [Mexican Americans] inclusion within whiteness, provided that they subsumed ethnic identities under their newly acquired white identity and its core value of white supremacy." This bargain, he argues, came at the cost of organizing across racial lines with African Americans. Foley, *Reflexiones 1997*, 63. Other relevant whiteness studies include Roediger, *Wages of Whiteness*; Ignatiev, *How the Irish Became White*; and Hale, *Making Whiteness*. More recently, Brian Behnken has argued that a similar disjuncture exists between Black and brown communities because of Mexican communities' failed claims to whiteness. See his "Movement in the Mirror" and *Fighting Their Own Battles*. Another school of thought focuses on evidence of organizing among Black and

brown communities—finding unity where the previous school of thought only found conflict. Carlos K. Blanton argues in his essay "George I. Sánchez, Ideology, and Whiteness in the Making of the Mexican American Civil Rights Movement, 1930–1960" that Sánchez and other Mexican American activists utilized "whiteness" as a form of legal opportunism rather than anti-Black racism. Instead of conflict, Blanton finds Black and brown communities linked in a shared experience of oppression. Still others find unity based on communities' shared experiences of racism. See, for example, Bernstein, *Bridges of Reform*; Rosas, *South Central Is Home*; Krochmal, *Blue Texas*; Pulido, *Black, Brown, Yellow, and Left*; Ogbar, "Puerto Rico en mi Corazón"; and Ogbar, "Rainbow Radicalism." Many of these works, like my own, move away from a success/failure model of analyzing these alliances and instead outline the contours of daily life where these communities met. Additionally, they emphasize the local particularities of these organizing efforts. Not surprisingly, much of the literature has focused on the West and Southwest, as these were the areas with the greatest Latino populations.

5. "Founding of SNCC," SNCC Digital Gateway, accessed September 21, 2022, https://snccdigital.org/events/founding-of-sncc/.

6. For more on the rich SNCC historiography, see Carson, *In Struggle*; Chafe, *Civilities and Civil Rights*; Charron, *Freedom's Teacher*; Crosby, *Civil Rights History*; Crosby, *Little Taste of Freedom*; Dittmer, *Local People*; Fleming, *Soon We Will Not Cry*; Forner, *Why the Vote Wasn't Enough*; Frye, *Cradle of Freedom*; Greenberg, *Circle of Trust*; Hale, *Freedom Schools*; Hamlin, *Crossroads at Clarksdale*; Jeffries, *Bloody Lowndes*; Kelen, *This Light of Ours*; Levy, *Civil War on Race Street*; Marshall, *Student Activism and Civil Rights*; McGuire, *At the Dark End of the Street*; Monteith, *SNCC's Stories*; Moye, *Ella Baker*; Moye, *Let the People Decide*; Payne, *I've Got the Light of Freedom*; Ransby, *Ella Baker*; Hogan, *Many Minds, One Heart*; and Lovelace, "Making the World in Atlanta's Image."

7. "SNCC Sends Marion Barry & Others to Political Conventions," SNCC Digital Library, accessed September 21, 2022, https://snccdigital.org/events/sncc-sends -marion-barry-others-to-political-conventions/; SNCC Founding Statement, Civil Rights Movement Archive, accessed September 21, 2022, www.crmvet.org /docs/snccı.htm; Ella Baker, "Bigger Than a Hamburger," *Southern Patriot*, May 1960.

8. Hogan, *Many Minds, One Heart*; Payne, *I've Got the Light of Freedom*.

9. Betita Martinez, "Liz Is Betita: A SNCC Memory, 2010," Civil Rights Movement Archive, www.crmvet.org/nars/stor/s_betita.htm.

10. For further discussion of her experience with segregation in Washington, DC, see Mártinez, "Neither Black nor White," 531–33; Mártinez interviews by Loretta Ross, 5–10.

11. Varela interview by author.

12. For information about YCS, see Varela, "Time to Get Ready," 556; Varela interview by author.

13. Varela, "Time to Get Ready," 557.

14. For more on the conservatism of Orange County, see McGirr, *Suburban Warriors*.

15. Ramirez, *Woman in the Zoot Suit*; Sanchez, *Becoming Mexican American*; Pitti, *Devil in Silicon Valley*; Flores, *Grounds for Dreaming*.

16. Zapata interview by author, March 21, 2012.

17. Ramirez, *Woman in the Zoot Suit*; Sanchez, *Becoming Mexican American*; Pitti, *Devil in Silicon Valley*; Flores, *Grounds for Dreaming*.

18. Bernstein, *Bridges of Reform*; Brilliant, *Color of America*; Flores, *Grounds for Dreaming*; Pawel, *Union of Their Dreams*; Pitti, *Devil in Silicon Valley*; Ruiz, *Cannery Women, Cannery Lives*.

19. Zapata interview by author, May 19, 2010.

20. Zapata interview by author, March 21, 2012; Zapata interview by author, May 19, 2010. For more on the connections between SNCC and the UFW, see Araiza, *To March for Others*.

21. Zapata interview by author, May 19, 2010.

22. Zapata interview by author, March 21, 2012.

23. Zapata interview by author, March 21, 2012.

24. Weise, *Corazón de Dixie*.

25. Zapata interview by author, April 18, 2010; Zapata interview by author, May 19, 2010.

26. Varela interview by author.

27. Varela interview by author; Varela, "Time to Get Ready."

28. Varela interview by author; Greenberg, *Circle of Trust*, 94; Varela, "Time to Get Ready," 555.

29. "The Road to Selma," SNCC Digital Gateway, accessed September 21, 2022, https://snccdigital.org/our-voices/learning-from-experience/part-1/.

30. Varela, "Time to Get Ready," 555.

31. Varela interview by author.

32. Araiza, *To March for Others*.

33. Varela interview by author.

34. Martinez, "Liz Is Betita."

35. Zapata interview by author, May 19, 2010.

36. Zapata interview by author, May 19, 2010.

37. *Eyes on the Prize: America's Civil Rights Years, 1954–1965*, directed by Orlando Bagwell et al., written by Henry Hampton and Julian Bond (Alexandria, VA: PBS Video, 2010), DVD.

38. *Nuestra Historia, Nuestra Voz: Latinxs at Duke*, exhibit, 2022, Chappel Family Gallery, Perkins Library, Duke University, Durham, NC; Barahona, "History of Latinx Students at Duke University."

39. Weaver, *Darkroom*, 86 (emphasis in original).

40. Cortez interview by author. For more on the history of the Congress of Racial Equality (CORE), see Frazier, *Harambee City*; Purnell, *Fighting Jim Crow*; Catsam, *Freedom's Main Line*; Arsenault, *Freedom Riders*; and Meier and Rudwick, *CORE*.

41. Cortez interview by author.

42. Cortez interview by author.

43. Ford, *Liberated Threads*; Ford, "SNCC Women."

44. Todd interview by junior and senior high school students of the D.C. Everest Area School District; Cortez interview by author.

45. Cortez interview by author.

46. Cortez interview by author.

47. Mártinez interviews by Loretta Ross.

48. For more on Freedom Summer, see Dittmer, *Local People*, 250–81; Hogan, *Many Minds, One Heart*, 156, 167, 269–71; Visser-Maessen, *Robert Parris Moses*; and Watson, *Freedom Summer*, 11–14, 171–76, 183–85.

49. Zapata interview by author, March 21, 2012.

50. Varela, "Time to Get Ready"; Varela interview by author.

51. "Mississippi Freedom Vote," SNCC Digital Gateway, accessed September 21, 2022, https://snccdigital.org/events/mississippi-freedom-vote/.

52. Sellers and Terrell, *River of No Return*.

53. Hogan, *Many Minds, One Heart*, 198, 202, 217.

54. Hogan, *Many Minds, One Heart*, 206.

55. For more on the Chicano movement, see Montejano, *Anglos and Mexicans*; García, *Mexican Americans*; Chávez, *"¡Mi Raza Primero!"*; Ruiz, *From Out of the Shadows*; López, *Racism on Trial*; Gómez-Quiñones and Vásquez, *Making Aztlán*; Oropeza, *Raza Si, Guerra No*; Blackwell, *¡Chicana Power!*; García, *Chicanismo*; and Mariscal, *Brown-Eyed Children of the Sun*.

56. Araiza, *To March for Others*.

57. "Why Filmstrips," SNCC Digital Gateway, accessed September 21, 2022, https://snccdigital.org/our-voices/learning-from-experience/part-4/.

58. "Why Filmstrips."

59. "Why Filmstrips."

60. "Why Filmstrips."

61. Chávez, *"¡Mi Raza Primero!"*; Gómez-Quiñones and Vásquez, *Making Aztlán*; López, *Racism on Trial*; Acuña, *Occupied America*.

62. Varela interview by author.

63. "International Connections," SNCC Digital Gateway, accessed September 21, 2022, https://snccdigital.org/inside-sncc/international-connections/.

64. Forman, *Making of Black Revolutionaries*, 447. For more on SNCC and internationalism, see Lovelace, "William Worthy's Passport"; and Tyson, *Radio Free Dixie*. For more on broader Black internationalism at this time, see Mealy, *Fidel and Malcolm X*; Plummer, "Castro in Harlem"; Cruse, "A Negro Looks at Cuba"; Tyson, *Radio Free Dixie*; and Bloom and Martin, *Black against Empire*.

65. Varela interview by author.

66. For more on SNCC and Black Power, see Jeffries, *Bloody Lowndes*; Tyson, *Radio Free Dixie*; Moye, *Let the People Decide*; Tyson, *Blood Done Sign My Name*; Ashmore, *Carry It On*; Crosby, *Little Taste of Freedom*; and Greene, *Our Separate Ways*.

67. Carson, *In Struggle*; Hogan, *Many Minds, One Heart*; Jeffries, *Bloody Lowndes*.

68. "An International Consciousness," SNCC Digital Gateway, accessed on September 21, 2022, https://snccdigital.org/our-voices/internationalism/part-1/.

69. "International Awareness," SNCC Digital Gateway, accessed on September 21, 2022, https://snccdigital.org/our-voices/emergence-Black-power/international/.

70. "Roots," SNCC Digital Gateway, accessed on September 21, 2022, https://snccdigital.org/our-voices/emergence-Black-power/roots/.

71. Carson, *In Struggle*, 192.

72. Mártinez interviews by Loretta Ross, 70; Carson, *In Struggle*; Forman, *Making of Black Revolutionaries*.

73. Elizabeth Mártinez, New York Staff Letter, April 5, 1966, Reel 47, Student Nonviolent Coordinating Committee Papers, University of Virginia Special Collections, Charlottesville.

74. Mártinez letter.

75. Ransby, *Ella Baker*, 344.

76. Forman, *Making of Black Revolutionaries*, 449.

77. Carson, *In Struggle*, 240.

78. "December 1966: SNCC Staff Meeting at Peg Leg BatesClub," SNCC Digital Gateway, accessed September 21, 2022, https://snccdigital.org/events/sncc-staff-meeting-peg-leg-bates-club/.

79. Ransby, *Ella Baker*, 300–303, 344.

80. Elizabeth (Betita) Mártinez, "Black, White, and Tan," June 1967, Reel 47, Student Nonviolent Coordinating Committee Papers, University of Virginia Special Collections, Charlottesville.

81. Mártinez, "Black, White, and Tan," 7–9; Mártinez, "Neither Black nor White."

82. Mártinez, "Black, White, and Tan," 7–9. For more on anti-Black racism throughout the region, see Torres-Saillant, "Tribulations of Blackness"; Gudmundson and Wolfe, *Blacks and Blackness*; García-Peña, *Borders of Dominicanidad*; Clealand, *Power of Race in Cuba*; Domínguez, *Race in Cuba*; Pappademos, *Black Political Activism*; de la Fuente, *Nation for All*; Andrews, *Afro-Latin America*; and Benson, *Antiracism in Cuba*.

83. Mártinez, "Black, White, and Tan," 4–9.

84. Varela interview by author.

85. Varcla interview by author.

86. Varela, "Time to Get Ready," 568; Mártinez letter.

87. Araiza, *To March for Others*, 59.

88. Araiza, "For Freedom of Other Men," 44–45; Mártinez, "Neither Black nor White," 534; Lester, "'Black Revolution Is Real'"; "Stokely Carmichael Speech for Organization of Latin American Solidarity (OLAS)" (Havana, Cuba, August 1967), Reel 11, Student Nonviolent Coordinating Committee Papers, University of Virginia Special Collections, Charlottesville.

89. Araiza, "For Freedom of Other Men," 44–45; Mártinez, "Neither Black nor White," 534; Lester, "'Black Revolution Is Real'"; "Stokely Carmichael Speech."

90. "Stokely Carmichael Speech."

91. "Stokely Carmichael Speech."

92. Joseph, *Stokely*; Jeffries, *Bloody Lowndes*.

93. Oropeza, *King of Adobe*.
94. "Maria Varela Meets Reies Tijerína at National Conference for New Politics," SNCC Digital Gateway, accessed February 8, 2021, https://snccdigital.org/events /maria-varela-meets-reies-tijerina-at-national-new-politics-conference/; Varela interview by author; Varela, "Time to Get Ready."
95. Araiza, *To March for Others*, 66.
96. For more on their role in Chicana feminist movements and Chicana feminism more broadly, see Araiza, *To March for Others*; Martínez, *500 Years of Chicana Women's History*; Holsaert, Noonan, Richardson, Robinson, Young, and Zellner, *Hands on the Freedom Plow*; López, *Racism on Trial* (Varela's involvement on 214); Mártinez, "'Chingón Politics' Die Hard"; "Maria Varela Meets Reies Tijerína"; Ruiz, *From Out of the Shadows* (Varela on 104–5, 144–45; Mártinez on 100, 105, 107, 149); and Blackwell, *¡Chicana Power!*. For more on Mártinez changing her name, see "Elizabeth (Betita Mártinez) Sutherland," SNCC Digital Gateway, accessed September 21, 2022, https://snccdigital.org/people/elizabeth-betita-martinez -sutherland/.
97. Varela, "Time to Get Ready," 568.
98. Mártinez, "Black, White, and Tan."
99. Araiza, *To March for Others*; Behnken, *Fighting Their Own Battles*; Behnken, *Struggle in Black and Brown*; Foley, *White Scourge*; Foley, *Quest for Equality*.

Chapter Four

1. Jose M. interview by Ana Trejo. All interviews by Ana Trejo cited in this book were conducted for her undergraduate capstone project at Duke University, "A (Not So) Magical Carpet Ride for the Latinx Community in Dalton, Georgia," in the author's possession.
2. Jose M. interview by Ana Trejo.
3. Jose M. interview by Ana Trejo.
4. Projected Growth in GA Schools, Western Interstate Commission for Higher Education/College Board, Series I, Box 2, Folder 5, Georgia Project Records, Richard B. Russell Library, University of Georgia, Athens (hereafter cited as GAPR).
5. Patton and Parker, *Carpet Capital*, 209, 231, 256.
6. Zúñiga and Hernández-León, *New Destinations*, 262.
7. Zúñiga and Hernández-León, "Appalachia Meets Aztlán," 259.
8. Zúñiga and Hernández-León, *New Destinations*; Davis, Deaton, Boyle, and Schick, *Voices from the Nueva Frontera*; Engstrom, "Industry, Social Regulation, and Scale"; Hernández-León and Zúñiga, "Mexican Immigrant Communities"; Murphy, Blanchard, and Hill, *Latino Workers*.
9. For more on how ideas about Latinos traveled through media, politics, and business, see Weise, *Corazón de Dixie*; Cadava, *Standing on Common Ground*; Cadava, *Hispanic Republican*; Mora, *Making Hispanics*; Dávila, *Latino Spin*; Allen, *Univision, Telemundo*; and Aldama, *Latinx TV*.
10. HoSang, *Racial Propositions*.

11. Flamming, *Creating the Modern South*, 110.
12. Zúñiga and Hernández-León, "Dalton Story," 40.
13. Zúñiga interview by author.
14. Hamann, "Georgia Project," 119, 22.
15. Zúñiga and Hernández-León, *New Destinations*, 259; Davis, Deaton, Boyle, and Schick, *Voices from the Nueva Frontera*, 5.
16. Murphy, Blanchard, and Hill, *Latino Workers*, 37.
17. Massey, *New Faces in New Places*; Massey, Durand, and Malone, *Beyond Smoke and Mirrors*; Minian, *Undocumented Lives*.
18. Weise, *Corazón de Dixie*, 128.
19. Murphy, Blanchard, and Hill, *Latino Workers*, 127.
20. Engstrom, "Industry, Social Regulation, and Scale"; Weise, *Corazón de Dixie*.
21. Zúñiga and Hernández-León, *New Destinations*, 50.
22. Griffith, "Rural Industry and Mexican Immigration," 50; Stull, Broadway, and Griffith, *Any Way You Cut It*.
23. Fink, *Maya of Morganton*; Striffler, *Chicken*; Mohl, "Latinization in the Heart of Dixie," 243.
24. Guerrero, *Nuevo South*; Weise, *Corazón de Dixie*; Stuesse, *Scratching Out a Living*; Marrow, *New Destination Dreaming*; Marrow, "On the Line."
25. Stuesse, *Scratching Out a Living*, 73.
26. Weise, *Corazón de Dixie*.
27. Zúñiga and Hernández-León, *New Destinations*, 262.
28. Stuesse, *Scratching Out a Living*, 87; Jones, *Browning of the New South*, 16.
29. Laura E. Helton and Angela Stuesse, "Low-Wage Legacies, Race, and the Golden Chicken in Mississippi: Where Contemporary Immigration Meets African American Labor History," *Southern Spaces*, December 31, 2013, https://southern spaces.org/2013/low-wage-legacies-race-and-golden-chicken-mississippi-where -contemporary-immigration-meets-african-american-labor-history/.
30. Helton quoted in Stuesse, *Scratching Out a Living*, 77.
31. Davis, Deaton, Boyle, and Schick, *Voices from the Nueva Frontera*, 6.
32. Weise, *Corazón de Dixie*.
33. Stuesse, *Scratching Out a Living*, 76.
34. Stuesse, *Scratching Out a Living*, 76.
35. Striffler, *Chicken*.
36. Guerrero, *Nuevo South*; Striffler, *Chicken*; Stuesse, *Scratching Out a Living*; Marrow, "On the Line"; Simon, *Hamlet Fire*; Stull, Broadway, and Griffith, *Any Way You Cut It*.
37. Striffler, *Chicken*; Helton and Stuesse, "Low-Wage Legacies."
38. Davis, Deaton, Boyle, and Schick, *Voices from the Nueva Frontera*, 17; Patton and Parker, *Carpet Capital*, 280.
39. Noriega interview by Ana Trejo.
40. Hamann, "Georgia Project," 120.
41. Joe Drape and Audra Melton, "'The Carpet Capital of the World' Is Now Soccer Town U.S.A.," *New York Times*, April 14, 2022.

42. Hamann, "Georgia Project," 124–26.
43. Patton and Parker, *Carpet Capital*, 209, 231, 291; Murphy, Blanchard, and Hill, *Latino Workers*, 47.
44. Cited in Patton and Parker, *Carpet Capital*, 280.
45. Hispanic Labor Migration and the Nation's Carpet Capital—Dalton, Georgia, Drs. Harold R. Trendell, Mark W. Patterson, and Garrett C. Smith, Department of Sociology, Geography and Anthropology, Kennesaw State University, 13, 15, GAPR (hereafter cited as Kennesaw State Report).
46. GA Project Clipping, 1999, Series VI, Box 1, Folder 5, GAPR.
47. Davis, Deaton, Boyle, and Schick, *Voices from the Nueva Frontera*, 68–74.
48. Davis, Deaton, Boyle, and Schick, *Voices from the Nueva Frontera*, 68–74.
49. Davis, Deaton, Boyle, and Schick, *Voices from the Nueva Frontera*, 76.
50. "Centro Latino," Series 11, Box 5, Folder 4, GAPR.
51. Davis, Deaton, Boyle, and Schick, *Voices from the Nueva Frontera*, 69.
52. Hernández-León and Zúñiga, "Mexican Immigrant Communities."
53. Hernández-León and Zúñiga, "Mexican Immigrant Communities," 19.
54. Centro Latino 2000 Donations, Centro Latino, Series 11, Box 5, Folder 4, GAPR.
55. Centro Latino Board of Directors, Centro Latino, Series 11, Box 5, Folder 4, GAPR.
56. Rafael Carballo, "Georgia Project vs. Dalton Schools hispanos: ¿Un problema u oportunidad?" *El Tiempo*, June 9, 1999.
57. Carballo, "Georgia Project vs. Dalton Schools."
58. Needs Assessment of the Hispanic Community in Dalton, October 28, 1997, 2, GAPR.
59. Needs Assessment of the Hispanic Community in Dalton, October 28, 1997, 6, GAPR.
60. Zúñiga interview by author.
61. Series 1, Box 2, Folder 21, GAPR.
62. GA Project Bilingual, 7, Series 11, Box 2, GAPR.
63. ACLA, Series 11, Box 4, Folder 37, GAPR.
64. GA Project Bilingual, Series 11, Box 2, GAPR.
65. GA Project Bilingual, 11, Series 11, Box 2, GAPR.
66. ACLA, Series 11, Box 4, Folder 37, GAPR.
67. Stuesse, *Scratching Out a Living*; Ribas, *On the Line*; McClain et al., "Racial Distancing in a Southern City."
68. McClain et al., "Racial Distancing in a Southern City."
69. Hoppenjans and Richardson, "Mexican Ways, African Roots," 518.
70. Jones, *Browning of the New South*; Brown and Jones, "Immigrant Rights Are Civil Rights."
71. The "hardworking" emphasis also exposed another deep fracture around race within the Latino community. While, to date, no research has been done on the presence of Afro-Latino populations in Dalton, Georgia, during this time, there were robust Afro-Latino populations elsewhere in the Southeast. In the 1980s–2000s, for example, Winston-Salem, North Carolina, was home to a growing Afro-Mexican population. Therefore, for some non-Black Latinos, the

anti-Blackness that was implied in the "hardworking" script included Black Latinos. For non-Black Latinos to invest so deeply in a category like "hardworking" that was imbued with anti-Blackness, toward both African American and Afro-Latino people, shows that even in the late 1990s and early 2000s "Latinidad" was a category defined by its relation to, or distance from, Blackness. In many ways the relative scholarly silences (with important exceptions) on contemporary Afro-Latino experiences in the South point to the power of this historical framework and the urgency of that research to help dismantle/better understand it. The experience of non-Black Latinos, as this book shows, has been triangulated between Black and white in many cases. So Afro-Latinos demonstrate the fractured nature of Latinidad and the limits of that category in understanding how race works in the South—and perhaps the United States more broadly. Vaughn and Vinson, "Unfinished Migrations"; Jones, *Browning of the New South.*

72. Needs Assessment of the Hispanic Community in Dalton, October 28, 1997, 6, GAPR.

73. Davis, Deaton, Boyle, and Schick, *Voices from the Nueva Frontera*, 35.

74. Davis, Deaton, Boyle, and Schick, *Voices from the Nueva Frontera*, 34–35.

75. Davis, Deaton, Boyle, and Schick, *Voices from the Nueva Frontera*, 77.

76. Carballo, "Georgia Project vs. Dalton Schools."

77. Zúñiga and Hernández-León, *New Destinations*, 262.

78. Hernández-León and Zúñiga, "'Making Carpet by the Mile.'"

79. Mitchell interview by Bob Short.

80. Hamman, "Georgia Project," 134.

81. Mitchell interview by Bob Short.

82. Davis, Deaton, Boyle, and Schick, *Voices from the Nueva Frontera*, 71.

83. Needs Assessment of the Hispanic Community in Dalton, October 28, 1997, 20, GAPR.

84. Zúñiga interview by author; Hamann interview by author; Mitchell interview by Bob Short; Davis, Deaton, Boyle, and Schick, *Voices from the Nueva Frontera*, 10.

85. Subseries A, Series 1, Box 1, Folder 1, GAPR.

86. Kennesaw State Report, 24.

87. Gil Klein, "Hispanics Fueling Boom in Old South," *Richmond-Times Dispatch*, September 5, 1999; "Poll Rates Funding Pick," *Daily Citizen-News* (Dalton, GA), April 24, 1997.

88. Sarah Waugh, "Language and Education," Latinx NC, *Story Map*, April 11, 2022, https://storymaps.arcgis.com/stories/a9442aef9ca54434b80fb8fb507b2797.

89. Davis, Deaton, Boyle, and Schick, *Voices from the Nueva Frontera*, 112; Accord, March 19, 1997, Series 1, Box 1, GAPR.

90. Accord, March 19, 1997, Series 1, Box 1, GAPR.

91. Davis, Deaton, Boyle, and Schick, *Voices from the Nueva Frontera*, 113; "History of the Georgia Project," *Georgia: The University of Georgia Magazine*, March 1999.

92. Engstrom, "Industry, Social Regulation, and Scale," 160.

93. Christina Lynch Quinn, "Mexico Trip Gives Cultural Insights," *Daily Citizen-News* (Dalton, GA), August 25, 1997, 1, Series 1, Box 1, GAPR.

94. Quinn, "Mexico Trip Gives Cultural Insights."

95. Davis, Deaton, Boyle, and Schick, *Voices from the Nueva Frontera*, 111–12.

96. "Georgia Project Committee Correspondence," 1996, Series 1, Subseries A, Box 1, Folder 1, GAPR.

97. Billy Bice to Dr. Zúñiga, September 25, 1996, Series 1, Box 1, Folder: GA Project Committee Correspondence, GAPR.

98. Davis, Deaton, Boyle, and Schick, *Voices from the Nueva Frontera*, 119.

99. Davis, Deaton, Boyle, and Schick, *Voices from the Nueva Frontera*, 119.

100. Zúñiga and Hernández-León, *New Destinations*, 249.

101. Needs Assessment of the Hispanic Community in Dalton, October 28, 1997, 14–15, GAPR.

102. Needs Assessment of the Hispanic Community in Dalton, October 28, 1997, 19, GAPR.

103. Needs Assessment of the Hispanic Community in Dalton, October 28, 1997, 3, GAPR.

104. "Business Involvement Aids Georgia Project," *Daily Citizen-News* (Dalton, GA), January 23, 1997, Series 1, Box 1, GAPR.

105. Odem and Lacy, *Latino Immigrants*; Weise, *Corazón de Dixie*.

106. Hamann, "Georgia Project," 147–48.

107. Davis, Deaton, Boyle, and Schick, *Voices from the Nueva Frontera*, 33–34; Leaders of the Hispanic Community in Dalton Individual Profiles, Series 1, Box 2, Folder 21, GAPR.

108. Kennesaw State Report, 16.

109. Kennesaw State Report, 15.

110. Goodman, *Deportation Machine*; Nevins, *Operation Gatekeeper and Beyond*; Rodriguez, "Constructing Mexican Atlanta"; Kanstroom, *Deportation Nation*.

111. Rodriguez, "Constructing Mexican Atlanta."

112. Zúñiga and Hernández-León, *New Destinations*, 264; Rodriguez, "Constructing Mexican Atlanta."

113. Davis, Deaton, Boyle, and Schick, *Voices from the Nueva Frontera*, 7.

114. Dudziak, *Cold War Civil Rights*.

115. Stuesse, *Scratching Out a Living*, 108.

116. Weise, *Corazón de Dixie*, 152.

117. Weise, *Corazón de Dixie*, 155.

118. Weise, *Corazón de Dixie*.

119. Jamie Jones, "Senator Praises Georgia Project," *Daily Citizen-News* (Dalton, GA), September 3, 1999.

120. Mitchell inteview by Bob Short.

121. "'Georgia Project' Boosts Ties with Hispanic Community," Series 1, Box 1, Folder "Georgia Project Committee Correspondence," GAPR.

122. Shirley J. Lorberbaum (Mohawk Industries) to Tommy Maybank (Maybank Textiles), May 29, 1998, Series 1, Subseries A, Box 1, Folder 22, GAPR.

123. Shirley J. Lorberbaum, Draft of Fundraising Letter, May 8, 1998, Series 1, Subseries A, Box 1, Folder 22, GAPR (emphasis in original).

124. Shirley J. Lorberbaum, Draft of Fundraising Letter.
125. Dávila, *Latino Spin*, 164.
126. Murphy, Blanchard, and Hill, *Latino Workers*, 50; Engstrom, "Industry, Social Regulation, and Scale."
127. "'Georgia Project' Boosts Ties with Hispanic Community."
128. Kennesaw State Report, 4.
129. "History of the Georgia Project"; Jamie Jones, "Hispanics Affect Carpet Industry," *Daily Citizen*, November 24, 2002. The Georgia Project, Series 1, Box 1, Folder 42, GAPR.
130. Jones, "Hispanics Affect Carpet Industry."
131. Zúñiga and Hernández-León, *New Destinations*, 266–68.
132. Murphy, Blanchard, and Hill, *Latino Workers*, 50.
133. "History of the Georgia Project."
134. Hayes Ferguson, "Immigrant Wave Valued for Strong Work Ethic," *Times-Picayune*, December 29, 1997.
135. Jose M. interview by Ana Trejo.
136. "History of the Georgia Project."
137. Guerrero, *Nuevo South*; Weise, *Corazón de Dixie*; Stuesse, *Scratching Out a Living*; Ribas, *On the Line*.
138. Nuñez, "Latino Pastoral Narrative."
139. Stull, Broadway, and Griffith, *Any Way You Cut It*, 154.
140. For the Southeast poultry industry, see Stull, Broadway, and Griffith, *Any Way You Cut It*, 140; Stuesse, *Scratching Out a Living*; Guerrero, *Nuevo South*; Weise, *Corazón de Dixie*; and Ribas, *On the Line*.
141. Stuesse, *Scratching Out a Living*, 94.
142. Jerry Grillo, "Carpet Maker to the World," *Georgia Trend Magazine*, July 1, 2006.
143. Davis, Deaton, Boyle, and Schick, *Voices from the Nueva Frontera*, 12; Needs Assessment of the Hispanic Community in Dalton, October 28, 1997, 6, GAPR.
144. Dávila quoted in Nuñez, "Latino Pastoral Narrative."
145. Griffith, "Rural Industry and Mexican Immigration," 66
146. Lippard and Gallagher, *Being Brown in Dixie*, 202.
147. Davis, Deaton, Boyle, and Schick, *Voices from the Nueva Frontera*, 43.
148. Hamann, "Georgia Project," 147.
149. Zúñiga and Hernández-León, *New Destinations*, 268.
150. Davis, Deaton, Boyle, and Schick, *Voices from the Nueva Frontera*, 56.
151. By this time "Latino" had started to circulate as a term used by both Latinos and non-Latinos. However, early on in the South, "Hispanic" was the most frequently used.
152. Tanuja Surpuriya, "Ga. Project Future on Line Tonight," *Daily Citizen-News* (Dalton, GA), June 14, 1999; Tanuja Surpuriya, "Ga. Project Survives," *Daily Citizen-News* (Dalton, GA), June 15, 1999.
153. Erwin Mitchell to Michael J. Bowers, May 20, 1996; Michael J. Bowers to Erwin Mitchell, June 11, 1996, Series I, Box 2, Folder 11, GAPR.
154. Davis, Deaton, Boyle, and Schick, *Voices from the Nueva Frontera*, 83.

155. Allene Magill, email message to Marioly Villareal, March 27, 2001; Marioly Villar-real, email message to Allene Magill, April 5, 2001; and Memorandum by Erwin Mitchell to the Executive Committee regarding DPS/Monterrey Teachers, May 11, 2001, Series II, Box 2, Folder 15, GAPR.

156. Davis, Deaton, Boyle, and Schick, *Voices from the Nueva Frontera*, 71.

157. Zúñiga and Hernández-León, *New Destinations*, 262.

158. "Assimilating Hispanic Students into the Mainstream Curriculum in the Dalton and Whitfield County Schools Systems," Grant Application to: Fund for the Improvement of Education, US Dept of Education, Erwin Mitchell, March 31, 2001, 10, Series I, Subseries A, Box 1, Folder 1, GAPR; Jacki Baines, "Citizenship Laws Need to Be Better Enforced" (letter to the editor), Series VI, Box 1, GAPR; "History of the Georgia Project"; David L. Kirp, "The Old South's New Face," *Nation*, June 26, 2000; Davis, Deaton, Boyle, and Schick, *Voices from the Nueva Frontera*, 83.

159. Zúñiga and Hernández-León, *New Destinations*, 249.

160. Jose M. interview by Ana Trejo.

Chapter Five

1. Jose Rico interview by Ariel Eure.

2. For more on the deployment of civil rights memory for contemporary immigrant struggles in the South, see Foster, "Post-Civil Rights in the Hold"; Márquez, "Juan Crow"; Johnson, "Immigration and Civil Rights"; Ferreti, "Let's Empty the Clip."

3. Jose Rico interview by Ariel Eure.

4. Kosta Harlan, "8 Undocumented Youth Arrested in Georgia as Hundreds March to Protest Education Ban," *Fight Back! News*, April 7, 2011, www.fightbacknews.org/2011/4/7/8-undocumented-youth-arrested-georgia-hundreds-march-protest-education-ban.

5. Jose Rico interview by Ariel Eure.

6. Micah Uetricht, "Seven Undocumented Youth Protest, Risk Deportation in Georgia," *Generation Progress* (blog), April 7, 2011, https://genprogress.org/eight-undocumented-youth-protest-risk-deportation-in-georgia/.

7. Beltrán, *Trouble with Unity*.

8. Zepeda-Millán, "Weapons of the (Not So) Weak."

9. Weise, *Fighting for Their Place*, 176.

10. Jones, *Browning of the New South*, 7.

11. The following data comes from the US censuses for 1990 through 2010. Census data, while providing access to a lot of information, often tends to disproportionately represent certain groups. Until 2010, the census was not offered in Spanish, so it is reasonable to assume that Latinos who only spoke Spanish did not participate in the census. Additionally, the categories in the census population questions referring to the Latino community often changed, reflecting the struggle the United States has faced to categorize Latinos within the Black/white racial binary. The 1930 census was the first to mention any aspect of the Latino community, including a "Mexican" racial category. After that, no mention

of Latinos appeared in the census population data until 1970, when the census asked if individuals came from "Mexican, Puerto Rican, Cuban, Central or South American, Other Spanish" descent. In the 1980, a question was included on if individuals were of "Spanish origin." Beginning in 1990, the census changed the category from "Spanish origin" to "Hispanic."

12. Alabama, Arkansas, Georgia, North Carolina, South Carolina, and Tennessee.

13. "The New Latino South: The Context and Consequences of Rapid Population Growth," Pew Research Center, Hispanic Trends Project (blog), July 26, 2005, www.pewresearch.org/hispanic/2005/07/26/the-new-latino-south/.

14. Mohl, "Globalization, Latinization"; Gill, *Latino Migration Experience*; Guerrero, "Impacting Arkansas."

15. Guerrero, *Nuevo South*, 153.

16. For more on the historical construction of the "illegal," see De Genova, "Spectacles of Migrant 'Illegality'"; De Genova, *Working the Boundaries*; Ngai, *Impossible Subjects*; Chavez, *Latino Threat*; and Santa Ana, *Brown Tide Rising*. For more on the historical construction of the "illegal" in the South in particular, see Ferreti, "Let's Empty the Clip"; and Guerrero, *Nuevo South*.

17. Julie Weise argues in chapter 5 of *Corazón de Dixie* that the anti-"illegal" rhetoric arrived in the South by way of California, Arizona, Fox News, and social media.

18. Notable exceptions to this trend include research by Ben Vinson III and Jennifer Jones on the Afro-Mexican populations in Winston-Salem, North Carolina.

19. For others on September 11 as a turning point in southern Latino history, see Marrow, *New Destination Dreaming*; and Rodriguez, "Constructing Mexican Atlanta."

20. For more on the historical connections between policing and immigration, see Hernandez, *Migra!*; Golash-Boza, *Deported*; Goodman, *Deportation Machine*; Kanstroom, *Deportation Nation*; Chavez, *Latino Threat*; Minian, *Undocumented Lives*; Santa Ana, *Brown Tide Rising*; Bustamante and Gamino, "'La Polimigra'"; Ordaz, *Shadow of El Centro*; Chávez-García, "Youth of Color"; and Chávez-García, *States of Delinquency*.

21. Behdad, *Forgetful Nation*; Ahmad, "Homeland Insecurities"; De Genova, "Production of Culprits"; Volpp, "Citizen and the Terrorist"; Dudziak, *September 11 in History*; Gonzales, *Reform without Justice*.

22. "National Security Entry-Exit Registration System (NSEERS)," Arab American Institute, accessed May 20, 2020, www.aaiusa.org/nseers; "Post-9/11 Backlash," South Asian Americans Leading Together, accessed September 22, 2022, https://saalt.org/policy-change/post-9-11-backlash/.

23. Coleman and Kocher, "Detention, Deportation, Devolution"; Massey, "Racial Formation in Theory and Practice"; Johnson, "September 11 and Mexican Immigrants"; Mariscal, "Homeland Security, Militarism"; Winders, "Bringing Back the (B)Order."

24. Coleman and Kocher, "Detention, Deportation, Devolution," 228.

25. Quoted in Odem and Lacy, *Latino Immigrants*, 145.

26. Hernández, "Pursuant to Deportation," 58.

27. Golash-Boza, "Parallels between Mass Incarceration and Mass Deportation," 492.
28. Bender, "Sight, Sound, and Stereotype," 1153; Johnson, "September 11 and Mexican Immigrants"; Mariscal, "Homeland Security, Militarism"; Coleman and Kocher, "Detention, Deportation, Devolution"; Massey, "Racial Formation in Theory and Practice"; Hernández, "Pursuant to Deportation"; Marrow, *New Destination Dreaming*; Jones, *Browning of the New South*.
29. Noriega interview by Ana Trejo.
30. Jose M. interview by Ana Trejo.
31. Winders, "Bringing Back the (B)Order"; Marrow, *New Destination Dreaming*.
32. Jones, *Browning of the New South*, 82.
33. Jones, *Browning of the New South*, 91.
34. Stuesse, *Scratching Out a Living*, 107.
35. Yazmin Garcia Rico interview by Eladio B. Bobadilla.
36. Zartha interview by Michael Fuhlhage.
37. Van Gelderen interview by Michael Fuhlhage.
38. Menjívar and Enchautegui, "Confluence of the Economic Recession"; Goodman, *Deportation Machine*; Golash-Boza, *Deported*.
39. Marrow, *New Destination Dreaming*.
40. "Empowering Local Law Enforcement to Combat Illegal Immigration," Hearing before the Subcommittee on Criminal Justice, Drug Policy, and Human Resources, of the Committee on Government Reform, House of Representatives, 109th Congress, Second Session, August 25, 2006, 103, accessed September 25, 2020, www.govinfo.gov/content/pkg/CHRG-109hhrg36029/html/CHRG-109hhrg36029.htm.
41. Jones, *Browning of the New South*, 85.
42. "Hatewatch," Southern Poverty Law Center, accessed April 30, 2020, www.splcenter.org/hatewatch; Odem and Lacy, *Latino Immigrants*, 146.
43. Weise, *Corazón de Dixie*.
44. Weise, *Corazón de Dixie*, 183.
45. Odem and Lacy, *Latino Immigrants*, 145.
46. Jones, *Browning of the New South*, 16.
47. Odem and Lacy, *Latino Immigrants*.
48. Jane Ruffin, "We Do Want Immigrants—Legal Ones," *Raleigh News and Observer*, February 12, 2006.
49. "Empowering Local Law Enforcement to Combat Illegal Immigration."
50. "Empowering Local Law Enforcement to Combat Illegal Immigration."
51. Chavez, *Latino Threat*; Beltrán, *Cruelty as Citizenship*; Gonzales, *Reform without Justice*.
52. Randy Capps, Marc R. Rosenblum, Muzaffar Chishti, and Cristina Rodríguez, "Delegation and Divergence: 287(g) State and Local Immigration Enforcement," Migration Policy Institute, January 2011, www.migrationpolicy.org/research/delegation-and-divergence-287g-state-and-local-immigration-enforcement.
53. Capps, Rosenblum, Chishti, and Rodríguez, "Delegation and Divergence."
54. Capps, Rosenblum, Chishti, and Rodríguez, "Delegation and Divergence."

55. Capps, Rosenblum, Chishti, and Rodríguez, "Delegation and Divergence"; "Empowering Local Law Enforcement to Combat Illegal Immigration."

56. For more on the links between racial profiling, hyperpolicing, and mass incarceration, see Alexander, *New Jim Crow*; Gilmore, *Golden Gulag*; Muhammad, *Condemnation of Blackness*; Berger, *Captive Nation*; Hernandez, *City of Inmates*; Thompson, "Why Mass Incarceration Matters"; Perkinson, *Texas Tough*; and Murch, *Living for the City*.

57. Sam Whitehead, "After Almost a Decade, an Immigration Enforcement Program Still Divides a Georgia Community," Georgia Public Broadcasting, March 21, 2017, www.gpb.org/news/2017/03/21/after-almost-decade-immigration-enforcement -program-still-divides-georgia-community.

58. Whitehead, "After Almost a Decade."

59. Browne and Odem, "'Juan Crow' in the Nuevo South?"

60. Quoted in Gill, *Latino Migration Experience*, 33.

61. Chavez, *Latino Threat*, 3, 6–7.

62. Guerrero, *Nuevo South*, 152.

63. In the wake of the attacks, xenophobia and anti-Arab racism grew. Many Muslim and Arab Americans immediately experienced increased policing in airports, suspicion from neighbors and coworkers, and vitriol in the streets. The Department of Homeland Security created the National Security Entry-Exist Registration Systems (NSEERS), which came to be known by many as the "Muslim Registry." It required nonimmigrant men and boys from predominantly Arab and Muslim-majority countries to report to an immigration office to be photographed, fingerprinted, and interviewed. NSEERS legalized racial profiling of Arab and Muslim Americans under the thinly veiled color-blind language of fighting the War on Terror. "National Security Entry-Exit Registration System (NSEERS)."

64. Sanchez, *Becoming Mexican American*.

65. Freedom of Information Act Library, Immigration and Customs Enforcement, accessed May 2, 2020, www.ice.gov/foia/library; Marrow, *New Destination Dreaming*.

66. Sanchez, *Becoming Mexican American*.

67. Mohl, "Politics of Expulsion."

68. The South was not alone in passing SB1070 copycat bills. At least twenty-four state legislatures have introduced versions of the controversial "show me your papers" bill since the original passed in the spring of 2010. Most of these bills, however, ultimately died before becoming law. Georgia, South Carolina, and Alabama were among the handful of successful states to pass SB1070-style legislation. Many of these laws featured language about crime, terrorism, and the need to obey the rule of law.

69. Robbie Brown, "Georgia Gives Police Added Power to Seek Out Illegal Immigrants," *New York Times*, May 13, 2011.

70. Seth Freed Wessler, "Welcome to the Wild, Wild South: Georgia Passes SB 1070 Copycat Bill," *Colorlines*, April 15, 2011, www.colorlines.com/articles/welcome -wild-wild-south-georgia-passes-sb-1070-copycat-bill.

71. *The Unafraid* (documentary film), directed by Anayansi Prado and Heather Courtney, 2018, https://gooddocs.net/products/the-unafraid.

72. Davis, Deaton, Boyle, and Schick, *Voices from the Nueva Frontera*.

73. Jim Davenport, "Gov. Nikki Haley Signs Illegal Immigration Police Checks Law," *Post and Courier* (Charleston, SC), June 26, 2011.

74. Asraa Mustufa, "South Carolina's Gov. Nikki Haley Makes Good on Anti-Immigrant Promises," *Colorlines*, June 30, 2011, www.colorlines.com/articles /south-carolinas-gov-nikki-haley-makes-good-anti-immigrant-promises.

75. "South Carolina's Gov. Nikki Haley Makes Good on Anti-Immigrant Promises."

76. Susan Eaton, "A New Kind of Southern Strategy," *Nation*, August 10, 2011, www .thenation.com/article/archive/new-kind-southern-strategy/.

77. Eaton, "A New Kind of Southern Strategy."

78. Brown and Jones, "Immigrant Rights Are Civil Rights."

79. Jose [pseud.] interview by author.

80. For more on the role of color in structuring race within Latino and Latin American communities, see Golash-Boza and Darity, "Latino Racial Choices"; Telles, *Pigmentocracies*; Hordge-Freeman and Veras, "Out of the Shadows"; White, "Salience of Skin Tone"; Bonilla-Silva, *White Supremacy*; and Araujo-Dawson, "Understanding the Complexities of Skin Color."

81. Zavaleta-Jimenez interview by Aliza Sir.

82. Zavaleta-Jimenez interview by Aliza Sir.

83. Weise, *Corazón de Dixie*, chap. 3.

84. Davenport, "Gov. Nikki Haley Signs Illegal Immigration Police Checks Law."

85. Brown, "Georgia Gives Police Added Power to Seek Out Illegal Immigrants."

86. Joe Sutton "Mississippi Lawmakers Pass Controversial Immigration Bill," CNN, March 16, 2012.

87. Stuesse, *Scratching Out a Living*; Engstrom, "Industry, Social Regulation, and Scale"; Mohl, "Globalization, Latinization"; Gill, *Latino Migration Experience*; Weise, *Corazón de Dixie*.

88. Mohl, "Globalization, Latinization."

89. Peggy Gargis, "Alabama Sets Nation's Toughest Immigration Law," Reuters, June 9, 2011, www.reuters.com/article/us-immigration-alabama/alabama-sets -nations-toughest-immigration-law-idUSTRE7584C920110609.

90. "Analysis of HB 56, 'Alabama Taxpayer and Citizen Protection Act,'" American Civil Liberties Union, accessed May 22, 2020, www.aclu.org/other/analysis-hb -56-alabama-taxpayer-and-citizen-protection-act.

91. Ferreti, "Let's Empty the Clip," 49.

92. Ferreti, "Let's Empty the Clip," 51.

93. Tim Henderson, "Why Hispanics Are Leaving Some Southern Counties," Pew, August 2, 2017, http://pew.org/2wiCaUR.

94. Carlito interview by author; Enrique [pseud.] interview by author; Karen [pseud.] interview by author; Maria [pseud.] interview by author.

95. "Alabama's Shame: HB 56 and the War on Immigrants," Southern Poverty Law

Center, February 1, 2012, www.splcenter.org/20120131/alabamas-shame-hb-56 -and-war-immigrants.

96. Roshell [pseud.] interview by author.

97. "Alabama's Shame."

98. "Alabama's Shame."

99. De Genova, "Spectacles of Migrant 'Illegality,'" 1182; De Genova, *Working the Boundaries.*

100. William Brown and Mary Odem, "Living across Borders: Guatemala Maya Im-migrants in the US South," *Southern Spaces*, February 16, 2011, https://southern spaces.org/2011/living-across-borders-guatemala-maya-immigrants-us-south/; Ramirez, "El Nuevo Bajio"; Stuesse, *Scratching Out a Living*; Ribas, *On the Line*; Fink, *Maya of Morganton*; Gill, *Latino Migration Experience*; Browne and Odem, "'Juan Crow' in the Nuevo South?"

101. Olivos and Sandoval, "Latina/o Identities"; Menjívar, *Fragmented Ties*; García, *Refugee Challenge*; Rodriguez and Menjívar, "Central American Immigrants."

102. Yashar, *Contesting Citizenship*; Grandin, *Blood of Guatemala*; Saldaña-Portillo, *Indian Given*; Speed, *Incarcerated Stories*; Wade, *Race and Ethnicity*; Golash-Boza and Bonilla-Silva, "Rethinking Race"; Dzidzienyo and Oboler, *Neither Enemies nor Friends*, 117–36; Castellanos, Nájera, and Aldama, *Comparative Indigeneities*; Mallon, *Decolonizing Native Histories.*

103. De Genova, "Spectacles of Migrant 'Illegality,'" 1180.

104. Gilmore, *Golden Gulag*; Robinson and Kelley, *Black Marxism*; Woods and Gilmore, *Development Arrested.*

105. Diane McWhorter, "Carry Me Home Alabama," *New York Times*, June 17, 2012.

106. "One of Alabama's Worst Times since Jim Crow," ACLU, October 13, 2011, YouTube, www.youtube.com/watch?v=fdt5MbmoKwE.

107. Márquez, "Juan Crow."

108. Willoughby-Herard, "'Whatever That Survived.'" Clyde Woods and Ruth Wilson Gilmore, *Development Arrested*, similarly argue that the economic landscape of the South today resulted from successive reconstitutions of the "plantation bloc" system. In the context of new legal realities like abolition, the passage of the Civil Rights Act, and the emergence of globalization, southern economic elites preserved labor systems that extended plantation logics long after the demise of chattel slavery.

109. Peña, *Translating Blackness.*

110. Jones, *Browning of the New South*, 70.

111. Jones, *Browning of the New South*, 188.

112. Enrique [pseud.] interview by author.

113. Collins, *Black Feminist Thought.*

114. Golash-Boza, "Parallels between Mass Incarceration and Mass Deportation"; Chavez, *Latino Threat.*

115. "Empowering Local Law Enforcement to Combat Illegal Immigration."

116. Hordge-Freeman and LoBlack, "'Cops Only See the Brown Skin'";

Hordge-Freeman and Veras, "Out of the Shadows." There are exciting develop-
ments in an oral history of Afro-Cubans in Miami by Dr. Devyn Spence Benson
and Dr. Danielle Clealand; Sawyer and Paschel, "'We Didn't Cross the Color
Line"; Nopper, "Why Black Immigrants Matter"; Molina, *How Race Is Made*;
Willoughby-Herard, "'Whatever That Survived.'"

117. Among the top birth countries for Black immigrants in 2014 were Guyana,
Dominican Republic, Mexico, Panama, and Cuba. See Carl Lipscombe, Juliana Morgan-Trostle, and Kexin Zheng, "The State of Black Immigrants," Black
Alliance for Just Immigration and NYU School of Law Immigrant Rights Clinic,
2016, https://stateofblackimmigrants.com/assets/sobi-fullreport-jan22.pdf.

118. Golash-Boza, "Parallels between Mass Incarceration and Mass Deportation."

119. Peña, *Translating Blackness*, 13–14.

120. Enrique [pseud.] interview by author.

121. Jose [pseud.] interview by author.

122. Stuesse, *Scratching Out a Living*; Ribas, *On the Line*.

123. Marrow, *New Destination Dreaming*, 124.

124. Marrow, *New Destination Dreaming*, 124.

125. Rodriguez interview by Rachel Osborn.

126. Rodriguez interview by Rachel Osborn.

127. Hernández, *Racial Innocence*.

128. Hooker, "Indigenous Inclusion/Black Exclusion"; Paschel, *Becoming Black Political
Subjects*; Rivera-Rideau, Jones, and Paschel, *Afro-Latin@s in Movement*.

129. "U.S. Hispanic Population Surpassed 60 Million in 2019, But Growth Has
Slowed," Pew Research Center, Hispanic Trends Project (blog), July 7, 2020, www
.pewresearch.org/fact-tank/2020/07/07/u-s-hispanic-population-surpassed-60
-million-in-2019-but-growth-has-slowed/.

Conclusion

1. Richard Enriquez interview by author.

2. Richard Enriquez interview by author; Rubio interview by Sarah Thuesen.

3. Rubio interview by Sarah Thuesen.

4. Rubio interview by Sarah Thuesen.

5. Rubio interview by Sarah Thuesen.

6. Ignatiev, *How the Irish Became White*; Roediger, *Wages of Whiteness*.

7. There is some work in this field by Frank Guridy, Vanessa Valdés, and Jennifer
Jones, but much more is still necessary. Pablo Jose López Oro at Smith College
is working on a project on the history of Afro-Latinos in the South, which will
certainly add a great deal to the field.

8. Roberto Lovato, "Juan Crow in Georgia," *Nation*, May 26, 2008, www.thenation
.com/article/archive/juan-crow-georgia/; Márquez, "Juan Crow."

BIBLIOGRAPHY

Interviews and Oral Histories

All interviews were conducted by the author unless otherwise noted.

Aguirre, Manuel. Oral history interview by Angela Macias, August 12, 2002. Voces Oral History Collection, University of Texas at Austin.

Campos, Juana. Interview by Hector Corporan, January 4, 1993. Anacostia Archives, Washington, DC.

Carlito, Delores. January 2, 2018.

Castro, Mauricio. June 12, 2017.

Cortez, Fatima. January 26, 2011.

de Leon, Robert. Oral history interview by Sonia Song-Ha Lee, July 21, 2005. In possession of Sonia Song-Ha Lee.

Diaz, Manny. Oral history interview by Sonia Song-Ha Lee, August 18, 2005. In possession of Sonia Song-Ha Lee.

Enrique [pseud.]. January 4, 2018.

Enriquez, Mary. March 6, 2012.

Enriquez, Richard. March 6, 2012.

Hamann, Edmund T. March 23, 2016.

Jose [pseud.]. January 4, 2018.

Karen [pseud.]. January 2, 2018.

M., Jose. Interview by Ana Trejo, August 6, 2021. In author's possession.

Maria [pseud.]. January 2, 2018.

Mártinez, Elizabeth (Betita). Oral history interviews by Loretta Ross, March 3 and August 6, 2006. Voices of Feminism Oral History Project, Sophia Smith Collection of Women's History, Smith College, Northampton, MA.

Mitchell, Erwin. Oral history interview by Bob Short, October 20, 2008. Russell Library for Political and Research Studies, University of Georgia, Athens.

Noriega, Carlos. Interview by Ana Trejo, August 10, 2021. In author's possession.

Pepe, Lori. February 20, 2019.

Ramírez, Lillian. Oral history interview by Raquel Garza, October 8, 2011. Voces Oral History Collection, University of Texas at Austin.

Rico, Jose. Oral history interview by Ariel Eure, April 11, 2011. New Roots: Voices from Carolina del Norte, Southern Historical Collection, University of North Carolina at Chapel Hill.

Rico, Yazmin Garcia. Oral history interview by Eladio B. Bobadilla, March 6, 2015. Southern Oral History Program Collection, University of North Carolina at Chapel Hill.

Rodriguez, Edgar. Oral history interview by Rachel Osborn, March 2, 2008. Southern Oral History Program Collection, University of North Carolina at Chapel Hill.

Roshell [pseud.]. January 5, 2018.

Rubio, Isabel. Oral history interview by Sarah Thuesen, August 17, 2006. Southern Oral History Program Collection, University of North Carolina at Chapel Hill.

Soto, Alice. Interview by Richard Enriquez, May 1, 1991. In author's possession.

Todd, Fatima Cortez. Oral history interview by junior and senior high school students of the D.C. Everest Area School District, 2012, D.C. Everest Oral History Project, Weston, WI. Accessed September 21, 2022.

Van Gelderen, Federico. Interview by Michael Fuhlhage, February 28, 2008. Southern Oral History Program Collection, University of North Carolina at Chapel Hill.

Varela, Maria. January 17, 2012.

Zapata, Luis. April 18, 2010; May 19, 2010; March 21, 2012.

Zartha, Rafael Prieto. Oral history interview by Michael Fuhlhage, March 28, 2008. Southern Oral History Program Collection, University of North Carolina at Chapel Hill.

Zavaleta-Jimenez, Irving. Oral history interview by Aliza Sir, April 4, 2013. Southern Oral History Program Collection, University of North Carolina at Chapel Hill.

Zúñiga, Victor. April 11, 2016.

Manuscript Collections and Archives

Athens, GA
    Richard B. Russell Library, University of Georgia
        Georgia Project Records
Chapel Hill, NC
    Wilson Library Special Collections, University of North Carolina at Chapel Hill
        Southern Historical Collection
        Southern Oral History Program Collection
            New Roots: Voices from Carolina del Norte
Charlottesville, VA
    University of Virginia Special Collections
        Student Nonviolent Coordinating Committee Papers
Columbia, SC
    South Caroliniana Library, University of South Carolina
Durham, NC
    Rubenstein Library, Duke University
        University Archives
Stanford, CA
    Stanford University Special Collections
        Ernesto Galarza Papers
Washington, DC
    Charles Sumner School Museum and Archives
    Smithsonian Institution Collection

Online Archival Sources

Gale Digital Database
   American Civil Liberties Union Papers
ProQuest History Vault
   National Association for the Advancement of Colored People Papers

Periodicals

Atlanta Daily World
Baltimore Afro-American
Charlotte (NC) Observer
Chicago Defender
Daily Citizen-News (Dalton, GA)
Daily Tar Heel (Chapel Hill, NC)
Dillon (SC) Herald
Enterprise Journal (McComb, MS)
Florence (SC) Morning News
Georgia: The University of Georgia
   Magazine
Georgia Trend Magazine
Harvard Law Review
Jackson (MS) Sun
Narratives
The Nation
New York Times
Norfolk Journal and Guide

North Carolina Catholic
Northwest Arkansas Times
Pittsburgh Courier
Post and Courier (Charleston, SC)
La Prensa (San Antonio, TX)
Raleigh (NC) News & Observer
Richmond-Times Dispatch
Southern Patriot
Southern Spaces
Sunday Oregonian
El Tiempo (Dalton, GA)
Time
Times (Louisiana)
Times-Picayune (New Orleans, LA)
Toledo Blade
Wall Street Journal
Washington Post Magazine
Washington Tribune

Books and Journal Articles

Abel, Elizabeth. *Signs of the Times: The Visual Politics of Jim Crow*. Berkeley: University of California Press, 2010.

Acuña, Rodolfo. *Occupied America: A History of Chicanos*. 8th ed. Boston: Pearson, 2015.

Ahmad, Muneer. "Homeland Insecurities: Racial Violence the Day after September 11." *Race/Ethnicity: Multidisciplinary Global Contexts* 4, no. 3 (2011): 337–50.

Alcoff, Linda Martín. "Is Latina/o Identity a Racial Identity?" In *Hispanics/Latinos in the United States*, edited by Jorge J. E. Gracia and Pablo de Greiff, 23–44. New York: Routledge, 2000.

———. "Latinos beyond the Binary." *Southern Journal of Philosophy* 47, no. S1 (2009): 112–28.

Aldama, Frederick Luis, ed. *Latinx TV in the Twenty-First Century*. Tucson: University of Arizona Press, 2022.

Alexander, Michelle. *The New Jim Crow*. New York: New Press, 2012.

Allen, Craig. *Univision, Telemundo, and the Rise of Spanish-Language Television in the United States*. Gainesville: University Press of Florida, 2020.

Allen, James. *Without Sanctuary: Lynching Photography in America*. Santa Fe, NM: Twin Palms, 1999.

Almaguer, Tomas. *Racial Fault Lines: The Historical Origins of White Supremacy in California*. With a new preface edition. Berkeley: University of California Press, 2008.

Alonzo, Juan J. *Badmen, Bandits, and Folk Heroes: The Ambivalence of Mexican American Identity in Literature and Film*. Tucson: University of Arizona Press, 2009.

Alvarez, Luis. *The Power of the Zoot: Youth Culture and Resistance during World War II*. Berkeley: University of California Press, 2008.

Amezcua, Mike. "Beautiful Urbanism: Gender, Landscape, and Contestation in Latino Chicago's Age of Urban Renewal." *Journal of American History* 104, no. 1 (2017): 97–119.

Anderson, Carol. *Eyes Off the Prize: The United Nations and the African American Struggle for Human Rights, 1994–1955*. Cambridge, UK: Cambridge University Press, 2003.

Andrews, George Reid. *Afro-Latin America: Black Lives, 1600–2000*. Cambridge, MA: Harvard University Press, 2016.

Aparicio, Frances R., and Susana Chávez-Silverman, eds. *Tropicalizations: Transcultural Representations of Latinidad*. Hanover, NH: Dartmouth College Press, 1997.

Araiza, Lauren. *To March for Others: The Black Freedom Struggle and the United Farm Workers*. Philadelphia: University of Pennsylvania Press, 2013.

Araujo-Dawson, Beverly. "Understanding the Complexities of Skin Color, Perceptions of Race, and Discrimination among Cubans, Dominicans, and Puerto Ricans." *Hispanic Journal of Behavioral Sciences* 37, no. 2 (2015): 243–56.

Aron, Cindy S. *Working at Play: A History of Vacations in the United States*. New York: Oxford University Press, 2001.

Arredondo, Gabriela F. *Mexican Chicago: Race, Identity and Nation, 1916–39*. Urbana: University of Illinois Press, 2008.

Arsenault, Raymond. *Freedom Riders: 1961 and the Struggle for Racial Justice*. New York: Oxford University Press, 2007.

Asch, Chris Myers, and George Derek Musgrove. *Chocolate City: A History of Race and Democracy in the Nation's Capital*. Chapel Hill: University of North Carolina Press, 2017.

Ashmore, Susan Youngblood. *Carry It On: The War on Poverty and the Civil Rights Movement in Alabama, 1964–1972*. Athens: University of Georgia Press, 2008.

Austin, Paula C. *Coming of Age in Jim Crow DC: Navigating the Politics of Everyday Life*. New York: New York University Press, 2019.

Ayers, Edward L. *The Promise of the New South: Life After Reconstruction*. 15th anniversary ed. New York: Oxford University Press, 2007.

Baldwin, James. *The Price of the Ticket: Collected Nonfiction, 1948–1985*. New York: St. Martin's, 1985.

Barber, Llana. *Latino City: Immigration and Urban Crisis in Lawrence, Massachusetts, 1945–2000*. Chapel Hill: University of North Carolina Press, 2017.

Barber, Lucy G. *Marching on Washington: The Forging of an American Political Tradition.* 2nd ed. Berkeley: University of California Press, 2002.

Bartley, Numan V. *The Rise of Massive Resistance: Race and Politics in the South during the 1950s.* Baton Rouge: Louisiana State University Press, 1999.

Bates, Beth Tompkins. *Pullman Porters and the Rise of Protest Politics in Black America, 1925–1945.* Chapel Hill: University of North Carolina Press, 2001.

Bebout, Lee. *Whiteness on the Border: Mapping the US Racial Imagination in Brown and White.* New York: New York University Press, 2016.

Behdad, Ali. *A Forgetful Nation: On Immigration and Cultural Identity in the United States.* Durham, NC: Duke University Press, 2005.

Behnken, Brian D. *Fighting Their Own Battles: Mexican Americans, African Americans, and the Struggle for Civil Rights in Texas.* Chapel Hill: University of North Carolina Press, 2011.

———. "The Movement in the Mirror: Civil Rights and the Causes of Black-Brown Disunity in Texas." In *The Struggle in Black and Brown: African American and Mexican American Relations during the Civil Rights Era*, edited by Brian D. Behnken, 49–77. Lincoln: University of Nebraska, 2011.

———, ed. *The Struggle in Black and Brown: African American and Mexican American Relations during the Civil Rights Era.* Lincoln: University of Nebraska Press, 2012.

Beltrán, Cristina. *Cruelty as Citizenship: How Migrant Suffering Sustains White Democracy.* Minneapolis: University of Minnesota Press, 2020.

———. *The Trouble with Unity: Latino Politics and the Creation of Identity.* New York: Oxford University Press, 2010.

Bender, Steven W. "Sight, Sound, and Stereotype: The War on Terrorism and Its Consequences for Latinas/os." *Oregon Law Review* 81, no. 4 (2002): 1153–78.

Benson, Devyn Spence. *Antiracism in Cuba: The Unfinished Revolution.* Chapel Hill: University of North Carolina Press, 2016.

Berg, Charles Ramírez. *Latino Images in Film: Stereotypes, Subversion, and Resistance.* Austin: University of Texas Press, 2002.

Berger, Dan. *Captive Nation: Black Prison Organizing in the Civil Rights Era.* Chapel Hill: University of North Carolina Press, 2014.

Berger, Dina. *The Development of Mexico's Tourism Industry: Pyramids by Day, Martinis by Night.* New York: Palgrave MacMillan, 2006.

Berger, Dina, and Andrew Grant Wood, eds. *Holiday in Mexico: Critical Reflections on Tourism and Tourist Encounters.* Durham, NC: Duke University Press, 2010.

Bernstein, Shana. *Bridges of Reform: Interracial Civil Rights Activism in Twentieth-Century Los Angeles.* Oxford, UK: Oxford University Press, 2011.

Berrey, Stephen A. *The Jim Crow Routine: Everyday Performances of Race, Civil Rights, and Segregation in Mississippi.* Chapel Hill: University of North Carolina Press, 2015.

Biondi, Martha. *To Stand and Fight: The Struggle for Civil Rights in Postwar New York City.* Cambridge, MA: Harvard University Press, 2006.

Blackwell, Maylei. *¡Chicana Power!: Contested Histories of Feminism in the Chicano Movement.* Austin: University of Texas Press, 2011.

Blanton, Carlos K. "George I. Sanchez, Ideology, and Whiteness in the Making of the Mexican American Civil Rights Movement, 1930–1960." *Journal of Southern History* 72, no. 3 (2006): 569–604.

———. *George I. Sánchez: The Long Fight for Mexican American Integration*. New Haven, CT: Yale University Press, 2015.

Blight, David W. *American Oracle: The Civil War in the Civil Rights Era*. Cambridge, MA: Harvard University Press, 2013.

———. *Race and Reunion: The Civil War in American Memory*. Cambridge, MA: Harvard University Press, 2002.

Bloom, Joshua, and Waldo E. Martin Jr. *Black against Empire: The History and Politics of the Black Panther Party*. With a new preface. Berkeley: University of California Press, 2016.

Blu, Karen I. *The Lumbee Problem: The Making of an American Indian People*. Lincoln: University of Nebraska Press, 2001.

Bonilla-Silva, Eduardo. *Racism without Racists: Color-Blind Racism and the Persistence of Racial Inequality in America*. 3rd ed. Lanham, MD: Rowman & Littlefield, 2009.

———. *White Supremacy and Racism in the Post-Civil Rights Era*. Boulder, CO: Lynne Rienner, 2001.

Borstelmann, Thomas. *The Cold War and the Color Line: American Race Relations in the Global Arena*. Cambridge, MA: Harvard University Press, 2003.

Bow, Leslie. *Partly Colored: Asian Americans and Racial Anomaly in the Segregated South*. New York: New York University Press, 2010.

Brilliant, Mark. *The Color of America Has Changed: How Racial Diversity Shaped Civil Rights Reform in California, 1941–1978*. New York, Oxford: Oxford University Press, 2012.

Brinson, Claudia Smith. *Stories of Struggle: The Clash over Civil Rights in South Carolina*. Columbia: University of South Carolina Press, 2020.

Brown, Flora Bryant. "NAACP Sponsored Sit-Ins by Howard University Students in Washington, D.C., 1943–1944." *Journal of Negro History* 85, no. 4 (Fall 2000): 274–86.

Brown, Hana, and Jennifer A. Jones. "Immigrant Rights Are Civil Rights." *Contexts* 15, no. 2 (2016): 34–39.

Browne, Irene, and Mary Odem. "'Juan Crow' in the Nuevo South? Racialization of Guatemalan and Dominican Immigrants in the Atlanta Metro Area." *Du Bois Review: Social Science Research on Race* 9, no. 2 (2012): 321–37.

Burgos, Adrian. *Playing America's Game: Baseball, Latinos, and the Color Line*. Berkeley: University of California Press, 2007.

Bustamante, Juan José, and Eric Gamino. "'La Polimigra': A Social Construct behind the 'Deportation Regime' in the Greater Northwest Arkansas Region." *Humanity and Society* 42, no. 3 (2018): 344–66.

Cadava, Geraldo. *The Hispanic Republican: The Shaping of an American Political Identity, from Nixon to Trump*. New York: HarperCollins, 2020.

———. *Standing on Common Ground: The Making of a Sunbelt Borderland*. Cambridge, MA: Harvard University Press, 2013.

Camarillo, Albert M. "Navigating Segregated Life in America's Racial Borderhoods, 1910s–1950s." *Journal of American History* 100, no. 3 (2013): 645–62.

Candelario, Ginetta E. B. *Black behind the Ears: Dominican Racial Identity from Museums to Beauty Shops.* Durham, NC: Duke University Press, 2007.

Caplan, Marvin. "Eat Anywhere!" *Washington History* 1, no. 1 (1989): 24–39.

Carson, Clayborne. *In Struggle: SNCC and the Black Awakening of the 1960s.* Cambridge, MA: Harvard University Press, 1995.

Castellanos, M. Bianet, Lourdes Gutiérrez Nájera, and Arturo J. Aldama. *Comparative Indigeneities of the Américas: Toward a Hemispheric Approach.* Tucson: University of Arizona Press, 2012.

Catsam, Derek Charles. "Early Economic Civil Rights in Washington, DC: The New Negro Alliance, Howard University, and the Interracial Workshop." In *The Economic Civil Rights Movement: African Americans and the Struggle for Economic Power*, edited by Michael Ezra, 46–57. London: Taylor & Francis, 2013.

———. *Freedom's Main Line: The Journey of Reconciliation and the Freedom Rides.* Lexington: University Press of Kentucky, 2009.

Chafe, William. *Civilities and Civil Rights: Greensboro, North Carolina, and the Black Struggle for Freedom.* New York: Oxford University Press, 1980.

Chamberlain, Charles D. *Victory at Home: Manpower and Race in the American South during World War II.* Athens: University of Georgia Press, 2003.

Charron, Katherine Mellen. *Freedom's Teacher: The Life of Septima Clark.* Chapel Hill: University of North Carolina Press, 2009.

Chávez, Ernesto. *"¡Mi Raza Primero!" (My People First!): Nationalism, Identity, and Insurgency in the Chicano Movement in Los Angeles, 1966–1978.* Berkeley: University of California Press, 2002.

Chavez, Karma R. *Queer Migration Politics: Activist Rhetoric and Coalitional Possibilities.* Urbana: University of Illinois Press, 2013.

Chavez, Leo. *The Latino Threat: Constructing Immigrants, Citizens, and the Nation.* 2nd ed. Stanford, CA: Stanford University Press, 2013.

Chávez-García, Miroslava. *States of Delinquency: Race and Science in the Making of California's Juvenile Justice System.* Berkeley: University of California Press, 2012.

———. "Youth of Color and California's Carceral State: The Fred C. Nelles Youth Correctional Facility." *Journal of American History* 102, no. 1 (2015): 47–60.

Cheng, Wendy. *The Changs Next Door to the Díazes: Remapping Race in Suburban California.* Minneapolis: University of Minnesota Press, 2013.

Clealand, Danielle Pilar. *The Power of Race in Cuba: Racial Ideology and Black Consciousness during the Revolution.* Oxford: Oxford University Press, 2017.

Cobb, James C. *Away Down South: A History of Southern Identity.* Oxford, UK: Oxford University Press, 2007.

———. *The Most Southern Place on Earth: The Mississippi Delta and the Roots of Regional Identity.* New York: Oxford University Press, 1994.

Cocks, Catherine. *Tropical Whites: The Rise of the Tourist South in the Americas.* Philadelphia: University of Pennsylvania Press, 2013.

Coleman, Mathew, and Austin Kocher. "Detention, Deportation, Devolution and Immigrant Incapacitation in the US, Post 9/11." *Geographical Journal* 177, no. 3 (2011): 228–37.

Collins, Patricia Hill. *Black Feminist Thought: Knowledge, Consciousness, and the Politics of Empowerment*. Rev. 10th anniversary ed. 2nd ed. London: Routledge, 1999.

Connolly, N. D. *A World More Concrete: Real Estate and the Remaking of Jim Crow South Florida*. Chicago: University of Chicago Press, 2016.

Cook, Robert. *Troubled Commemoration: The American Civil War Centennial, 1961–1965*. Baton Rouge: Louisiana State University Press, 2007.

Coulthard, Glen Sean. *Red Skin, White Masks: Rejecting the Colonial Politics of Recognition*. Minneapolis: University of Minnesota Press, 2014.

Coward, John M. *Indians Illustrated: The Image of Native Americans in the Pictorial Press*. Urbana: University of Illinois Press, 2016.

Cox, Karen L., ed. *Destination Dixie: Tourism and Southern History*. Gainesville: University Press of Florida, 2014.

———. *Dreaming of Dixie: How the South Was Created in American Popular Culture*. Chapel Hill: University of North Carolina Press, 2011.

Crenshaw, Kimberlé, Neil Gotanda, Gary Peller, and Kendall Thomas, eds. *Critical Race Theory: The Key Writings That Formed the Movement*. New York: New Press, 1996.

Crespino, Joseph. *Strom Thurmond's America*. New York: Hill and Wang, 2012.

Crosby, Emilye, ed. *Civil Rights History from the Ground Up: Local Struggles, a National Movement*. Athens: University of Georgia Press, 2011.

———. *A Little Taste of Freedom: The Black Freedom Struggle in Claiborne County, Mississippi*. Chapel Hill: University of North Carolina Press, 2005.

Cruse, Harold. "A Negro Looks at Cuba." In *The Essential Harold Cruse: A Reader*, edited by William Jelani Cobb, 8–20. New York: Palgrave, 2002.

Cruz-Janzen, Marta I. "Madre Patria (Mother Country): Latino Identity and Rejections of Blackness." *Trotter Review* 17, no. 1 (2007): 79–92.

Dailey, Jane, Glenda Elizabeth Gilmore, and Bryant Simon, eds. *Jumpin' Jim Crow: Politics from Civil War to Civil Rights*. Princeton, NJ: Princeton University Press, 2000.

Dash, J. Michael. *The Other America: Caribbean Literature in a New World Context*. Charlottesville: University of Virginia Press, 1998.

Dávila, Arlene. *Latinos, Inc.: The Marketing and Making of a People*. Berkeley: University of California Press, 2001.

———. *Latino Spin: Public Image and the Whitewashing of Race*. New York: New York University Press, 2008.

———. "The Latin Side of Madison Avenue: Marketing and the Language That Makes Us 'Hispanics.'" In *Mambo Montage: The Latinization of New York*, edited by Agustín Laó-Montes and Arlene Dávila, 411–24. New York: Columbia University Press, 2001.

Davis, Angela Y. *Women, Race and Class*. New York: Knopf Doubleday, 1983.

Davis, Donald E., Thomas M. Deaton, David P. Boyle, and Jo-Anne Schick, eds. *Voices from the Nueva Frontera: Latino Immigration in Dalton, Georgia*. Knoxville: University of Tennessee Press, 2009.

De Genova, Nicholas. "The Production of Culprits: From Deportability to Detainability in the Aftermath of 'Homeland Security.'" *Citizenship Studies* 11, no. 5 (2007): 421–48.

———. "Spectacles of Migrant 'Illegality': The Scene of Exclusion, the Obscene of Inclusion." *Ethnic and Racial Studies* 36, no. 7 (2013): 1180–98.

———. *Working the Boundaries: Race, Space, and "Illegality" in Mexican Chicago*. Durham, NC: Duke University Press, 2005.

De Genova, Nicholas, and Ana Yolanda Ramos-Zayas. *Latino Crossings: Mexicans, Puerto Ricans, and the Politics of Race and Citizenship*. New York: Taylor & Francis, 2003.

de la Cadena, Marisol. "Reconstructing Race: Racism, Culture and Mestizaje in Latin America." *NACLA Report on the Americas* 34, no. 6 (2001): 16–23.

de la Fuente, Alejandro. *A Nation for All: Race, Inequality, and Politics in Twentieth-Century Cuba*. Chapel Hill: University of North Carolina Press, 2001.

De León, Arnoldo. *They Called Them Greasers: Anglo Attitudes toward Mexicans in Texas, 1821–1900*. Austin: University of Texas Press, 1983.

Deloria, Philip J. *Playing Indian*. New Haven, CT: Yale University Press, 1999.

Denning, Michael. *The Cultural Front: The Laboring of American Culture in the Twentieth Century*. London: Verso, 2010.

de Oca Ricks, Maria Montes. "Ernesto Galarza." In *Dictionary of Literary Biography, Chicano Writers, Second Series*, Vol. 122, edited by Francisco A. Lomelí and Carl R. Shirley. Detroit, MI: Gale Research, 1992.

de Onís, Catalina (Kathleen) M. "What's in an 'x'? An Exchange about the Politics of 'Latinx.'" *Chiricú Journal: Latina/o Literatures, Arts, and Cultures* 1, no. 2 (2017): 78–91.

Devlin, Rachel. *A Girl Stands at the Door: The Generation of Young Women Who Desegregated America's Schools*. New York: Basic Books, 2018.

Dilworth, Leah. *Imagining Indians in the Southwest: Persistent Visions of a Primitive Past*. Washington, DC: Smithsonian Institution Scholarly Press, 1997.

Dittmer, John. *Local People: The Struggle for Civil Rights in Mississippi*. Urbana: University of Illinois Press, 1995.

Dochuk, Darren. *From Bible Belt to Sunbelt: Plain-Folk Religion, Grassroots Politics, and the Rise of Evangelical Conservatism*. New York: W. W. Norton, 2010.

Domínguez, Esteban Morales. *Race in Cuba: Essays on the Revolution and Racial Inequality*. New York: Monthly Review, 2012.

Donato, Rubén, and Jarrod Hanson. "'Porque Tenían Sangre de "NEGROS"': The Exclusion of Mexican Children from a Louisiana School, 1915–1916." *Association of Mexican American Educators Journal* 11, no. 1 (2017): 125–45.

Dowling, Julie A. *Mexican Americans and the Question of Race*. Austin: University of Texas Press, 2014.

Duany, Jorge. "Reconstructing Racial Identity: Ethnicity, Color, and Class among Dominicans in the United States and Puerto Rico." *Latin American Perspectives* 25, no. 3 (1998): 147–72.

Dubin, Steven C. "Symbolic Slavery: Black Representations in Popular Culture." *Social Problems* 34, no. 2 (1987): 122–40.

Du Bois, W. E. B. *Dusk of Dawn (The Oxford W. E. B. Du Bois)*. New York: Oxford University Press, 2014.

Du Bois, W. E. B., and David Levering Lewis. *Black Reconstruction in America, 1860–1880*. New York: Free Press, 1998.

Duck, Leigh Anne. *The Nation's Region: Southern Modernism, Segregation, and U.S. Nationalism*. Athens: University of Georgia Press, 2006.

Dudziak, Mary L. *Cold War Civil Rights: Race and the Image of American Democracy*. Princeton, NJ: Princeton University Press, 2011.

———, ed. *September 11 in History: A Watershed Moment?* Durham, NC: Duke University Press, 2003.

Dunbar-Ortiz, Roxanne. *An Indigenous Peoples' History of the United States*. Boston: Beacon Press, 2015.

Dzidzienyo, Anani, and Suzanne Oboler. *Neither Enemies nor Friends: Latinos, Blacks, Afro-Latinos*. New York: Palgrave Macmillan, 2005.

Estes, Nick. *Our History Is the Future: Standing Rock versus the Dakota Access Pipeline, and the Long Tradition of Indigenous Resistance*. London: Verso, 2019.

Fahs, Alice, and Joan Waugh, eds. *The Memory of the Civil War in American Culture*. Chapel Hill: University of North Carolina Press, 2004.

Fairbanks, Robert B. *The War on Slums in the Southwest: Public Housing and Slum Clearance in Texas, Arizona, and New Mexico, 1935–1965*. Philadelphia: Temple University Press, 2014.

Feimster, Crystal N. *Southern Horrors: Women and the Politics of Rape and Lynching*. Cambridge, MA: Harvard University Press, 2011.

Fernández, Delia. "Becoming Latino: Mexican and Puerto Rican Community Formation in Grand Rapids, Michigan, 1926–1964." *Michigan Historical Review* 39, no. 1 (2013): 71–100.

Fernández, Johanna. *The Young Lords: A Radical History*. Chapel Hill: University of North Carolina Press, 2020.

Fernández, Lilia. *Brown in the Windy City: Mexicans and Puerto Ricans in Postwar Chicago*. Chicago: University of Chicago Press, 2014.

Fields, Barbara J. "Whiteness, Racism, and Identity." *International Labor and Working-Class History* 60 (Fall 2001): 48–56.

Fields, Karen E., and Barbara J. Fields. *Racecraft: The Soul of Inequality in American Life*. London: Verso, 2014.

Figueroa, Mónica G. Moreno. "Distributed Intensities: Whiteness, Mestizaje and the Logics of Mexican Racism." *Ethnicities* 10, no. 3 (2010): 387–401.

Fink, Leon. *The Maya of Morganton: Work and Community in the Nuevo New South*. Chapel Hill: University of North Carolina Press, 2003.

Flamming, Douglas. *Creating the Modern South: Millhands and Managers in Dalton, Georgia, 1884–1984*. Chapel Hill: University of North Carolina Press, 1992.

Fleming, Cynthia Griggs. *Soon We Will Not Cry: The Liberation of Ruby Doris Smith Robinson*. Lanham, MD: Rowman & Littlefield, 1998.

Flores, Juan, and Miriam Jiménez Román. "Triple-Consciousness? Approaches to

Afro-Latino Culture in the United States." *Latin American and Caribbean Ethnic Studies* 4, no. 3 (2009): 319–28.

Flores, Lori A. *Grounds for Dreaming: Mexican Americans, Mexican Immigrants, and the California Farmworker Movement.* New Haven, CT: Yale University Press, 2018.

Foley, Neil. *Quest for Equality: The Failed Promise of Black-Brown Solidarity.* Cambridge, MA: Harvard University Press, 2010.

———. *Reflexiones 1997: New Directions in Mexican American Studies.* Austin: Center for Mexican American Studies, University of Texas at Austin, 1998.

———. *The White Scourge: Mexicans, Blacks, and Poor Whites in Texas Cotton Culture.* Berkeley: University of California Press, 1999.

Ford, Tanisha C. *Liberated Threads: Black Women, Style, and the Global Politics of Soul.* Chapel Hill: University of North Carolina Press, 2017.

———. "SNCC Women, Denim, and the Politics of Dress." *Journal of Southern History* 79, no. 3 (2013): 625–59.

Forman, James. *The Making of Black Revolutionaries.* Seattle: University of Washington Press, 1997.

Forner, Karlyn. *Why the Vote Wasn't Enough for Selma.* Durham, NC: Duke University Press, 2017.

Foster, Gaines M. *Ghosts of the Confederacy: Defeat, the Lost Cause, and the Emergence of the New South, 1865–1913.* New York: Oxford University Press, 1988.

Frazier, Nishani. *Harambee City: The Congress of Racial Equality in Cleveland and the Rise of Black Power Populism.* Fayetteville: University of Arkansas Press, 2017.

Frye, Gaillard. *Cradle of Freedom: Alabama and the Movement That Changed America.* Tuscaloosa: University of Alabama Press, 2004.

Galarza, Ernesto. *Barrio Boy: With Connections.* Austin, TX: Holt McDougal, 1999.

Gallagher, Gary. *Causes Won, Lost, and Forgotten: How Hollywood and Popular Art Shape What We Know about the Civil War.* Chapel Hill: University of North Carolina Press, 2013.

García, Ignacio M. *Chicanismo: The Forging of a Militant Ethos among Mexican Americans.* 3rd ed. Tucson: University of Arizona Press, 1997.

———. *White But Not Equal: Mexican Americans, Jury Discrimination, and the Supreme Court.* Tucson: University of Arizona Press, 2009.

García, María Cristina. *The Refugee Challenge in Post-Cold War America.* New York: Oxford University Press, 2020.

García, Mario T. *Mexican Americans: Leadership, Ideology, and Identity, 1930–1960.* New Haven, CT: Yale University Press, 1991.

García-Peña, Lorgia. *The Borders of Dominicanidad: Race, Nation, and Archives of Contradiction.* Durham, NC: Duke University Press, 2016.

———. "Translating Blackness." *Black Scholar* 45, no. 2 (2015): 10–20.

———. *Translating Blackness: Latinx Colonialities in Global Perspective.* Durham, NC: Duke University Press, 2022.

Gaytán, Marie Sarita. "'Una Copita Amigo': Ethnic Mexicans, Consumer Culture, and the American Marketplace." *Latino Studies* 14, no. 4 (2016): 458–81.

Gill, Hannah. *The Latino Migration Experience in North Carolina: New Roots in the Old North State*. 2nd ed. Chapel Hill: University of North Carolina Press, 2018.

Gilmore, Glenda Elizabeth. *Defying Dixie: The Radical Roots of Civil Rights, 1919–1950*. New York: W. W. Norton, 2009.

Gilmore, Ruth Wilson. *Golden Gulag: Prisons, Surplus, Crisis, and Opposition in Globalizing California*. Berkeley: University of California Press, 2007.

Glotzer, Paige. *How the Suburbs Were Segregated: Developers and the Business of Exclusionary Housing, 1890–1960*. New York: Columbia University Press, 2020.

Golash-Boza, Tanya Maria. *Deported: Immigrant Policing, Disposable Labor and Global Capitalism*. New York: New York University Press, 2015.

———. "The Parallels between Mass Incarceration and Mass Deportation: An Intersectional Analysis of State Repression." *Journal of World-Systems Research* 22, no. 2 (2016): 484–509.

Golash-Boza, Tanya, and Eduardo Bonilla-Silva. "Rethinking Race, Racism, Identity and Ideology in Latin America." *Ethnic and Racial Studies* 36, no. 10 (2013): 1485–89.

Golash-Boza, Tanya, and William Darity. "Latino Racial Choices: The Effects of Skin Colour and Discrimination on Latinos' and Latinas' Racial Self-Identifications." *Ethnic and Racial Studies* 31, no. 5 (2008): 899–934.

Goldsby, Jacqueline. *A Spectacular Secret: Lynching in American Life and Literature*. Chicago: University of Chicago Press, 2006.

Goldstein, Eric L. *The Price of Whiteness: Jews, Race, and American Identity*. Princeton, NJ: Princeton University Press, 2008.

Goluboff, Risa L. *The Lost Promise of Civil Rights*. Cambridge, MA: Harvard University Press, 2010.

Gomez, Laura E. *Manifest Destinies: The Making of the Mexican American Race*. New York: New York University Press, 2008.

Gómez-Quiñones, Juan, and Irene Vásquez. *Making Aztlán: Ideology and Culture of the Chicana and Chicano Movement, 1966–1977*. Albuquerque: University of New Mexico Press, 2014.

Gonda, Jeffrey D. *Unjust Deeds: The Restrictive Covenant Cases and the Making of the Civil Rights Movement*. Chapel Hill: University of North Carolina Press, 2015.

Gonzales, Alfonso. *Reform without Justice: Latino Migrant Politics and the Homeland Security State*. Oxford, UK: Oxford University Press, 2014.

Gonzalez, Gilbert G. *Chicano Education in the Era of Segregation*. Denton: University of North Texas Press, 2013.

Goodman, Adam. *The Deportation Machine: America's Long History of Expelling Immigrants*. Princeton, NJ: Princeton University Press, 2020.

Gracia, Jorge, ed. *Forging People: Race, Ethnicity, and Nationality in Hispanic American and Latinx Thought*. Notre Dame, IN: University of Notre Dame Press, 2011.

Grandin, Greg. *The Blood of Guatemala: A History of Race and Nation*. Durham, NC: Duke University Press, 2000.

Green, Constance McLaughlin. *The Secret City: A History of Race Relations in the Nation's Capital*. Princeton, NJ: Princeton University Press, 1967.

Greenbaum, Susan D. *More Than Black: Afro-Cubans in Tampa*. Gainesville: University Press of Florida, 2002.

Greenberg, Cheryl, ed. *A Circle of Trust: Remembering SNCC*. New Brunswick, NJ: Rutgers University Press, 1998.

Greene, Christina. *Our Separate Ways: Women and the Black Freedom Movement in Durham, North Carolina*. Chapel Hill: University of North Carolina Press, 2005.

Griffith, David. "Rural Industry and Mexican Immigration and Settlement in North Carolina." In *New Destinations: Mexican Immigration in the United States*, edited by Victor Zúñiga and Rubén Hernández-León, 244–73. New York: Russell Sage, 2005.

Grillo, Evelio. *Black Cuban, Black American: A Memoir*. Houston, TX: Arte Público, 2000.

Gross, Ariela J. *What Blood Won't Tell: A History of Race on Trial in America*. Cambridge, MA: Harvard University Press, 2008.

Gudmundson, Lowell, and Justin Wolfe, eds. *Blacks and Blackness in Central America: Between Race and Place*. Durham, NC: Duke University Press, 2010.

Guerrero, Perla M. *Nuevo South: Latinas/os, Asians, and the Remaking of Place*. Austin: University of Texas Press, 2017.

Guglielmo, Thomas A. *White on Arrival: Italians, Race, Color, and Power in Chicago, 1890–1945*. New York: Oxford University Press, 2004.

Guidotti-Hernández, Nicole M. "Affective Communities and Millennial Desires: Latinx, or Why My Computer Won't Recognize Latina/o." *Cultural Dynamics* 29, no. 3 (2017): 141–59.

Guridy, Frank Andre. *Forging Diaspora: Afro-Cubans and African Americans in a World of Empire and Jim Crow*. Chapel Hill: University of North Carolina Press, 2010.

Gutiérrez, David G. *Walls and Mirrors: Mexican Americans, Mexican Immigrants, and the Politics of Ethnicity*. Berkeley: University of California Press, 1995.

Hale, Grace Elizabeth. "'For Colored' and 'For White': Segregating Consumption in the South." In *Jumpin' Jim Crow: Southern Politics from Civil War to Civil Rights*, edited by Jane Dailey, Glenda Elizabeth Gilmore, and Bryant Simon, 162–82. Princeton, NJ: Princeton University Press, 2000.

———. *Making Whiteness: The Culture of Segregation in the South, 1890–1940*. New York: Vintage, 1999.

———. *A Nation of Outsiders: How the White Middle Class Fell in Love with Rebellion in Postwar America*. New York: Oxford University Press, 2011.

Hale, Jon N. *The Freedom Schools: Student Activists in the Mississippi Civil Rights Movement*. New York: Columbia University Press, 2016.

Hall, Jacquelyn Dowd. *Revolt against Chivalry: Jessie Daniel Ames and the Women's Campaign Against Lynching*. New York: Columbia University Press, 1993.

Hamilton, Tikia. "The Cost of Integration: The Contentious Career of Garnet C. Wilkinson." *Washington History* 30, no. 1 (Spring 2018): 50–60.

Hamlin, Francoise N. *Crossroads at Clarksdale: The Black Freedom Struggle in the Mississippi Delta after World War II*. Chapel Hill: University of North Carolina Press, 2012.

Hartman, Saidiya V. *Scenes of Subjection: Terror, Slavery, and Self-Making in Nineteenth-Century America*. New York: Oxford University Press, 1997.

Hernández, David Manuel. "Pursuant to Deportation: Latinos and Immigrant Detention." *Latino Studies* 6 (2008): 35–63.

Hernandez, Kelly Lytle. *City of Inmates: Conquest, Rebellion, and the Rise of Human Caging in Los Angeles, 1771–1965.* Chapel Hill: University of North Carolina Press, 2017.

———. *Migra!: A History of the U.S. Border Patrol.* Berkeley: University of California Press, 2010.

Hernández, Tanya Katerí. "Afro-Mexicans and the Chicano Movement: The Unknown Story." *California Law Review* 92, no. 5 (2004): 1537–51.

———. "Latino AntiBlack Bias and the Census Categorization of Latinos: Race, Ethnicity, or Other?" In *AntiBlackness,* edited by Moon-Kie Jung and João H. Costa Vargas, 283–97. Durham, NC: Duke University Press, 2021.

———. *Racial Innocence: Unmasking Latino Anti-Black Bias and the Struggle for Equality.* Boston: Beacon, 2022.

Hernández-León, Rubén, and Víctor Zúñiga. "'Making Carpet by the Mile': The Emergence of a Mexican Immigrant Community in an Industrial Region of the U.S. Historic South." *Social Science Quarterly* 81, no. 1 (2000): 49–66.

———. "Mexican Immigrant Communities in the South and Social Capital: The Case of Dalton, Georgia." Working paper, Center for Comparative Immigration Studies, University of California, San Diego, December 2, 2002. https://escholarship.org/uc/item/9r5749mm.

Hewitt, Nancy A. *Southern Discomfort: Women's Activism in Tampa, Florida, 1880s–1920s.* Urbana: University of Illinois Press, 2003.

Hinnershitz, Stephanie. *A Different Shade of Justice: Asian American Civil Rights in the South.* Chapel Hill: University of North Carolina Press, 2017.

Hobbs, Allyson. *A Chosen Exile: A History of Racial Passing in American Life.* Cambridge, MA: Harvard University Press, 2016.

Hoffnung-Garskof, Jesse. *A Tale of Two Cities: Santo Domingo and New York after 1950.* Princeton, NJ: Princeton University Press, 2007.

Hogan, Wesley. *Many Minds, One Heart: SNCC's Dream for a New America.* Chapel Hill: University of North Carolina Press, 2007.

Hollis, Tim. *Dixie before Disney: 100 Years of Roadside Fun.* Jackson: University Press of Mississippi, 1999.

Holsaert, Faith S., Martha Prescod Norman Noonan, Judy Richardson, Betty Garman Robinson, Jean Smith Young, and Dorothy M. Zellner, eds. *Hands on the Freedom Plow: Personal Accounts by Women in SNCC.* Urbana: University of Illinois Press, 2012.

Holt, Thomas C. "Marking: Race, Race-Making, and the Writing of History." *American Historical Review* 100, no. 1 (1995): 1–20.

———. *The Problem of Race in the Twenty-First Century.* Cambridge, MA: Harvard University Press, 2002.

Hooker, Juliet. "Hybrid Subjectivities, Latin American Mestizaje, and Latino Political Thought on Race." *Politics, Groups, and Identities* 2, no. 2 (2014): 188–201.

———. "Indigenous Inclusion/Black Exclusion: Race, Ethnicity and Multicultural Citizenship in Latin America." *Journal of Latin American Studies* 37, no. 2 (2005): 285–310.

———. *Theorizing Race in the Americas: Douglass, Sarmiento, Du Bois, and Vasconcelos.* New York: Oxford University Press, 2019.

Hoppenjans, Lisa, and Ted Richardson. "Mexican Ways, African Roots." In *The Afro-Latin@ Reader: History and Culture in the United States,* edited by Miriam Jiménez Román and Juan Flores, 512–19. Durham, NC: Duke University Press, 2010.

Hordge-Freeman, Elizabeth, and Angelica LoBlack. "'Cops Only See the Brown Skin, They Could Care Less Where It Originated': Afro-Latinx Perceptions of the #BlackLivesMatter Movement." *Sociological Perspectives* 64, no. 4 (2021): 518–35.

Hordge-Freeman, Elizabeth, and Edlin Veras. "Out of the Shadows, into the Dark: Ethnoracial Dissonance and Identity Formation among Afro-Latinxs." *Sociology of Race and Ethnicity* 6, no. 2 (2020): 146–60.

Horne, Gerald. *The Apocalypse of Settler Colonialism: The Roots of Slavery, White Supremacy, and Capitalism in 17th Century North America and the Caribbean.* New York: Monthly Review, 2018.

HoSang, Daniel Martinez. *Racial Propositions: Ballot Initiatives and the Making of Postwar California.* Berkeley: University of California Press, 2010.

Ignatiev, Noel. *How the Irish Became White.* New York, London: Routledge, 2008.

Innis-Jiménez, Michael. *Steel Barrio: The Great Mexican Migration to South Chicago, 1915–1940.* New York: New York University Press, 2013.

Jacobson, Matthew Frye. *Whiteness of a Different Color: European Immigrants and the Alchemy of Race.* Cambridge, MA: Harvard University Press, 1999.

James, C. L. R. *The Black Jacobins: Toussaint L'Ouverture and the San Domingo Revolution.* 2nd ed. New York: Vintage, 1989.

Jeffries, Hasan Kwame. *Bloody Lowndes: Civil Rights and Black Power in Alabama's Black Belt.* New York: New York University Press, 2009.

Jenkins, Destin, and Justin Leroy, eds. *Histories of Racial Capitalism.* New York: Columbia University Press, 2021.

Johnson, Benjamin Heber. *Revolution in Texas: How a Forgotten Rebellion and Its Bloody Suppression Turned Mexicans into Americans.* New Haven, CT: Yale University Press, 2005.

Johnson, Kevin R. "Immigration and Civil Rights: Is the New Birmingham the Same as the Old Birmingham Symposium: Noncitizen Participation in the American Polity." *William and Mary Bill of Rights Journal* 21, no. 2 (2012): 367–98.

———. "September 11 and Mexican Immigrants: Collateral Damage Comes Home." *DePaul Law Review* 52 (2003): 849–70.

Johnson, Stephen. *Burnt Cork: Traditions and Legacies of Blackface Minstrelsy.* Amherst : University of Massachusetts Press, 2012.

Johnson, Walter, and Robin D. G. Kelley, eds. *Race Capitalism Justice.* Boston: Boston Review, 2017.

Jones, Jennifer A. *The Browning of the New South.* Chicago: University of Chicago Press, 2019.

Joseph, Peniel E. *Stokely: A Life.* New York: Civitas Books, 2016.

Jung, John. *Chopsticks in the Land of Cotton: Lives of Mississippi Delta Chinese Grocers.* Yin & Yang, 2011.

Jung, Moon-Kie, and João H. Costa Vargas, eds. *Antiblackness*. Durham, NC: Duke University Press, 2021.

Kanstroom, Daniel. *Deportation Nation: Outsiders in American History*. Cambridge, MA: Harvard University Press, 2010.

Kelen, Leslie, ed. *This Light of Ours: Activist Photographers of the Civil Rights Movement*. Jackson: University Press of Mississippi, 2012.

King, P. Nicole. "Behind the Sombrero: Identity and Power at South of the Border, 1949–2001." In *Dixie Emporium: Tourism, Foodways, and Consumer Culture in the American South*, edited by Anthony J. Stanonis, 148–75. Athens: University of Georgia Press, 2008.

———. *Sombreros and Motorcycles in a Newer South: The Politics of Aesthetics in South Carolina's Tourism Industry*. Jackson: University Press of Mississippi, 2012.

King, Tiffany Lethabo. *The Black Shoals: Offshore Formations of Black and Native Studies*. Durham, NC: Duke University Press, 2019.

Krochmal, Max. *Blue Texas: The Making of a Multiracial Democratic Coalition in the Civil Rights Era*. Chapel Hill: University of North Carolina Press, 2016.

Kruse, Kevin M. *White Flight: Atlanta and the Making of Modern Conservatism*. Princeton, NJ: Princeton University Press, 2007.

Larsen, Nella, and Emily Bernard. *Passing*. Edited by Thadious M. Davis. New York: Penguin Classics, 2003.

Lassiter, Matthew D. *The Silent Majority: Suburban Politics in the Sunbelt South*. Princeton, NJ: Princeton University Press, 2007.

Lassiter, Matthew D., and Joseph Crespino, eds. *The Myth of Southern Exceptionalism*. New York: Oxford University Press, 2009.

Lau, Peter F. *Democracy Rising: South Carolina and the Fight for Black Equality since 1865*. Lexington: University Press of Kentucky, 2006.

Lee, Sonia Song-Ha. *Building a Latino Civil Rights Movement: Puerto Ricans, African Americans, and the Pursuit of Racial Justice in New York City*. Chapel Hill: University of North Carolina Press, 2014.

Lester, Julius. "'Black Revolution Is Real': Stokely in Cuba." *The Movement* 3, no. 9 (September 1967).

Levy, Peter B. *Civil War on Race Street: The Civil Rights Movement in Cambridge, Maryland*. Gainesville: University Press of Florida, 2003.

Lewis, George. *The White South and the Red Menace: Segregationists, Anticommunism, and Massive Resistance, 1945–1965*. Gainesville: University Press of Florida, 2004.

Lippard, Cameron D., and Charles A. Gallagher, eds. *Being Brown in Dixie: Race, Ethnicity, and Latino Immigration in the New South*. Boulder, CO: Lynne Rienner, 2010.

Lippi-Green, Rosina. *English with an Accent: Language, Ideology and Discrimination in the United States*. 2nd ed. London: Routledge, 2011.

Loewen, James W. *The Mississippi Chinese: Between Black and White*. 2nd ed. Long Grove, IL: Waveland, 1988.

López, Ian F. Haney. *Racism on Trial: The Chicano Fight for Justice*. Cambridge, MA: Belknap Press of Harvard University Press, 2004.

———. *White by Law: The Legal Construction of Race*. 10th anniversary ed. New York: New York University Press, 2006.

López Oro, Paul Joseph. "Garifunizando Ambas Américas: Hemispheric Entanglements of Blackness/Indigeneity/AfroLatinidad." *Postmodern Culture* 31, no. 1 (2020), 1-29.

———. "A Love Letter to Indigenous Blackness." *NACLA Report on the Americas* 53, no. 3 (2021): 248-54.

Lott, Eric. *Love and Theft: Blackface Minstrelsy and the American Working Class*. New York: Oxford University Press, 2013.

Lovelace, H. Timothy, Jr. "Making the World in Atlanta's Image: The Student Nonviolent Coordinating Committee, Morris Abram, and the Legislative History of the United Nations Race Convention." *Law and History Review* 32, no. 2 (2014): 385-429.

———. "William Worthy's Passport: Travel Restrictions and the Cold War Struggle for Civil and Human Rights." *Journal of American History* 103, no. 1 (2016): 107-31.

Lowery, Malinda Maynor. *The Lumbee Indians: An American Struggle*. Chapel Hill: University of North Carolina Press, 2018.

———. *Lumbee Indians in the Jim Crow South: Race, Identity, and the Making of a Nation*. Chapel Hill: University of North Carolina Press, 2010.

Loza, Mireya. *Defiant Braceros: How Migrant Workers Fought for Racial, Sexual, and Political Freedom*. Chapel Hill: University of North Carolina Press, 2016.

Lozano, Rosina. *An American Language: The History of Spanish in the United States*. Oakland: University of California Press, 2018.

Mallon, Florencia E. *Decolonizing Native Histories: Collaboration, Knowledge, and Language in the Americas*. Durham, NC: Duke University Press, 2011.

Marable, Manning. *Race, Reform, and Rebellion: The Second Reconstruction and Beyond in Black America, 1945-2006*. 3rd ed. Jackson: University Press of Mississippi, 2007.

Mariscal, George. *Brown-Eyed Children of the Sun: Lessons from the Chicano Movement, 1965-1975*. Albuquerque: University of New Mexico Press, 2005.

Mariscal, Jorge. "Homeland Security, Militarism, and the Future of Latinos and Latinas in the United States." *Radical History Review* 2005, no. 93 (2005): 39-52.

Márquez, Benjamin. *Lulac: The Evolution of a Mexican American Political Organization*. Austin: University of Texas Press, 1993.

Márquez, Cecilia. "Juan Crow and the Erasure of Blackness in the Latina/o South." *Labor* 16, no. 3 (2019): 79-85.

Marquez, John David. "Juan Crow: Progressive Mutations of the Black-White Binary." In *Critical Ethnic Studies: A Reader*, edited by Nada Elia, Jodi Kim, Shana L. Redmond, Dylan Rodriguez, Sarita Echavez See, and David Hernández, 43-62. Durham, NC: Duke University Press, 2016.

Marrow, Helen B. *New Destination Dreaming: Immigration, Race, and Legal Status in the Rural American South*. Stanford, CA: Stanford University Press, 2011.

———. "On the Line: Latino Life in New Immigrant Destinations after 2005." *Contemporary Sociology* 46, no. 3 (2017): 265-73.

Marshall, James P. *Student Activism and Civil Rights in Mississippi: Protest Politics and the*

Struggle for Racial Justice, 1960–1965. Baton Rouge: Louisiana State University Press, 2013.

Mártinez, Elizabeth. "Chingón Politics' Die Hard: Reflections on the First Chicano Activist Reunion." In *Living Chicana Theory*, edited by Carla Trujillo, 123–27. Berkeley, CA: Third Women, 1997.

Martínez, Elizabeth "Betita." *500 Years of Chicana Women's History/500 Años de La Mujer Chicana.* New Brunswick, NJ: Rutgers University Press, 2008.

Mártinez, Elizabeth (Betita) Sutherland. "Neither Black nor White in a Black-White World." In *Hands on the Freedom Plow: Personal Accounts by Women in SNCC*, edited by Faith S. Holsaert, Martha Prescod Norman Noonan, Judy Richardson, Betty Garman Robinson, Jean Smith Young, and Dorothy M. Zellner, 531–39. Urbana: University of Illinois, 2010.

Martinez, Monica Muñoz. *The Injustice Never Leaves You: Anti-Mexican Violence in Texas.* Cambridge, MA: Harvard University Press, 2018.

Massey, Douglas S., ed. *New Faces in New Places: The Changing Geography of American Immigration.* New York: Russell Sage, 2008.

———. "Racial Formation in Theory and Practice: The Case of Mexicans in the United States." *Race and Social Problems* 1, no. 1 (2009): 12–26.

Massey, Douglas S., Jorge Durand, and Nolan J. Malone. *Beyond Smoke and Mirrors: Mexican Immigration in an Era of Economic Integration.* New York: Russell Sage, 2003.

Masur, Kate. *An Example for All the Land: Emancipation and the Struggle over Equality in Washington, D.C.* Chapel Hill: University of North Carolina Press, 2010.

Matos, Yalidy. "A Legacy of Exclusion: The Geopolitics of Immigration and Latinas/os in the South." *Labor* 16, no. 3 (2019): 87–93.

McClain, Paula D., Niambi M. Carter, Victoria M. DeFrancesco Soto, Monique L. Lyle, Jeffrey D. Grynaviski, Shayla C. Nunnally, Thomas J. Scotto, J. Alan Kendrick, Gerald F. Lackey, and Kendra Davenport Cotton. "Racial Distancing in a Southern City: Latino Immigrants' Views of Black Americans." *Journal of Politics* 68, no. 3 (2006): 571–84.

McGirr, Lisa. *Suburban Warriors: The Origins of the New American Right.* Princeton, NJ: Princeton University Press, 2002.

McGuire, Danielle L. *At the Dark End of the Street: Black Women, Rape, and Resistance— A New History of the Civil Rights Movement from Rosa Parks to the Rise of Black Power.* New York: Vintage, 2011.

McMillen, Neil R. *The Citizens' Council; Organized Resistance to the Second Reconstruction, 1954–64.* Urbana: University of Illinois Press, 1971.

McNamara, Sarah. "Borderland Unionism: Latina Activism in Ybor City and Tampa, Florida, 1935–1937." *Journal of American Ethnic History* 38, no. 4 (2019): 10–32.

McNeil, Genna Rae. "Community Initiative in the Desegregation of District of Columbia Schools, 1947–1954: A Brief Historical Overview of Consolidated Parent Group, Inc. Activities from Bishop to Bolling." *Howard Law Journal* 23, no. 1 (1980): 25–42.

McPherson, Tara. *Reconstructing Dixie: Race, Gender, and Nostalgia in the Imagined South.* Durham, NC: Duke University Press, 2003.

McQuirter, Marya Annette. "'Our Cause Is Marching On': Parent Activism, Browne

Junior High School, and the Multiple Meanings of Equality in Post-War Washing-ton." *Washington History* 16, no. 2 (2004): 66–82.

McRae, Elizabeth Gillespie. *Mothers of Massive Resistance: White Women and the Politics of White Supremacy*. New York: Oxford University Press, 2020.

Mealy, Rosemari. *Fidel and Malcolm X: Memories of a Meeting*. Baltimore, MD: Black Classic, 2013.

Meier, August, and Elliott Rudwick. *CORE: A Study in the Civil Rights Movement, 1942–1968*. New York: Oxford University Press, 1973.

Menchaca, Martha. "The Anti-Miscegenation History of the American Southwest, 1837 to 1970: Transforming Racial Ideology into Law." *Cultural Dynamics* 20, no. 3 (2008): 279–318.

Mendieta, Eduardo. "The Making of New Peoples: Hispanicizing Race." In *Hispanics/Latinos in the United States*, edited by Jorge J. E. Gracia and Pablo de Greiff, 45–49. New York: Routledge, 2000.

Menjívar, Cecilia. *Fragmented Ties: Salvadoran Immigrant Networks in America*. Berkeley: University of California Press, 2000.

Menjívar, Cecilia, and María E. Enchautegui. "Confluence of the Economic Recession and Immigration Laws in the Lives of Latino Immigrant Workers in the United States." In *Immigrant Vulnerability and Resilience: Comparative Perspectives on Latin American Immigrants during the Great Recession*, edited by María Aysa-Lastra and Lorenzo Cachón, 105–26. Cham, Switzerland: Springer International, 2015.

Merrill, Dennis. *Negotiating Paradise: U.S. Tourism and Empire in Twentieth-Century Latin America*. Chapel Hill: University of North Carolina Press, 2009.

Milian, Claudia. *Latining America: Black-Brown Passages and the Coloring of Latino/a Studies*. Athens: University of Georgia Press, 2013.

———. *LatinX*. Minneapolis: University of Minnesota Press, 2019.

Mills, Charles W. *The Racial Contract*. Ithaca, NY: Cornell University Press, 1999.

Minian, Ana Raquel. *Undocumented Lives: The Untold Story of Mexican Migration*. Cambridge, MA: Harvard University Press, 2020.

Mintz, Sidney Wilfred. *Caribbean Transformations*. New York: Columbia University Press, 1989.

Mohl, Raymond A. "Globalization, Latinization, and the Nuevo New South." *Journal of American Ethnic History* 22, no. 4 (2003): 31–66.

———. "Latinization in the Heart of Dixie: Hispanics in Late-Twentieth-Century Alabama." *Alabama Review* 55, no. 4 (2002): 243–74.

———. "The Politics of Expulsion: A Short History of Alabama's Anti-Immigrant Law, HB 56." *Journal of American Ethnic History* 35, no. 3 (2016): 42–67.

Molina, Natalia. *Fit to Be Citizens? Public Health and Race in Los Angeles, 1879–1939*. Berkeley: University of California Press, 2006.

———. *How Race Is Made in America: Immigration, Citizenship, and the Historical Power of Racial Scripts*. Berkeley: University of California Press, 2014.

———. "The Power of Racial Scripts: What the History of Mexican Immigration to the United States Teaches Us about Relational Notions of Race." *Latino Studies* 8, no. 2 (2010): 156–75.

Molina, Natalia, Daniel Martinez HoSang, and Ramón A. Gutiérrez, eds. *Relational Formations of Race: Theory, Method, and Practice*. Berkeley: University of California Press, 2019.

Monteith, Sharon. *SNCC's Stories: The African American Freedom Movement in the Civil Rights South*. Athens: University of Georgia Press, 2020.

Montejano, David. *Anglos and Mexicans in the Making of Texas, 1836–1986*. Austin: University of Texas Press, 1987.

Moore, Winfred B., Jr., and Orville Vernon Burton, eds. *Toward the Meeting of the Waters: Currents in the Civil Rights Movement of South Carolina during the Twentieth Century*. Columbia: University of South Carolina Press, 2008.

Mora, G. Cristina. *Making Hispanics: How Activists, Bureaucrats, and Media Constructed a New American*. Chicago: University of Chicago Press, 2014.

Morgan, Edmund S. *American Slavery, American Freedom*. New York: W. W. Norton, 2003.

Morgan, Jennifer L. *Laboring Women: Reproduction and Gender in New World Slavery*. Philadelphia: University of Pennsylvania Press, 2004.

Moye, Todd. *Ella Baker: Community Organizer of the Civil Rights Movement*. Lanham, MD: Rowman & Littlefield, 2013.

———. *Let the People Decide: Black Freedom and White Resistance Movements in Sunflower County, Mississippi, 1945–1986*. Chapel Hill: University of North Carolina Press, 2004.

Muhammad, Khalil Gibran. *The Condemnation of Blackness: Race, Crime, and the Making of Modern Urban America*. Cambridge, MA: Harvard University Press, 2011.

Murphy, Arthur, Colleen Blanchard, and Jennifer Hill, eds. *Latino Workers in the Contemporary South*. Athens: University of Georgia Press, 2001.

Murphy, Mary-Elizabeth B. *Jim Crow Capital: Women and Black Freedom Struggles in Washington, D.C., 1920–1945*. Chapel Hill: University of North Carolina Press, 2018.

Murch, Donna Jean. *Living for the City: Migration, Education, and the Rise of the Black Panther Party in Oakland, California*. Chapel Hill: University of North Carolina Press, 2010.

Nevins, Joseph. *Operation Gatekeeper and Beyond: The War On "Illegals" and the Remaking of the U.S.–Mexico Boundary*. 2nd ed. New York: Routledge, 2010.

Ngai, Mae. *Impossible Subjects: Illegal Aliens and the Making of Modern America*. Princeton, NJ: Princeton University Press, 2005.

Nickerson, Michelle, and Darren Dochuk, eds. *Sunbelt Rising: The Politics of Space, Place, and Region*. Philadelphia: University of Pennsylvania Press, 2014.

Nopper, Tamara. "Why Black Immigrants Matter: Refocusing the Discussion on Racism and Immigrant Enforcement." In *Keeping Out the Other: A Critical Introduction to Immigration Enforcement Today*, edited by David C. Brotherton and Philip Kretsedemas, 204–38. New York: Columbia University Press, 2008.

Nuñez, Gabriela. "The Latino Pastoral Narrative: Backstretch Workers in Kentucky." *Latino Studies* 10, no. 1 (2012): 107–27.

Nunley, Tamika Y. *At the Threshold of Liberty: Women, Slavery, and Shifting Identities in Washington, D.C.* Chapel Hill: University of North Carolina Press, 2021.

Oboler, Suzanne. *Ethnic Labels, Latino Lives: Identity and the Politics of (Re)Presentation in the United States*. Minneapolis: University of Minnesota Press, 1995.

Odem, Mary E., and Elaine Lacy, eds. *Latino Immigrants and the Transformation of the U.S. South*. Athens: University of Georgia Press, 2009.

Ogbar, Jeffrey O. G. "Puerto Rico en mi Corazón: The Young Lords, Black Power and Puerto Rican Nationalism in the U.S., 1966-1972." *CENTRO: Journal of the Center for Puerto Rican Studies* 18, no. 1 (Spring 2006): 148-69.

———. "Rainbow Radicalism: The Rise of Radical Ethnic Nationalism." In *The Black Power Movement: Rethinking the Civil Rights-Black Power Era*, edited by Peniel E. Joseph, 193-228. New York: Routledge Press, 2006.

Olivos, Edward M., and Gerardo F. Sandoval. "Latina/o Identities, the Racialization of Work, and the Global Reserve Army of Labor: Becoming Latino in Postville, Iowa." *Ethnicities* 15, no. 2 (2015): 190-210.

Omi, Michael, and Howard Winant. *Racial Formation in the United States: From the 1960s to the 1990s*. 2nd ed. New York: Routledge, 1994.

Ordaz, Jessica. *The Shadow of El Centro: A History of Migrant Incarceration and Solidarity*. Chapel Hill: University of North Carolina Press, 2021.

Oropeza, Lorena. *The King of Adobe: Reies López Tijerina, Lost Prophet of the Chicano Movement*. Chapel Hill: University of North Carolina Press, 2019.

———. *Raza Si, Guerra No: Chicano Protest and Patriotism during the Viet Nam War Era*. Berkeley: University of California Press, 2005.

Orozco, Cynthia E. *No Mexicans, Women, or Dogs Allowed: The Rise of the Mexican American Civil Rights Movement*. Austin: University of Texas Press, 2009.

Ortiz, Paul. *Emancipation Betrayed: The Hidden History of Black Organizing and White Violence in Florida from Reconstruction to the Bloody Election of 1920*. Berkeley: University of California Press, 2005.

Oshinsky, David M. *Worse Than Slavery: Parchman Farm and the Ordeal of Jim Crow Justice*. New York: Free Press, 1997.

Otero, Lydia R. *La Calle: Spatial Conflicts and Urban Renewal in a Southwest City*. 3rd ed. Tucson: University of Arizona Press, 2010.

Owsley, Frank Lawrence. "Review of *The Myth of the Lost Cause, 1865-1900*, by Rollin G. Osterweis." *Mississippi Quarterly* 27, no. 4 (1974): 511-13.

Pacifico, Michele F. "'Don't Buy Where You Can't Work': The New Negro Alliance of Washington." *Washington History* 6, no. 1 (1994): 66-88.

Pappademos, Melina. *Black Political Activism and the Cuban Republic*. Chapel Hill: University of North Carolina Press, 2012.

Parker, Christopher S. *Fighting for Democracy: Black Veterans and the Struggle against White Supremacy in the Postwar South*. Princeton, NJ: Princeton University Press, 2009.

Paschel, Tianna S. *Becoming Black Political Subjects: Movements and Ethno-Racial Rights in Colombia and Brazil*. Princeton, NJ: Princeton University Press, 2016.

Pascoe, Peggy. *What Comes Naturally: Miscegenation Law and the Making of Race in America*. New York: Oxford University Press, 2010.

Patton, Randall L., and David B. Parker. *Carpet Capital: The Rise of a New South Industry*. Athens: University of Georgia Press, 1999.

Pawel, Miriam. *Union of Their Dreams*. London: Bloomsbury, 2010.

Payne, Charles M. *I've Got the Light of Freedom: The Organizing Tradition and the Mississippi Freedom Struggle*. 2nd ed. Berkeley: University of California Press, 2007.

Perales, Monica. *Smeltertown: Making and Remembering a Southwest Border Community*. Chapel Hill: University of North Carolina Press, 2010.

Perea, Juan F. "The Black/White Binary Paradigm of Race: The 'Normal Science' of American Racial Thought." *California Law Review*, no. 5 (1997): 1213–58.

Perez, Gina. *The Near Northwest Side Story: Migration, Displacement, and Puerto Rican Families*. Berkeley: University of California Press, 2004.

Pérez, Raúl. "Brownface Minstrelsy: 'José Jiménez,' the Civil Rights Movement, and the Legacy of Racist Comedy." *Ethnicities* 16, no. 1 (2016): 40–67.

Perkinson, Robert. *Texas Tough: The Rise of America's Prison Empire*. New York: Picador, 2010.

Phillips, Katrina. *Staging Indigeneity: Salvage Tourism and the Performance of Native American History*. Chapel Hill: University of North Carolina Press, 2021.

Phillips, Kimberley L. *War! What Is It Good For? Black Freedom Struggles and the U. S. Military from World War II to Iraq*. Chapel Hill: University of North Carolina Press, 2012.

Pitti, Stephen J. *The Devil in Silicon Valley: Northern California, Race, and Mexican Americans*. 3rd ed. Princeton, NJ: Princeton University Press, 2004.

Plummer, Brenda Gayle. "Castro in Harlem: A Cold War Watershed." In *Rethinking the Cold War*, edited by Allen Hunter, 133–55. Philadelphia: Temple University Press, 1998.

———. *Rising Wind: Black Americans and U.S. Foreign Affairs, 1935–1960*. Chapel Hill: University of North Carolina Press, 2009.

Pulido, Laura. *Black, Brown, Yellow, and Left: Radical Activism in Los Angeles*. Berkeley: University of California Press, 2006.

Purnell, Brian. *Fighting Jim Crow in the County of Kings: The Congress of Racial Equality in Brooklyn*. Lexington: University Press of Kentucky, 2015.

Quan, Robert Seto, and Julian B. Roebuck. *Lotus among the Magnolias: The Mississippi Chinese*. Jackson: University Press of Mississippi, 2007.

Raiford, Leigh Renee. *Imprisoned in a Luminous Glare: Photography and the African American Freedom Struggle*. Chapel Hill: University of North Carolina Press, 2011.

Ramirez, Catherine. *The Woman in the Zoot Suit: Gender, Nationalism, and the Cultural Politics of Memory*. Durham, NC: Duke University Press, 2009.

Ramírez, Dixa. *Colonial Phantoms: Belonging and Refusal in the Dominican Americas, from the 19th Century to the Present*. New York: New York University Press, 2018.

Ransby, Barbara. *Ella Baker and the Black Freedom Movement: A Radical Democratic Vision*. Chapel Hill: University of North Carolina Press, 2005.

"Recent Cases." *George Washington Law Review* 18, no. 4 (1949–50): 557–90.

Ribas, Vanesa. *On the Line: Slaughterhouse Lives and the Making of the New South*. Oakland: University of California Press, 2015.

Ritterhouse, Jennifer. *Growing Up Jim Crow: How Black and White Southern Children Learned Race.* Chapel Hill: University of North Carolina Press, 2006.

Rivera-Rideau, Petra R., Jennifer A. Jones, and Tianna Paschel, eds. *Afro-Latin@s in Movement: Critical Approaches to Blackness and Transnationalism in the Americas.* New York: Palgrave Macmillan, 2016.

Rivero, Yeidy M. "Erasing Blackness: The Media Construction of 'Race' in Mi Familia, the First Puerto Rican Situation Comedy with a Black Family." *Media, Culture, and Society* 24, no. 4 (2002): 481–97.

Roberts, Brian. *Blackface Nation: Race, Reform, and Identity in American Popular Music, 1812–1925.* Chicago: University of Chicago Press, 2017.

Robinson, Cedric J., and Robin D. G. Kelley. *Black Marxism: The Making of the Black Radical Tradition.* 2nd ed. Chapel Hill: University of North Carolina Press, 2000.

Rochmes, Daniel A., and G. A. Elmer Griffin. "The Cactus That Must Not Be Mistaken for a Pillow: White Racial Formation among Latinos." *Souls* 8, no. 2 (2006): 77–91.

Rodriguez, Clara E. *Latin Looks: Images of Latinas and Latinos in the U.S. Media.* Boulder, CO: Westview, 1997.

Rodriguez, Juana Maria. *Queer Latinidad: Identity Practices, Discursive Spaces.* New York: New York University Press, 2003.

Rodriguez, Nestor P., and Cecilia Menjívar. "Central American Immigrants and Racialization in a Post–Civil Rights Era." In *How the United States Racializes Latinos,* edited by José A. Cobas, Jorge Duany, and Joe R. Feagin, 183–99. London: Routledge, 2015.

Rodríguez-Silva, Ileana M. *Silencing Race: Disentangling Blackness, Colonialism, and National Identities in Puerto Rico.* New York: Palgrave Macmillan, 2012.

Roediger, David R. *The Wages of Whiteness: Race and the Making of the American Working Class.* London, New York: Verso, 2007.

Rogin, Michael. *Blackface, White Noise: Jewish Immigrants in the Hollywood Melting Pot.* Berkeley: University of California Press, 1996.

Román, Miriam Jiménez, and Juan Flores, eds. *The Afro-Latin@ Reader: History and Culture in the United States.* Durham, NC: Duke University Press, 2010.

Rosa, Jonathan. *Looking Like a Language, Sounding Like a Race: Raciolinguistic Ideologies and the Learning of Latinidad.* New York: Oxford University Press, 2019.

Rosaldo, Renato. "Imperialist Nostalgia." *Representations,* no. 26 (1989): 107–22.

Rosas, Abigail. *South Central Is Home: Race and the Power of Community Investment in Los Angeles.* Stanford, CA: Stanford University Press, 2019.

Rothstein, Richard. *The Color of Law: A Forgotten History of How Our Government Segregated America.* New York: Liveright, 2018.

Roy, Beth. *Bitters in the Honey: Tales of Hope and Disappointment across Divides of Race and Time.* Fayetteville: University of Arkansas Press, 1999.

Rugh, Susan. *Are We There Yet? The Golden Age of American Family Vacations.* Lawrence: University Press of Kansas, 2010.

Ruiz, Jason. *Americans in the Treasure House: Travel to Porfirian Mexico and the Cultural Politics of Empire.* Austin: University of Texas Press, 2014.

Ruiz, Vicki L. *Cannery Women, Cannery Lives: Mexican Women, Unionization, and the*

California Food Processing Industry, 1930–1950. Albuquerque: University of New Mexico Press, 1987.

———. *From Out of the Shadows: Mexican Women in Twentieth-Century America*. 10th anniversary ed. New York: Oxford University Press, 2008.

———. "South by Southwest: Mexican Americans and Segregated Schooling, 1900–1950." *OAH Magazine of History* 15, no. 2 (2001): 23–27.

Saldaña-Portillo, María Josefina. *Indian Given: Racial Geographies across Mexico and the United States*. Durham, NC: Duke University Press, 2016.

Sanchez, George J. *Becoming Mexican American: Ethnicity, Culture, and Identity in Chicano Los Angeles, 1900–1945*. New York: Oxford University Press, 1995.

San Miguel, Guadalupe. *"Let All of Them Take Heed": Mexican Americans and the Campaign for Educational Equality in Texas, 1910–1981*. Austin: University of Texas Press, 1987.

Santa Ana, Otto. *Brown Tide Rising: Metaphors of Latinos in Contemporary American Public Discourse*. Austin: University of Texas Press, 2002.

Sawyer, Mark Q., and Tianna S. Paschel. "'WE DIDN'T CROSS THE COLOR LINE, THE COLOR LINE CROSSED US': Blackness and Immigration in the Dominican Republic, Puerto Rico, and the United States." *Du Bois Review: Social Science Research on Race* 4, no. 2 (2007): 303–15.

Saxton, Alexander. *The Rise and Fall of the White Republic: Class Politics and Mass Culture in Nineteenth-Century America*. New York: Verso, 2003.

Schulman, Bruce J. *From Cotton Belt to Sunbelt: Federal Policy, Economic Development, and the Transformation of the South, 1938–1980*. New York: Oxford University Press, 1991.

Sears, John F. *Sacred Places: American Tourist Attractions in the Nineteenth Century*. Amherst: University of Massachusetts Press, 1999.

Sellers, Cleveland, and Robert Terrell. *The River of No Return: The Autobiography of a Black Militant and the Life and Death of SNCC*. Jackson: University Press of Mississippi, 1990.

Sexton, Jared. *Amalgamation Schemes: Antiblackness and the Critique of Multiracialism*. Minneapolis: University of Minnesota Press, 2008.

———. "People-of-Color-Blindness: Notes on the Afterlife of Slavery." *Social Text* 28, no. 2 103 (2010): 31–56.

Sharpe, Christina. *In the Wake: On Blackness and Being*. Durham, NC: Duke University Press, 2016.

Shermer, Elizabeth Tandy. *Sunbelt Capitalism: Phoenix and the Transformation of American Politics*. Philadelphia: University of Pennsylvania Press, 2015.

Simon, Bryant. *The Hamlet Fire: A Tragic Story of Cheap Food, Cheap Government, and Cheap Lives*. New York: New Press, 2017.

———. "Race Reactions: African American Organizing, Liberalism, and White Working-Class Politics in Postwar South Carolina." In *Jumpin' Jim Crow: Southern Politics from Civil War to Civil Rights*, edited by Jane Dailey, Glenda Elizabeth Gilmore, and Bryant Simon, 239–59. Princeton, NJ: Princeton University Press, 2000.

Simpson, Audra. *Mohawk Interruptus: Political Life across the Borders of Settler States.* Durham, NC: Duke University Press, 2014.

Singh, Nikhil. *Black Is a Country: Race and the Unfinished Struggle for Democracy.* Cambridge, MA: Harvard University Press, 2005.

Smallwood, Stephanie E. *Saltwater Slavery: A Middle Passage from Africa to American Diaspora.* Cambridge, MA: Harvard University Press, 2008.

Smith, Carol A. "The Symbolics of Blood: Mestizaje in the Americas." *Identities* 3, no. 4 (1997): 495–521.

Smith, Heather A., and Owen J. Furuseth, eds. *Latinos in the New South: Transformations of Place.* Aldershot, England: Ashgate, 2006.

Sokol, Jason. *There Goes My Everything: White Southerners in the Age of Civil Rights, 1945–1975.* New York: Vintage, 2007.

Somerville, Siobhan B. *Queering the Color Line: Race and the Invention of Homosexuality in American Culture.* Durham, NC: Duke University Press, 2000.

Speed, Shannon. *Incarcerated Stories: Indigenous Women Migrants and Violence in the Settler-Capitalist State.* Chapel Hill: University of North Carolina Press, 2019.

Spillers, Hortense J. "Mama's Baby, Papa's Maybe: An American Grammar Book." *Diacritics* 17, no. 2 (1987): 65–81.

Starnes, Richard D. "Creating a 'Variety Vacationland' Tourism Development in North Carolina, 1930–1990." In *Southern Journeys: Tourism, History, and Culture in the Modern South,* edited by Richard D. Starnes, 145–46. Tuscaloosa: University Alabama Press, 2003.

——, ed. *Southern Journeys: Tourism, History, and Culture in the Modern South.* Tuscaloosa: University Alabama Press, 2003.

Strachan, Ian Gregory. *Paradise and Plantation: Tourism and Culture in the Anglophone Caribbean.* Charlottesville: University of Virginia Press, 2003.

Striffler, Steve. *Chicken: The Dangerous Transformation of America's Favorite Food.* New Haven, CT: Yale University Press, 2007.

Strum, Philippa. *Mendez v. Westminster: School Desegregation and Mexican-American Rights.* Lawrence: University Press of Kansas, 2010.

Stuesse, Angela. *Scratching Out a Living: Latinos, Race, and Work in the Deep South.* Oakland, CA: University of California Press, 2016.

Stull, Donald D., Michael J. Broadway, and David Craig Griffith, eds. *Any Way You Cut It: Meat Processing and Small-Town America.* Lawrence: University Press of Kansas, 1995.

Taylor, Keeanga-Yamahtta. *From #BlackLivesMatter to Black Liberation.* Chicago: Haymarket Books, 2016.

Telles, Edward. *Pigmentocracies: Ethnicity, Race, and Color in Latin America.* Chapel Hill: University of North Carolina Press, 2014.

Theoharis, Jeanne, and Komozi Woodard, eds. *Freedom North: Black Freedom Struggles Outside the South, 1940–1980.* New York: Palgrave Macmillan, 2003.

Thompson, Heather Ann. "Why Mass Incarceration Matters: Rethinking Crisis, Decline, and Transformation in Postwar American History." *Journal of American History* 97, no. 3 (2010): 703–34.

Thompson, Krista A. *An Eye for the Tropics: Tourism, Photography, and Framing the Caribbean Picturesque*. Durham, NC: Duke University Press, 2007.

Torres-Saillant, Silvio. "The Tribulations of Blackness: Stages in Dominican Racial Identity." *Callaloo* 23, no. 3 (2000): 1086–111.

Tyson, Timothy B. *Blood Done Sign My Name: A True Story*. New York: Crown, 2005.

———. "Dynamite and 'The Silent South': A Story from the Second Reconstruction in South Carolina." In *Jumpin' Jim Crow: Southern Politics from Civil War to Civil Rights*, edited by Jane Dailey, Glenda Elizabeth Gilmore, and Bryant Simon, 275–79. Princeton, NJ: Princeton University Press, 2000.

———. *Radio Free Dixie: Robert F. Williams and the Roots of Black Power*. Chapel Hill: University of North Carolina Press, 2001.

Varela, Maria. "Time to Get Ready." In *Hands on the Freedom Plow: Personal Accounts by Women in SNCC*, edited by Faith S. Holsaert, Martha Prescod Norman Noonan, Judy Richardson, Betty Garman Robinson, Jean Smith Young, and Dorothy M. Zellner, 552–71. Urbana: University of Illinois Press, 2010.

Vaughn, Bobby, and Ben Vinson III. "Unfinished Migrations: From the Mexican South to the American South—Impressions on Afro-Mexican Migration to North Carolina." In *Beyond Slavery: The Multilayered Legacy of Africans in Latin America and the Caribbean*, edited by Darién J. Davis, 223–45. New York: Rowman & Littlefield, 2007.

Vickers, Scott B. *Native American Identities: From Stereotype to Archetype in Art and Literature*. Albuquerque: University of New Mexico Press, 1998.

Villanueva, Nicholas, Jr. *The Lynching of Mexicans in the Texas Borderlands*. Albuquerque: University of New Mexico Press, 2018.

Vinson, Ben, III. *Before Mestizaje: The Frontiers of Race and Caste in Colonial Mexico*. Cambridge, UK: Cambridge University Press, 2017.

Visser-Maessen, Laura. *Robert Parris Moses: A Life in Civil Rights and Leadership at the Grassroots*. Chapel Hill: University of North Carolina Press, 2016.

Volpp, Leti. "The Citizen and the Terrorist." In *September 11 in History: A Watershed Moment?*, edited by Mary L. Dudziak, 147–62. Durham, NC: Duke University Press, 2003.

Von Eschen, Penny M. *Race against Empire: Black Americans and Anticolonialism, 1937–1957*. Rev. ed. Ithaca, NY: Cornell University Press, 1997.

von Vacano, Diego A. *The Color of Citizenship: Race, Modernity and Latin American/Hispanic Political Thought*. New York: Oxford University Press, 2012.

Wade, Peter. *Race and Ethnicity in Latin America*. London: Pluto, 1997.

———. *Race and Ethnicity in Latin America*. 2nd ed. London: Pluto, 2010.

Walker, Anders. *The Ghost of Jim Crow: How Southern Moderates Used Brown v. Board of Education to Stall Civil Rights*. Oxford, UK: Oxford University Press, 2009.

Waters, Mary C. *Ethnic Options: Choosing Identities in America*. Berkeley: University of California Press, 1990.

Watson, Bruce. *Freedom Summer: The Savage Season That Made Mississippi Burn and Made America a Democracy*. New York: Penguin Group, 2010.

Weaver, Lila Quintero. *Darkroom: A Memoir in Black and White*. 2nd ed. Tuscaloosa: University Alabama Press, 2012.

Webb, Clive. "A Tangled Web: Black-Jewish Relations in the Twentieth-Century South." In *Jewish Roots in Southern Soil: A New History*, edited by Marcie Ferris and Mark I. Greenberg, 192–209. Waltham, MA: Brandeis, 2006.

Weise, Julie M. *Corazón de Dixie: Mexicanos in the U.S. South since 1910*. Chapel Hill: University of North Carolina Press, 2015.

———. *Fighting for Their Place: Mexicans and Mexican Americans in the U.S. South, 1910–2008*. New Haven, CT: Yale University, 2009.

———. "Introduction: Immigration History and the End of Southern Exceptionalism." *Journal of American Ethnic History* 38, no. 4 (2019): 5–9.

Weston, Mary Ann D. *Native Americans in the News: Images of Indians in the Twentieth Century Press*. Westport, CT: Praeger, 1996.

White, Karletta M. "The Salience of Skin Tone: Effects on the Exercise of Police Enforcement Authority." *Ethnic and Racial Studies* 38, no. 6 (2015): 993–1010.

Whitten, Norman E., and Arlene Torres. *Blackness in Latin America and the Caribbean: Eastern South America and the Caribbean*. Bloomington: Indiana University Press, 1998.

Wilderson, Frank B., III. *Red, White, and Black: Cinema and the Structure of U.S. Antagonisms*. Durham, NC: Duke University Press, 2010.

Williams, Eric, Colin A. Palmer, and William A. Darity. *Capitalism and Slavery*. 3rd ed. Chapel Hill: University of North Carolina Press, 2021.

Willis, Deborah. *Reflections in Black: A History of Black Photographers, 1840 to the Present*. New York: W. W. Norton, 2000.

Willis-Thomas, Deborah, and Deborah Willis, eds. *Picturing Us: African American Identity in Photography*. New York: New Press, 1996.

Willoughby-Herard, Tiffany. "More Expendable Than Slaves? Racial Justice and the After-Life of Slavery." *Politics, Groups, and Identities* 2, no. 3 (2014): 506–21.

———. "'The Whatever That Survived': Thinking Racialized Immigration through Blackness and the Afterlife of Slavery." In *Relational Formations of Race: Theory, Method, and Practice*, edited by Natalia Molina, Daniel Martinez HoSang, and Ramón A. Gutiérrez, 145–62. Berkeley: University of California Press, 2019.

Wilson, Charles Reagan. *Baptized in Blood: The Religion of the Lost Cause, 1865–1920*. 2nd ed. Athens: University of Georgia Press, 2009.

Winders, Jamie. "Bringing Back the (B)Order: Post-9/11 Politics of Immigration, Borders, and Belonging in the Contemporary US South." *Antipode* 39, no. 5 (2007): 920–42.

———. "Changing Politics of Race and Region: Latino Migration to the US South." *Progress in Human Geography* 29, no. 6 (2005): 683–99.

———. *Nashville in the New Millennium: Immigrant Settlement, Urban Transformation, and Social Belonging*. New York: Russell Sage, 2013.

———. "Representing the Immigrant Social Movements, Political Discourse, and Immigration in the U.S. South." *Southeastern Geographer* 51, no. 4 (2011): 596–614.

Wood, Andrew Grant, ed. *The Business of Leisure: Tourism History in Latin America and the Caribbean*. Lincoln: University of Nebraska Press, 2021.

Woods, Clyde, and Ruth Wilson Gilmore. *Development Arrested: The Blues and Plantation Power in the Mississippi Delta*. 2nd ed. London: Verso, 2017.

Woodward, C. Vann. *Origins of the New South, 1877–1913: A History of the South*. Rev. ed. Baton Rouge: Louisiana State University Press, 1951.

———. *The Strange Career of Jim Crow*. Commemorative ed. New York: Oxford University Press, 2001.

Woolfolk, Odessa. Afterword to *Black Workers' Struggle for Equality in Birmingham*, edited by Horace Huntley and David Montgomery. Urbana: University of Illinois Press, 2004.

Yancey, George. *Who Is White? Latinos, Asians, and the New Black/Nonblack Divide*. Boulder, CO: Lynne Rienner, 2003.

Yashar, Deborah J. *Contesting Citizenship in Latin America: The Rise of Indigenous Movements and the Postliberal Challenge*. Cambridge, UK: Cambridge University Press, 2005.

Zamora, Emilio. *Claiming Rights and Righting Wrongs in Texas: Mexican Workers and Job Politics during World War II*. College Station: Texas A&M University Press, 2009.

Zepeda-Millán, Chris. "Weapons of the (Not So) Weak: Immigrant Mass Mobilization in the US South." *Critical Sociology* 42, no. 2 (2016): 269–87.

Zúñiga, Víctor, and Rubén Hernández-León. "Appalachia Meets Aztlán: Mexican Immigration and Intergroup Relations in Dalton, Georgia." In *New Destinations: Mexican Immigration in the United States*, edited by Victor Zúñiga and Rubén Hernández-León, 244–73. New York: Russell Sage, 2005.

———. "The Dalton Story: Mexican Immigration and Social Transformation in the Carpet Capital of the World." In *Latino Immigrants and the Transformation of the U.S. South*, edited by Mary E. Odem and Elaine Lacy, 34–50. Athens: University of Georgia Press, 2009.

———, eds. *New Destinations: Mexican Immigration in the United States*. New York: Russell Sage, 2006.

Theses and Dissertations

Araiza, Lauren. "For Freedom of Other Men: Civil Rights, Black Power, and the United Farm Workers, 1965–1973." PhD diss., University of California Berkeley, 2006.

Barahona, Elizabeth. "The History of Latinx Students at Duke University." Undergraduate thesis, Duke University, 2018.

Engstrom, James Denton. "Industry, Social Regulation, and Scale: The Carpet Manufacturing Complex of Dalton, Georgia." PhD diss., Clark University, 1998.

Erdman, Jennifer L. "'Diplomacy, American Style:' Discrimination against Non-White Diplomats during the 1950s and 1960s and the Effect on the Cold War." PhD diss., Howard University, 2015.

Ferreti, Gwendolyn. "Let's Empty the Clip: State-Level Immigration Restriction and Community Resistance." PhD diss., University of Texas at Austin, 2016.

Foster, Theodore Roosevelt. "Post-Civil Rights in the Hold: Neoliberalism, Race and the Politics of Historical Memory in the Deep South." PhD diss., Northwestern University, 2019.

Guerrero, Perla M. "Impacting Arkansas: Vietnamese and Cuban Refugees and Latina/o Immigrants, 1975–2005." PhD diss., University of Southern California, 2010.

Hamann, Edmund Tappan. "The Georgia Project: A Binational Attempt to Reinvent a School District in Response to Latino Newcomers." PhD diss., University of Pennsylvania, 1999.

Koser, Laura. "Planned by Pedro: South of the Border, 1950–2001." Master's thesis, University of South Carolina, 2004.

Márquez, Cecilia. "Strange Career of Juan Crow: Latinxs and the Making of the U.S. South, 1940–2000." PhD diss., University of Virginia, 2016.

Ramirez, Yuridia. "El Nuevo Bajio and the New South: Race, Region, and Mexican Migration since 1980." PhD diss., Duke University, 2018.

Rodriguez, Iliana Yamileth. "Constructing Mexican Atlanta, 1980–2016." PhD diss., Yale University, 2020.

INDEX

Printed in the USA
CPSIA information can be obtained
at www.ICGtesting.com
LVHW012310191023
761576LV00004B/374